Although Central Europe is an area of prime importance in the world's future, we know very little of what is going on there. Even prior to the war we had scant knowledge of what was happening behind the scenes in the Central European countries — Hungary, Czechoslovakia, Austria, Yugoslavia, Rumania — except for the snap-judgements of itinerant correspondents plus an occasional analysis from one of the sounder journalists.

John Montgomery was appointed to his ministerial post by President Roosevelt to find out what precisely was going on in that tinder-box region of Europe. He lived in Hungary for eight years, knew and liked Hungarians of every political persuasion, class and interest — and his unusually well-informed book is of the utmost importance to all who are interested in foreign relations, modern history and the politics of our time.

With the rise of Hitler and Stalin the Central European countries became pawns in a colossal struggle for power. Caught between Germany and Russia, each country tried to preserve as much of its independence as possible — but each inevitably went down to defeat. Hungary, of course, was one of the major targets in this power-battle, and her rôle as a victim of this conflict has been widely misunderstood. *Hungary, The Unwilling Satellite* is the first book to present an authentic record of that country's history during the last fifteen years — a history which it is

[Continued on back flap]

HUNGARY

THE UNWILLING
SATELLITE

For a second time within a decade, a small European country, Hungary, is being turned into a satellite of an overwhelmingly strong neighbor.

While the present enslavement of Hungary by the Soviets is being carried out under repeated protests of the American government and public opinion, the true story of Hungary's nazification has never been presented to Americans.

My main objective in writing this book is my desire to remedy—even if belatedly—this omission.

I wish particularly to thank Mrs. Thea Wheelwright for the fine job she did in editing the manuscript, and Mr. J. McA. Smiley for the excellent maps he provided.

J. F. M.

HUNGARY

THE UNWILLING SATELLITE

VISTA BOOKS
Morristown, NJ
1993

Copyright by John Flournoy Montgomery

TO MY WIFE

Originally published by Devin-Adair Company, 1947

REPRINT EDITION PUBLISHED 1993 BY

VISTA BOOKS
P.O. Box 1766
Morristown, NJ 07962-1766

ISBN: 0-9628422-1-4

Library of Congress Card Catalog Number
93-60576

PRINTED IN THE U. S. A.

Contents

Preface

When once the Americans have taken up an idea, whether it be well or ill founded, nothing is more difficult than to eradicate it from their minds.

ALEXIS DE TOCQUEVILLE
Democracy in America, 1835

The statement in George Washington's farewell address that: "The nation which indulges towards another an habitual hatred or an habitual fondness is in some degree a slave. It is a slave to its animosity or to its affection, either of which is sufficient to lead it astray from its duty and its interest," is less frequently quoted than his warning against the entangling of "our peace and prosperity in the toils of European ambition, rivalship, interest, humor or caprice." Yet though it be true that our first President could hardly foresee our international commitments as the strongest world power, his statement concerning "habitual hatred" and "habitual fondness" is at present even more timely than in our nation's childhood.

Habitual hatred and fondness have done us immense harm, and they are just now the gravest threat to our peace and security. Hatred and fondness are emotions, not concepts. Hence to foster them harmonizes well with the thought that Americans cannot be asked to sacrifice their lives and fortunes save for ideals. Millions of my compatriots are wont to proclaim this doctrine with ostentatious self-esteem. Yet I venture to say that one could cite no surer evidence of our political immaturity.

A foreigner, whom I know as a keen observer of

1

Churchill's and Roosevelt's foreign policies, once re-marked to me that obviously the British could be led into war whereas the Americans must be maneuvered. This was not flattering and I was inclined to resent it. However, sincere self-examination may oblige us to find some truth in that verdict. Our stature is that of an adult, even a giant, but we are comparatively new in international relations, and therefore, our mental attitude in this field is more often than not that of an adolescent.

Afraid of being called cynics, most people do not desire to admit the truth that in default of a law-enforcing agency, international law is virtually non-existent and the relations of sovereign states are, in general, such as hold between gangsters—dominated by interests, not by sentiments. The idea that we are just now on the threshold of a better era is refuted by the fact that the second World War has immensely in-creased the power of the most perfectly totalitarian na-tion.

As a nation advances, it becomes increasingly aware that it is profitable to take other nations' interests into consideration. This is but an improved way of defend-ing and promoting one's own interests; it does not change the nature of international affairs.

Do not believe that the United States took part in two world wars just to live up to its ideals. The United States entered into both these wars to defend its vital interests. It may be said that in doing so it misjudged its interests. It may be said that it failed to protect them. These objections are open to discussion, but the fact remains that America took part in these wars for the utterly material reason that England's defeat would have jeopardized America's safety and prosperity. This, rightly or wrongly, was America's real motive.

We are not the only nation which feels that it must have its wars idealized. The old battle cries of "For God, For King, For Country!" were more truthful than our modern slogans, but even in those times the war lords found it advisable to fill their soldiers with the belief that God was with them and against the enemy. Riding the wave of miraculous progress, our age has substituted doctrines for deity.

It can readily be understood why we Americans have gone to such lengths to hide our interests in idealistic wrappings. Our experience in international relations is naturally much shorter than that of the Old World. Just as a horse, coming from an endless line of ancestors, need not be taught which herb is healthy and which one is poisonous, peoples of the Old World know almost instinctively the limits of terms like "alliance," "enemy," "oppression" or "peace." They know that beauty is relative to the beholder's eye; while we are still believers in the absolute. They have oppressed others and been oppressed. They have been the aggressors and the attacked. They have fought with everyone and against everyone. They are skeptical; we are still gullible. They realize that, knowing little of the past and less of the present, men know nothing of the future. We think that we are masters of our destiny. This faith is a source of strength but also of great error. He who looks too far ahead may easily stumble.

We shall not be on an equal footing with Old World nations until we acquire their sense of relativity. Hence our so-called idealists are the worst enemies of our national success. They blindfold us. They are responsible for our losing the peace after winning the war. They are the manufacturers of habitual hatred and habitual fondness. They make our diplomacy rigid and inadaptable.

As businessmen we know that co-operation need not be based on personal friendship; nor need we hate our competitor. We know that he is not necessarily a wrongdoer. In his way he may be right, just as we are right in our way. Our interests clash, that is all. As a nation we are still lacking this wisdom.

When, after the first World War, American and British scholars began to reveal that the war guilt had by no means been one-sided, our approach to their writings was chiefly emotional. Had we been a mature people, we should have been able to say: "Perhaps we were not crusaders after all, but we fought on the right side anyway, because we defended our interests." I admit that every nation would find it hard to attain that measure of aloofness. But even a slight admixture of it to our diplomacy would have sufficed to produce a more intelligent peace than the one patched up in the suburbs of Paris.

Convinced that we had fought on the side of the angels, we not only allowed our allies to put in practice the secret treaties they had withheld from our knowledge; we even made ourselves the champions of some of their most destructive designs. To top all that, we let them prescribe for us on which nations we had to bestow our habitual hatred and on which nations our habitual fondness.

The first World War, like the second one, was a struggle between two coalitions. I believe that not many Americans have ever considered that within a coalition there may be defenders of a bad cause along with defenders of a good one. Yet it is a general truth. He who fights against a coalition might easily be fighting on the wrong side and at the same time on the right side. This is not a reflection for generals, but it ought to be one for peacemakers.

We know now that, as the English historian G. P. Gooch put it, "the First War was an East European quarrel. Germany was dragged in by Austria; England and France by Russia." In other words, if we want to establish the original war guilt, we have first to consider the responsibilities of Russia and Austria-Hungary, whose respective allies were not given much choice. There is little doubt that Russia was more imperialistic than the Danubian monarchy, which had been on the defense against modern nationalism ever since the French Revolution.

To us, the first war appeared primarily as a conflict between Germany and our allies in western Europe because it was there that our troops fought. Austria-Hungary to us was a German satellite, and the part played by Russian autocracy was soon and conveniently forgotten. We were not burdened with knowledge of eastern European history and snatched gratefully the simple formulae offered by foreign propagandists. Since Germany was the enemy, Germany was wrong; since Germany was wrong, her Austro-Hungarian ally was wrong too. Since Russia was about to quit, why bother with her? France, Italy, England and Japan were certainly right.

Am I exaggerating? I do not think so. When Hitler began to make himself the heir of the Hapsburgs, Americans began to wake up. Since then I have been told by innumerable individuals that we should not have destroyed the old Austria—"but what else could we do?" they add. By way of justification they cite the "fact" that the Danubian empire was "ramshackle": It would not have held together anyway because, they say, modern nationalism had rendered it obsolete. Had we not been so informed by Hungarian, Slovakian, Croatian, Czech, Italian, Rumanian and even German-Austrian nationalists among our immigrants and visitors? If all of them had the same complaint, was that not sufficient proof? It did not occur to these Americans that the complaint might prove merely that no matter how ramshackle in appearance, the empire had kept any one of these races from chaining the others. Once the empire was dissolved these nations did not want its restoration. Americans do not seem to be aware that the most fervent longing of modern nationalists is not for freedom but for mastery. Austria-Hungary seemed ramshackle to Americans. Russia, just as heterogeneous as she, did not, because the czars, more reactionary than the Hapsburgs, had kept their subjects illiterate.

Making good use of our impression that we had participated in a principally Western conflict, our allies and associates laid down for us laws of habitual hatred and fondness concerning eastern Europe. We responded by being obedient and trustful, like draft oxen under the yoke. The English and French had already developed the conception of Latin-Slavic co-operation against non-Slavs and non-Latins. The German-Austrians and the Magyars were neither Slavic nor Latin. Hence these two were treated as vanquished and guilty while the Slavs of Austria-Hungary were nominated victors, although with exceedingly few exceptions they had defended the Hapsburg empire for four and a half years with no less fervor and tenacity than had the others. We Americans were ordered to love Czechoslovakia, Rumania and Yugoslavia and to applaud the ill-treatment meted out to Hungarians and German-Austrians. We did. We bowed reverently to the fact that one racially mixed community, Austria-Hungary, was replaced and absorbed by a number of states, three of which, namely Czechoslovakia, Yugoslavia and Rumania, were no less mixed than the dissected empire had been, whereas two states, Hungary and German-speaking Austria, suffered amputation of their best provinces.

I say we bowed to this settlement. To be quite exact, we did not care. The limited attention we gave to Europe hardly crossed the Rhine. If it suited the British and French to put millions of German-Austrians and Hungarians under Czech rule, Hungarians under Rumanian, and Croats under Serbian domination, why should we be squeamish?

But having helped our allies to win, we had our share of responsibility in the results of victory. We should not have washed our hands of all the injustice committed in the name of national self-determination, and yet we did. The fact that others, nearer to the spot, were no wiser than we may exculpate us, but it does not mean that we acted wisely. Peace treaties involve recognition of new factors that have been introduced by war; they also should involve a consulting together on the part of *all* the belligerents as to how best to set the world in working order again. Our desire to dictate the peace deprived us of much needed advice and criticism from experts among the countries most affected.

Even before Hitler shocked us into realizing our blunders, the truth had dawned upon some Americans who visited the dismembered empire. Businessmen, having visited first Croatia and then Serbia, or first Transylvania and then old Rumania, would ask me in bewilderment why advanced races had been put under the rule of comparatively backward ones. I could not find a satisfactory answer. Apparently in 1919 Christian statesmen had not yet discovered—as we now seem to have discovered—a method of chasing millions of provisionless people over the border without the slightest regard for family ties.

It is amazing how endurable have been those habitual hatreds and fondnesses produced in the first World War and then foisted on us by our allies. The explanation is propaganda—an amount of propaganda unthinkable at the time of Washington's warning. People deprived of their livelihood by their neighbors never even had a hearing. At the same time, those who profited by the victors' arbitrary discrimination showered us with an unceasing flow of propaganda. Especially does this refer to the Czechs, who took some of the best agricultural parts of Hungary and the richest industrial parts of German-speaking Austria. Many millions of dollars were spent every year in various kinds of propaganda—the object of which was to keep what had been seized.

All of this may sound like past history, outrun by events of incomparable magnitude. In reality it is living history. The same habitual hatreds and fondnesses are still alive and have already begun to shackle us and to make us blind to our own interests. I am not speaking of Germany and Japan, although these are cases where a policy of permanent hatred would be the source of most fateful blundering. I am speaking of the eastern half of Europe which includes one half of central Europe.

Again, as in 1919, we are asked to consider the Slavs our natural friends and the non-Slavs our natural enemies. But Slavism now means something quite different from what it meant after the other war. Then it referred to small and separate nations, to Poles, Czechs and Serbs. Now it refers to the largest continuous empire on earth, which, controlled by a dictator, stretches from the Pacific Ocean into the heart of Germany, having reduced to the position of satellites all the Slavic races which had not been under the scepter of the czars—all Poland, Bohemia, Slovakia, Serbia, Croatia, Slovenia and Bulgaria. At the same time, we are expected to contribute, at least by acquiescence, to the chaining of those elements in the Soviet sphere which are non-Slav, principally Hungary, Rumania and German-speaking Austria.

With great foresight, Russian, Czech and southern Slav-communist propagandists, drawing from seemingly inexhaustible funds, prepared the ground for this policy before the second World War ended in Europe. A shrewd distinction has been dinned into our ears— a distinction between Hitler's victims and his collaborators and satellites. How many Americans remember that Dr. Edouard Benes was swept out of office as president of Czechoslovakia by an irresistible wave of pro-German collaborationism which even rotted his own

National Socialist Party, whose champions, Beran and Chvalkovsky, he had nominated as premier and foreign minister? How many remember that the Slovaks, described for twenty years as members of the one Czechoslovak race, sided with Hitler in his war against Russia and declared war on Poland and America? Very few, it is safe to say. But everyone seems to believe that "feudal and fascist Hungary" was Hitler's enthusiastic ally. Again, few remember that the Moscow Declaration, signed by us in 1943, reminded Austria, Hitler's first victim, of her responsibility in having participated in the war. The labels "victim," "collaborator" and "satellite" have even been interchangeable. As long as it suited Moscow, Bulgaria was called a satellite of Hitler. When she became a satellite of Russia, it was acknowledged that she had been Hitler's victim. The same happened to Croatia.

It is not the purpose of this book to offer new objects of fondness or hatred. I am not asking anyone to like Hungarians and German-speaking Austrians and to despise Czechs, Croats and Serbs. Events to come may compel us to accept such an about-face in self-interest. But the less emotionally we act, the better we shall fare.

I have known many of these different races and ethnic groups and have found all to have attractive and charming traits. I reserve my own aversion for narrowminded, boisterous, intolerant jingoes, whether they speak Rumanian, Czech, German, Hungarian, Serbian, or any other tongue. In this I hope the reader will join me. It is best to reject the master race mania wherever it is met, and it is not confined to any one country. First of all, it is well to recognize that much so-called leftism is simply camouflaged nationalism.

Ethnic democracy, that is, racial equality within a country, is more important than democratic elections and cannot be replaced by the latter. Soviet Russia's habit of calling herself a democracy will perhaps compel us to discontinue the use of this term. As long as we do use it, it must not mislead us.

Many people think that it is useless to protest if one is face to face with accomplished facts that cannot be changed without another world war. My reply is that facts are really accomplished only when recognized as permanent, and that to consider another world war as the only remedy is to put into practice a defeatism which is not yet warranted.

Having been United States Minister to Hungary from 1933 to 1941, my regular post of observation in those critical years was Budapest. It was a unique post because the Magyars, neither Teuton nor Slav, were always aware of being between the two fires of German and Russian imperialism. During those years, most of us saw only one fire, the German one. Hungary's vision was far ahead of ours. Had we listened to Hungarian statesmen, we should perhaps have been able to limit Stalin's triumph in the hour of Hitler's fall.

Hungary, between the two wars, was a small country, and from my watchtower on the Danube my eyes could roam over her neighbors and neighbors' neighbors, over Austria, Czechoslovakia, Poland, Rumania, Bulgaria, Yugoslavia, Germany and Italy. The Department of State encouraged my travel across many borders. Anticipating what I want to show in this book, I might say that what I witnessed was a tragic and insoluble conflict between fear and honor, in which fear was bound to win. It is an undeniable fact that on many occasions those who had been treated as step-children by the Western powers in 1919 showed more loyalty to the Allied cause than their spoiled favorites did.

Would it not have been better if we had opposed the arbitrary discrimination indulged in by the surgeons of 1919, who thereby afforded Hitler his most powerful arguments? Offered a second chance, we ought to set ourselves strongly and firmly against a repetition which this time would allow Slavic imperialism to run amuck.

J. F. M.

August 1947

Part One

What Price Independence?

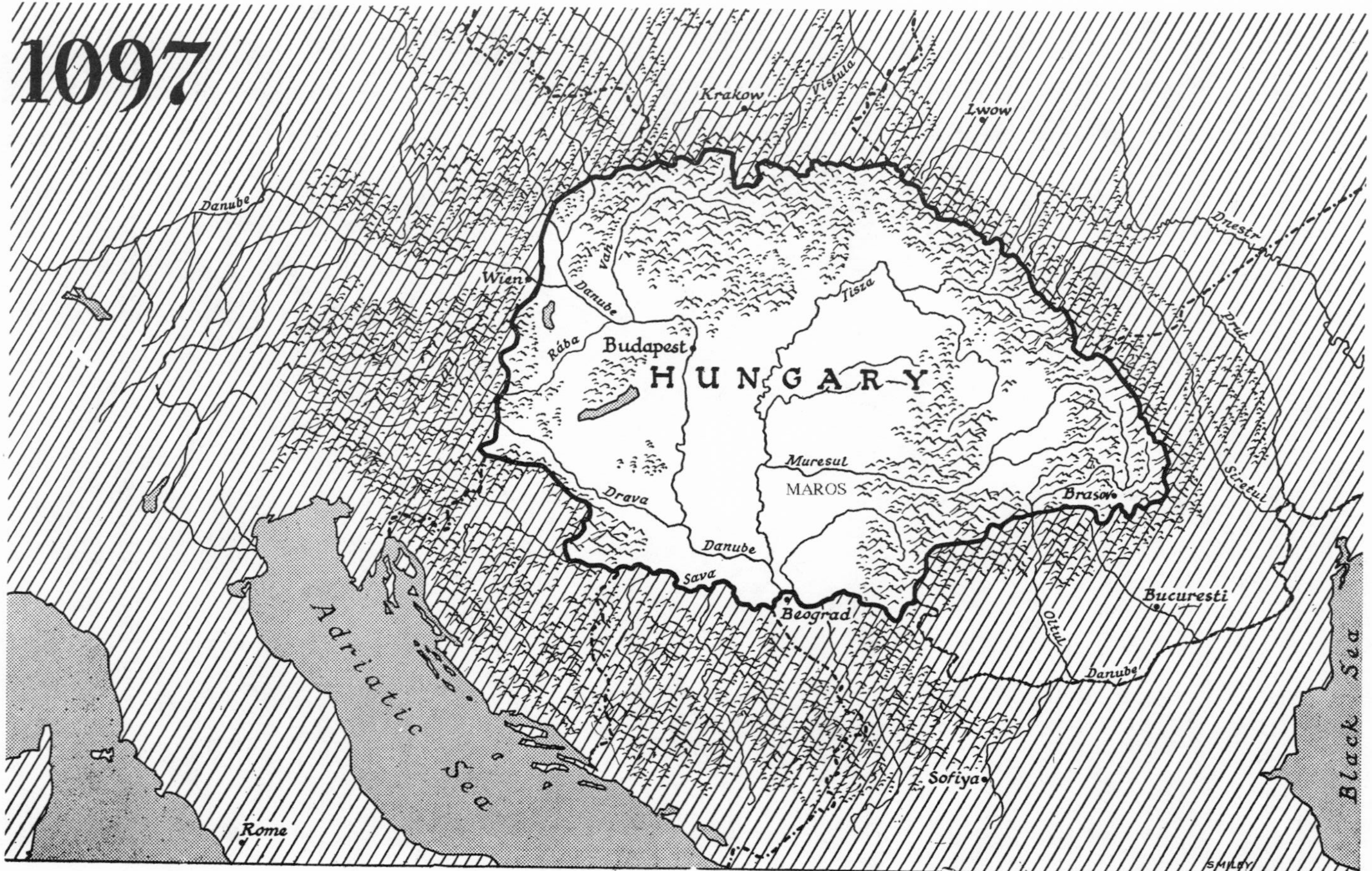
1097
Krakow
Vistula
Lwow
Danube
Wien
Danube
Vah
Rába
Budapest
HUNGARY
Tisza
Dnestr
Prut
Siretul
Muresul
MAROS
Brasov
Drava
Danube
Sava
Beograd
Bucuresti
Oltul
Danube
Adriatic Sea
Sofiya
Rome
Black Sea
SMILEY

1

THE PREWAR LINE-UP IN
CENTRAL EUROPE

~~~~~~

W HEN I looked down for the first time from the
Fishermen's Bastion next to the Coronation
Church on Castle Hill in Buda, I thought of what another envoy, Otto von Bismarck, had written to his
wife in 1852 when he was in Buda on a special mission
for the King of Prussia:

> The Emperor was so gracious as to offer me quarters
> in his castle, and here I am sitting in a large, vaulted
> hall at the open window into which enter the peals
> of the evening bells down in Pest. The view is en-
> chanting. The castle towers high on the hill. When
> I look down, there is first the Danube, over-arched
> by the Chain Bridge; then follows the city of Pest,
> and behind it there stretches the endless plain, van-
> ishing hazily in the blue-red evening vapor. To the
> left of Pest, my eyes can wander upstream; on its
> right bank, the Danube is first hemmed by the city
> of Buda, and then there are mountains, blue, bluer,
> finally brown-red in the glowing evening sky. In the
> middle of the two cities, there is the broad mirror of
> water, broken by the Chain Bridge and a wooded
> island. If only you were here for a moment to see
> with me the dead silver of the Danube, the dark
> mountains against the pale-red background and the
> lights of Pest glittering up to me; Vienna would go
> down in your appreciation compared with Buda-

Pest. You see, I am a worshipper of natural beauty. Now I must appease my stirred blood with a cup of tea. I don't know where I got that song that does not leave me alone today: 'Over the blue mountain, over the white seafoam, come thou beloved one, come to thy lonely home.'

This nostalgic song he quoted in English. No doubt Bismarck was enthralled by the irresistible charms of the Hungarian siren. I could easily share his emotions. It is undeniable that European city builders on the whole have made use of the favors of nature more successfully than we Americans, and of this the twin cities of Buda and Pest were an outstanding example.

I say "were" instead of "are" and I do so with a heavy heart. Today the outlook from the Fishermen's Bastion is not fascinating but saddening. The Royal Palace where Bismarck wrote that letter is in shambles, the Coronation Church is gutted. All six bridges have gone, and with them the lovely Szechenyi Chain Bridge. Margaret Island is devastated and the Corso, scene of mirth, grace and elegance, is no more. Eleven weeks of fighting, preceded by air bombardments, transformed many districts, rich and poor, into deserts of wreckage and rubble. Worst of all, hunger still stalks the capital of an agricultural country in which, before the Russians looted it, not even the destitute had lacked for daily bread.

Having known Hungary before the catastrophe, I have suffered an irreparable loss. Yet I am grateful that I was allowed to have a last glance at a great achievement to which the Western world owed a good deal of its security, alas, without acknowledging its debt. When we look at the map and find Europe a tiny appendix of the Asiatic mainland, we cannot help admiring the courage and tenacity of those who, through the centuries, prevented the submersion of Europe. One of the outposts holding out against immense pressure were the Magyars, though they had come from Asia themselves.

I saw Hungary in peace, but I cannot say that I saw her in normal times. "Normalcy" ended in 1914, and what was left of Hungary after the first World War was but a shadow of herself. As a result of Hitler's rise to power in 1933 Budapest had suddenly attained great importance on the international chessboard, and when I was asked to go there as American minister, I accepted my mission with eager expectation.

Before going there in July, 1933, I spent thirty days of preparatory study in the State Department and learned that while Hungary was a puppet of Italy and had no independence of action, she was of importance as a listening post. Italy had left the peace conferences of the suburbs of Paris dissatisfied after the first World War. For that reason she became the chief antagonist of France and those who had participated in the distribution of Europe, that is, Poland, Yugoslavia, Rumania and Czechoslovakia, who naturally agreed with France's policy of anti-revisionism. Those who had lost by the treaties of Versailles and Trianon naturally leaned toward Italy. The Germans did so rather reluctantly because they were playing for higher stakes and had a poor opinion of Italy's strength and ultimate reliability. The Austrians, on the other hand, regarded Italy as an anti-revisionist power because she refused to disgorge Southern Tyrol which had been taken from Austria. Only the Hungarians could look to Italy wholeheartedly as there was no clash of interests. Italy wanted revision at the expense of Yugoslavia, a member of the Little Entente, whose chief, and sometimes it seemed sole, aim was to keep Hungary under strict control.

Between Rome and Budapest there was common ground, but subsequent events proved that it is not true that Hungary was an Italian vassal. The idea that Hungary's policy was solely determined by Rome is a gross mistake. In foreign affairs, nothing is more alluring and more misleading than oversimplification. Not for a moment did the Hungarians renounce their right to make their own decisions—of course, within the limitations of a small, unarmed power. For a time, they were pretty well tied up with Italy because there was nothing else to do, but with the rise of Germany, this situation changed. Up to the time when Germany and Italy were pushed together by the force of events, Hungary could and did balance herself between the two. If Italy wanted her to do something she did not want to do, she told them that she could not because of Germany; and if Germany wanted her to do something she did not want to do, she told them the same thing about Italy. This policy in the hands of a clever diplomat like Kalman de Kanya gave Hungary, during most of the time that I was there, considerable liberty of action.

The nations on the European continent, including Russia, recognized the danger of Nazi Germany sooner than England or the United States. The general reaction was fear. In strong countries and in those which considered themselves strong, that fear was adulterated by hope of profit through the approaching turn of events. The Soviets regarded Hitler as their icebreaker who would destroy democracy, prosperity and freedom to their final advantage. Mussolini, overrating Italy's position and his own skill, thought that he would remain the senior partner in the new adventure. But France and the minor nations around Germany were subject to unadulterated fear. While England and America talked of peace, they commenced to think about war, and it became plain that the alternative was subjugation.

If England kept aloof, there seemed to be no need for any foreign policy. If there was to be a new war between the great powers, the supreme task of every weak country was to remain neutral, if possible. Apart from that, the most important thing was to be on the winning side. Who of the small neutral nations wanted Germany to win? It can be said with certainty that until June of 1941, when Germany attacked Russia, none of them wanted a German victory. There was good reason to believe that not even Mussolini wanted Hitler's victory to be complete. All the nations of Europe knew that a German triumph would mark the end of their sovereignty, but at this point we must distinguish between nations that had been the beneficiaries of the first World War and naturally were afraid of German success which would not only deprive them of their territorial gains but even of their sovereignty; and nations that had been ill-treated by the peace stipulations and found it more difficult to make up their minds. It is true that the latter preferred independence and narrow frontiers to dependence and wider ones, but at the same time they feared a German victory. To become dependent on Germany would be a hard fate. Yet, since Germany seemed to be invincible, they could not court complete disaster by openly opposing her. On the other hand, it was the natural instinct of the profiteers of the first World War openly to oppose Germany.

The whole picture was finally blurred by the German invasion of Russia. That happened after I left Hungary, but it was not unexpected. It was apparent that it was only a matter of time before the two tyrants would be at each other's throats. Russian communism is practically the same system as German national socialism. As they used to say in Budapest, the only difference between Nazism and Bolshevism is that it is colder in Russia. Both envisioned world conquest and were not only perfectly ruthless, but used the same methods. Americans, being farther from Russia and more or less blinded by their hate of Hitlerism, did not share this point of view with Europeans. This accounts for the fact that we did not make greater efforts to prevent pan-Slavism from succeeding pan-Germanism. The people of central and eastern Europe knew only too well that if the Germans were locusts, the Russians were super-locusts, impoverished by a planned economy which had put guns before butter, not since 1933, but since 1917.

It is, therefore, surprising that the Hungarians sympathized with the cause of the Allies to such a great extent as they did. It is undeniable that they did not receive encouragement from the democracies. We did not promise them anything—we only threatened. Yet with stout hearts and great political wisdom, they clung to the tradition of belonging to the Christian civilization of the Occident although they seemed to be destined for the un-Christian civilization of the Orient.

It is an undeniable fact that Hitler's best collaborators in the second World War were the Czechs, the Slovaks and the Rumanians. Hungary held out longest against German demands, indeed, until the spring of 1944. Foreign propaganda, however, supported by our OWI, succeeded in distorting historic facts by telling our public that the regimes in Bohemia, Slovakia and Rumania were not representative of their peoples' wishes whereas the Hungarian regime was. This allegation is highly questionable. Dr. Hacha, who surrendered Czechoslovakia, was constitutionally elected president after the resignation of Dr. Benes, who sent his congratulations upon the election. Father Tiso, the head of Slovakia, certainly enjoyed the adherence of the majority of his Catholic peasantry. In Rumania, the regime of King Carol and Marshal Antonescu was not what you would call democratic, but the movement which had swept it into power had been genuinely Rumanian. If, for argument's sake, we say that Hacha, Tiso and Antonescu were less representative than Horthy, would it justify the conclusion that Hungary's limited collaboration was more blameworthy than the unlimited collaboration of the others? If we accept the view that nations are not responsible for the actions of puppet regimes but are responsible for those of representative governments, then we should really prefer abject rather than partial surrender to tyrants. It sounds absurd, but at Teheran, Yalta and Potsdam, this preference was adopted as the policy of the major powers, including the United States of America.

2

HUNGARY'S SO-CALLED FEUDALISM

A<small>N</small> A<small>MERICAN</small> author and radio commentator recently explained to a friend of mine why the Russian occupation of Hungary was a very salutary event. "You know," he said, "Hungarian landowners are entitled to kill their serfs." This commentator had never set foot on Hungarian soil, but there was no doubt in his mind as to the truth of this statement. Stories about feudal Hungary were planted incessantly after the first World War in order to calm the world's conscience, which was a little troubled by the fact that in the name of national self-determination, more than three million Magyars had been put under Czech, Rumanian and Serbian rule. Now their feudal lords could no longer chop off their heads.

Feudalism is historically the medieval European system based on the relation of vassals and lords, arising from the holding of land in feud. Since feudalism is tied up with absolute monarchy, it is often forgotten that the crown and the lords were natural antagonists. The lords—or barons—could increase their prerogatives only at the expense of the crown. In the resulting struggle the crown often came to be allied with the common people against the nobility. Yet the net result was that the nobles were the champions of political liberties because the rights they won for themselves were afterward claimed by the common man. In the Holy Roman Empire the nobles were very successful in wresting concessions from the imperial crown. The Hungarian magnates never attained a similar position: In a small country the crown can assert itself more effectively. In the Holy Roman Empire the lords were for a long time the only politically vocal stratum of society; but the magnates in Hungary—which never belonged to the Roman Empire—were exposed to strong pressure from below, exerted by a very broad layer of minor nobles, the so-called gentry, which resembled the squirearchy of England and played a similar part in public affairs. Hence, unless we stretch political terms until they are completely disfigured, Hungary was never a feudal polity.

Hungary had a badly balanced distribution of its arable land. Many magnates owned large estates which were legally entailed and could neither be sold nor mortgaged. According to Hungarian official statements which I have usually found reliable, quoted by Victor Bator in the *American Hungarian Observer* of November 19, 1944, about three-quarters of all landholders owned in 1935 about one-tenth of the land. This sounds less startling when compared with Denmark, where "68% of all agricultural holdings under ten hectares (the hectare being equivalent to nearly two and a half acres) account for 11% of the land," and with Holland where "13.6% of the land is held by 61% of the proprietors." Bator writes:

> The true picture concerning big properties in Hungary is as follows: the arable area (including pasture land) is 13,142,122 yokes, that is 7,556,650 hectares. Out of this 1,225,325 hectares constitute the area of holdings of more than 575 hectares which are owned by private individuals and by the Church. This is

15.2% of the arable land. . . . It is pure misrepresentation to state that half or more than one-third of the land is owned by a few hundred landowners. Actually the area of large estates in private ownership is 1,530,000 hectares, that is, 14% of the arable land.

These figures show that the term "feudal Hungary" is, to say the least, highly exaggerated. To them should be added the following reflections: Extravagant ownership of the soil by aristocratic families would render a country feudal only if that ownership involved economic and political power. It did in Hungary before World War I, because agricultural products could be sold at a profit within the customs barriers of the Austro-Hungarian Empire, and the Hapsburg kings of Hungary preferred the aristocrats—often foreigners who had received their titles for service rendered to the dynasty—to the gentry, or simple noblemen. Whereas the aristocrats very often were on the side of the dynasty against the national interest, the nobles, who were descendants of the original conquerors of Hungary, identified themselves with the national cause. All this changed after the first World War. The aristocrats had invested their money lavishly in war loans which were entirely worthless after the defeat. The ruthless dissection of the old empire deprived them of their markets. In addition, with the rest of agricultural Europe, Hungary suffered because of the low prices brought about by the mechanization of North and South American farming. The effect on the aristocratic landowners was worse than on their untitled fellow sufferers because they were unable to sell or mortgage their entailed property. No longer propped up by the crown, the aristocrats saw their political influence dwindle after the first World War. Furthermore, they lost their most traditional profession, that of service in the armed forces. Hungary was allowed only a token army and the proud Hussar regiments, which had covered themselves with military glory for five centuries, lay buried under the ruins of the old monarchy.

The gentry took possession of Hungary after the fall of the Hapsburgs. By the time I was appointed there, in July 1933, the aristocrats had little or no political importance. I do not consider that the transition from aristocratic leadership to gentry and civil service rule was necessarily a blessing for either Hungary or her neighbors. I have mentioned that the Hapsburgs preferred the magnates, or titled noblemen, to the gentry. Franz Josef knew that in a multiracial empire surrounded by hostile neighbors, the most valuable elements were those who, owing to their upbringing and international family connections, stood above nationalism. The gentry have had a double function in Hungarian history—a positive one in keeping the nation alive and conscious of itself, and a negative one in being ultranationalistic. Thus they partly created the dangers against which they had to struggle.

Many people think that the existence of the Upper House, the House of Magnates, was sufficient to warrant Hungary being called a feudal country. When I was in Budapest, the Upper House was composed of the four Hungarian Hapsburgs, the two Keepers of the Crown, the supreme judges, the prelates and supreme dignitaries of the churches, the president of the National Bank, thirty-eight high aristocrats elected by

their peers, seventy-six men designated by the counties
and municipal cities, thirty-six representatives of the
chambers of agriculture, industry, commerce, lawyers,
notaries, universities, Heroes' Order, Academy of Sci-
ence and the stock exchange, forty lifelong members
nominated by the Regent, one physician, one indus-
trialist and one agriculturalist. It can be seen from thiᵣ
that the aristocrats were in the small minority. Great
Britain retains the sediments of feudalism by preserv-
ing the right of the king to create new peerages on the
advice of his government. In Hungary the Regent was
not entitled to bestow nobilities and, therefore, the
vanishing of aristocratic influence became quite patent.
Count Stephen Bethlen, prime minister during the
first decade without a king, had no estates and did not
represent the supposed interests of his class. Count
Teleki, though equally a member of one of the oldest
families, was also estateless, a quiet, soft-spoken scien-
tist, by no means fitting the pattern of feudal lordship.

All that was left of economic feudalism was in many
cases a brilliant front which covered indebtedness, if
not outright poverty. The attitude of the Hungarian
toward money was that its only function is to be spent.
Hungarian hospitality was something proverbial in
Europe. The Hungarian gentleman generally lived beyond his income, but he always entertained some way
or other, even if it meant coffee and roll dinners for
him during the following week.

Thus palaces built in the great day of the nobles and
magnates had been equipped with tremendous recep-
tion rooms and ballrooms on a par with those in the
Waldorf Astoria. These were not, of course, permanent

homes; when it came to bedrooms most of them had only one; but as the owner of one of them remarked, forty people could sleep in it. Likewise, they had only one bath, if any. The distribution of space between entertaining quarters and living quarters in these Budapest palaces is a true indication of the accent the average Hungarian puts on entertaining. There were, of course, a number of permanent homes, with lots of bedrooms, in Budapest; but most of the well-equipped homes were in the country.

Some of the Budapest palaces were still occupied by their owners while we were there, though most of them were for rent. No one could figure out how the servants in these palaces were paid. One nice thing about entertaining in Budapest was that you could get all the trained butlers and footmen you wanted, for despite their impoverishment noblemen always had more servants than they needed and were glad to offer their services.

The custom of tipping in Hungary far surpassed the American brand. For example, when you rode in the elevator of a building, you owed the operator twenty centimes. If by any chance you did not pay him, he would follow you out into the street, if necessary, to collect it. When you went into anyone's home and gave up your hat, you were supposed to pay a pengo to the maid for its return. If you were a dinner guest, you owed considerably more, depending on your financial status. You paid this money when you got your coat and hat to go home. The money thus received was split up by the household staff, everyone getting his particular share. It naturally followed that the most sought-after positions were in the homes of those who were continually entertaining. No one ever complained about the number of guests you had.

Labor conditions in Hungary have been badly misrepresented in America. Industrial labor was organized in Hungary preceding the first World War and had obtained by the time I arrived there a similar status to that of American labor gained through the New Deal. Nevertheless, relationships between management and labor, especially in smaller enterprises, had retained some of its paternal characteristics, which frankly I would not consider a disadvantage.

While industrial labor enjoyed in Hungary all the social security which a poor country could afford to provide, the situation was very different with agricultural labor. First of all, the major part of agricultural labor was not unionized and health and old-age insurance were granted them only to a very small degree. Real poverty could be observed among agricultural labor mainly because there were not enough jobs for them.

Accusations of Hungarian feudalism often arose abroad because these questions were handled in an antiquated paternal fashion leaving too much leeway to the individual landowner, who was considered responsible for agricultural labor within his domain. Agricultural labor usually concluded contracts with the landowners on a yearly basis, which gave them more security, but on the other hand their salaries were paid to a large extent in kind, which meant that in bad years they earned less than they would if working on a wage basis.

The general spirit of the Hungarian employer was

certainly not anti-labor. When, after the conclusion of the Trianon Treaty, living conditions became bad and jobs hard to find, the landowners voluntarily put a considerable part of their agricultural machinery out of use in order to provide more jobs to manual labor. This rule prevailed while I was in Hungary. Although it was self-imposed with the idea of helping labor, it was a shortsighted policy based upon a misapprehension—common in America also—that the more people who do the job the better.

The relationship between employer and employee differed from anything we know in America—unless we hark back to early plantation life—in that the employer had to supply everything in the way of clothes, laundry and payment of doctors' and dentists' bills, not only for the worker himself, but for his whole family. The employer was the banker. If anything happened and the worker's family needed money, he naturally came to his employer for help, and he got it—with no strings attached.

If you hire anyone in the United States, no matter how many years he works for you, you are free to discharge him if he does something deserving such treatment. Not so in Hungary. It was a very difficult proposition to dismiss a worker in Hungary, no matter what he had done, without making some provision for his future. We had a gardener who did nothing but dress up and sit in front of the house. His wife did all the work. We complained vigorously to the landlord. Finally he got us another gardener—but he could not *discharge* the first one; he simply transferred him to his country estate.

Some of the Hapsburgs themselves were impover-

ished by the claims of their employees. Archduke
Frederick, who had been commander in chief of the
Austro-Hungarian armies, was, before the first World
War, the richest man in the Hapsburg realm. At the
time I was in Hungary, he still had about forty thousand acres of land. When Austria and Czechoslovakia
expropriated his huge palaces and estates and the
famous art gallery which he owned in Vienna, they dis-
charged all his employees. These went back to Hungary, where the archduke, very honorably, considered
it his duty to support them. For this immense burden
even his large estate could not earn enough. Yet in his
will he bound his heirs to keep on supporting this mass
of dependents, even though he must have known that
they could only end in bankruptcy.

Every diplomat had to take the Hapsburg archdukes
in Hungary into consideration in the years preceding
World War II when some of the powers were flirting
with the idea of restoration. There was Archduke
Joseph and his wife, Augusta, who occupied a large
palace across from the prime ministry and not far from
the Royal Palace. Every chief of mission, after present-
ing his credentials, was expected to call on them and to
entertain them at least once a year. It was quite an
ordeal because Archduchess Augusta, to put it quite
frankly, did not know when to go home. If you had
them for dinner, everybody planned to stay the night,
because no one could leave until the archduke and
archduchess left. They did not play bridge; they only
played king and queen, and it was very boring. Most
people entertained them for lunch; while you had to
give up the afternoon to it, it was better than being up
all night. Augusta smoked cigars. I discovered that she

would never under any circumstances leave until she finished her cigar; offering small cigars and passing them only once had the effect of making her leave earlier. It was not considered fair to invite your diplomatic colleagues to a luncheon or a dinner for this royal pair without telling them in advance, and it was generally a matter of trading. If you stuck one of your diplomatic friends for a royal luncheon, he stuck you in return. One had to go to quite a few during the winter.

Joseph and Augusta had a son named Joseph Francis, who was not particularly bright, but his wife was a charming girl, the Princess Anna, also called Monica. We liked to entertain young Joseph on account of his wife. We were not, however, compelled by etiquette to entertain them every year or at all; and since we had so much entertaining to do, we had them only now and then.

Albrecht, the son of the Archduke Frederick, was very popular with Americans; we saved him for them and entertained him four or five times a year. He lived very simply and seemed to be more interested in carrying out his father's wishes than in pomp or ceremony. He had been brought up as an agriculturist and in this field he was somewhat of an expert. But there was some devil in him which always defeated him when he tried anything else. He was brilliant and as nice a person as you would want to meet socially, but absolutely eccentric and undisciplined. Whenever success seemed to be in his grasp he did something silly. In the end, after ups and downs in a campaign to make him king of Hungary, he sold himself to national socialist Germany —probably with ideas of getting back some of his father's estates.

I never met his father, as he lived in a gamekeeper's house up in the little town of Moson, near the Austrian border. I saw him several times, dressed in peasant costume, standing in the doorway of his home which was right on the street, smoking a long pipe and probably waiting to talk to a passerby. He was the most popular archduke of all with the protocol division of the Foreign Office because he never came to Budapest; but his death created the worst problem they had ever known. He had been a field marshal, a commander in chief, and an archduke. The funeral was attended by his nephew, the exiled King of Spain; by numerous archdukes; by all the surviving Austro-Hungarian field marshals; by personal representatives of Hitler; by members of the House of Savoy; by the diplomatic corps; by a son of the exiled German emperor; by representatives of the governments of Germany, Italy and Austria, and, of course, by the Regent of Hungary and his wife. In addition, there were members of the Hungarian government and delegates of the German and Austrian armies. Practically the whole Hungarian army was present.

The problem was taken over by Istvan de Barczy, chief of protocol of the prime ministry—Mr. Protocol himself—and he worked a miracle. Nobody felt slighted or neglected; everything went off just as if it had been rehearsed. It was really a great show, and I am sure that all the fuss would have amused the old man if he had seen it.

The setting was a tiny church in a small town. There had been snow, and the streets were very deep in slush. After the service, everybody formed in correct order behind the silver coffin. Frederick, due to one or all of his positions, was by tradition entitled to have a knight in armor follow his coffin. He received his due. I was told that this presented quite a problem, because no suitable armor could be found until someone suggested the Budapest Opera. The knight who followed Frederick's coffin wore the armor of Lohengrin.

The whole regiment of cavalry rode out in front, and the horses did their best to transform the slush into a perfumed carpet. But where they marched, Madame Horthy and all the ladies in their little open shoes marched too.

While entertaining archdukes was quite a problem, it had its useful side. Hungarians have been brought up on royalty. They might make fun of the archdukes, but they still have respect for them. There were few Hungarians who were not delighted to be invited to the same luncheon which bored the diplomats so exceedingly. This was especially true of the many ministers and politicians who came in from the country. If you really wanted to make a friend of almost any of the cabinet ministers, an invitation to lunch or dinner with one of the archdukes never failed.

3

ADMIRAL HORTHY'S POSITION AS REGENT

O N MARCH 15, 1939, a gala performance was given at the Royal Opera in Budapest in celebration of Hungary's Day of Independence, equivalent to our Fourth of July. It happened that Hitler had chosen this particular day for taking over Bohemia. Naturally considerable tension was felt in Budapest.

It was customary for these performances to be given under the auspices and for the benefit of some organization. Since the prime minister, Count Paul Teleki, was head of the Boy Scouts, on this night they were in charge. The Regent, most of the cabinet ministers, diplomats and local dignitaries were present. I made it a point to go every year, and on this occasion I attended with my daughter, son-in-law and some friends.

Before the prelude, a little Boy Scout came out and started to recite a speech, but he had scarcely got started when there was an unexpected interruption. This took the form of chanting in unison—what I later learned was "Justice for Szalasi!" Szalasi being the leader of the Hungarian Arrowcross Party, or Nazis, this was obviously some sort of demonstration against Horthy and Teleki.

My son-in-law and I left our box to see what was happening. We were near the stairs and, having located the noise as coming from the gallery, we went up. The chanting was interspersed with terrific shouts; we could not imagine what was happening. When I got to the top of the stairs I was astonished to find that the shouts were coming from the Regent. Two or three men were on the floor and he had another by the throat, slapping his face and shouting what I learned afterward was: "So you would betray your country, would you?" The Regent was alone, but he had the situation in hand. When he had thrown his man down, he began to mumble to himself, brushing off his clothes with his hands; and passed us down the stairs without saying a word. Meanwhile, there was great excitement

among the guards. The Regent's box led out into a
room where they were stationed. They had not heard
the Arrowcross demonstration. All they knew was that
all of a sudden the door of the Regent's box had
opened and he had rushed out like a shot before they
could get to their feet. The whole episode happened so
quickly that they had no idea where he was until he
came back.

A few days later, the Regent asked me to call,
thanked me for having come to his aid and presented
me with his picture. I was a little surprised at his de-
duction, but did not see any reason to contradict him.

The whole incident was typical not only of the
Regent's deep hatred of alien doctrine, but of the kind
of man he is. Although he was around seventy-two
years of age, it did not occur to him to ask for help; he
went right ahead like a skipper with a mutiny on his
hands.

Likewise, he never permitted Hitler to treat him as
the dictator treated the heads of other states. In August
1938, when Hitler, after seizing Austria and bringing
the German army to the Hungarian frontiers, invited
the Regent to become his military ally against the
Czechs, the Admiral replied, according to de Kanya,
who was then chairman of the foreign affairs committee
in the Upper House: "You will get another world war
and you will lose it, because you have no sea power."
Then when Hitler began to scream, the Admiral rose
and asked him not to forget that he, the leader of an
infant state, was speaking to the head of a thousand-
year-old sovereign state; and told him that unless he
was treated as such, he would leave at once. Hitler
calmed down immediately and after that treated the

Regent with respect, although the incident made him hate Horthy intensely and no doubt had a great deal to do with some of the things that happened later.

The Admiral had learned as a youngster in the Naval Academy at Pola to behave with poise and dignity. The statement that Hungary was a kingdom without a king and had as its head an admiral without a navy was often made. While it was true that Hungary never had a navy, Austria-Hungary had one and Admiral Horthy had been its commander in chief until 1918.

The official language of the Naval Academy at that time was German and Horthy, although the scion of a Magyar family, never spoke his mother tongue without a slight Austro-German accent. Like most Hungarians, though, he spoke many languages well enough to carry on a conversation without difficulty.

To call Horthy "Regent" as we and the British understand the term, is not quite correct. A better title would be "Lieutenant of the Realm," although in Hungarian his official title meant "Governor." Hungary, as contrasted with England and nearly every other kingdom, had always put the crown above its wearer: The king really served as regent for the crown in which rested the sublime power carried down through the ages from the time of King Stephen.

Hailing from the eastern slopes of the Ural Mountains, the migrating Magyars, who were of Finno-Ugrian origin, crossed the Carpathians in the winter of 895 to 896 A.D., led by their chieftain, Arpad, who was responsible to a council of their seven tribes.

His great-grandson, Duke Geza, was determined to rule over a Western nation, not a loose federation of eastern tribes. To this end, he educated his son Stephen in the new religion of the West and married him to the Bavarian princess Gizella. Stephen, who succeeded Geza in 997 and ruled until 1038, converted the pagan tribes of Hungary to Christianity. A brilliant warrior and wise legislator, he forced his faith upon his subjects, convinced that only through Christianity could Hungary become a Western power. In the year 1000 he sent an ambassador to Pope Sylvester II, to ask for a crown which would establish the fact that Stephen was not a vassal of the Holy Roman Empire. At that time, only three persons—the Holy Roman Emperor, the Pope and the Emperor at Constantinople—had the right to crown a king in Europe. By applying to the Pope, Stephen kept clear of political entanglements, both in the east and west.

Sylvester sent Stephen a crown and the apostolic cross, to be carried before him on state occasions as a symbol of his new title "Apostolic King." With the coronation of its medieval king, who after his death was sainted, Hungary became the most eastern of the western lands. This is the origin of the "millennial crown" around which the Magyars have built a comprehensive doctrine. Theoretically the king was elected and only became king when he was crowned by the nation. Actually, it was as regent for the crown that the nation bestowed upon him such royal powers as the right to confer nobility upon his subjects. At the same time, the crown set limits to his rights. The territory was not his but the crown's—hence he could not alienate it.

This doctrine was by no means a dead letter. By accepting the crown the king was bound to the constitution. For this reason, Franz Josef underwent the coronation only after completing his unconstitutional experiments. His presumptive successor, the Archduke Franz Ferdinand, was resolved to make changes that would have satisfied the Croats at the expense of the Magyars before accepting the crown.

It was because of this that the Serbian government had him murdered in 1914, fearing lest he destroy their plan of luring the Croats away from Austria-Hungary. The events which followed upon his murder led to the installation of Admiral Horthy as regent of a throneless Hungary.

After the collapse of the Austro-Hungarian armed forces and dissolution of the Hapsburg Empire following the war precipitated by Franz Ferdinand's death, the November 1918 Hungarian revolution established a weak and incompetent government under the leadership of Count Michael Karolyi. Due to internal disorder and pressure exercised on Hungary by her neighbors, this government was unable to maintain itself. In March 1919, the French army of occupation, in contravention to the treaty of armistice, ordered large parts of Hungary to be ceded to Rumania. The resulting desperation of the Hungarian people was exploited by Michael Karolyi, who handed over power to the communist agent, Bela Kun. Just released from prison, the latter organized an outright Bolshevik government on the Russian pattern.

It collapsed after a reign of 133 days of terror. The entire nation had been opposed to it. The peasantry, for instance, had refused to deliver food and all other supplies to the cities. Only by sheer force and terrorism could this government maintain itself, even tempo-

rarily. At the approach of the Rumanian army Bela
Kun and his associates—among them, Mathias Rakossi,
virtual dictator of present-day Hungary—fled from
Budapest to Vienna whence they traveled to Moscow.

Counterrevolutionaries stepped in, as Bela Kun and
his followers fled, and revoked the republic which
Count Karolyi had proclaimed before turning Hungary over to the communists. Hungary became again a
kingdom, but the throne stayed empty. Instead of a
king they chose to have a regent and wanted a man who
would be acceptable to the West. It is little known that
Horthy was chosen regent largely by the grace of Great
Britain. The British method of supporting him was
subtle and circuitous. Admiral Trowbridge, who
headed an Allied mission to Budapest, let it be known
that Horthy would be a good choice. Probably the
British navy had a stronger say in the matter than the
Foreign Office. Horthy had always expressed profound
admiration for the British navy.

Thus Hungary had a crown without a king—had the
benefits of a monarchy without its risks. The illusion
was ideal in a nation with a strong monarchist tradition. To all practical purposes, Hungarians had a
republic; but every so often the Guardians of the
Crown—who as such held the highest positions in
Hungary—met with the prime minister to perform an
ancient ceremony. Each had a key to the crown vault.
When all three keys had been turned, the door was
opened and the crown was examined to make sure that
it was still intact. All this was done under the surveillance of the crown guards, who watched over it twenty-
four hours of the day. The vault was carefully locked
at the end of the ceremony, a guard resumed his posi-

tion from which the crown vault was visible, and the eternal vigil went on.

It can be seen from this that the crown was much more important than the king and that Regent Horthy's position was not as odd as it might be in some other country. He did not have the prerogatives that a crowned king would have had. The government was not responsible to him, but to parliament. Until February, 1935, when the Government Party adopted a new Regency Bill, he could not sanction or refuse to sanction laws; he could only ask for reconsideration. In fact, his position was quite different from that of a regent as we understand it.

Horthy took his oath to the constitution very seriously; he never overstepped his authority. Looking back, there are times when I wish he had been less scrupulous, but his critics cannot have it both ways.

Although the young emperor, King Charles, had made him admiral and commander in chief of the Austro-Hungarian navy, all his devotion belonged to the memory of Franz Josef, whose aide he had been. He was already regent when Charles staged his two unsuccessful attempts to regain the throne. In March 1921, he appeared in Budapest and asked Horthy to yield his power to him. The Admiral persuaded him to return to Switzerland. In October of the same year, Charles came by air and landed near the Austrian border where he was welcomed by a small number of faithful followers, chiefly former army officers; and with them he marched on the capital. The Hungarian war minister, informed of the event, left his office and went for a walk. But Horthy ordered Captain Gombos, whom we shall see again as premier, to meet force with force. The king's detachment was dispersed, he fell into captivity and, as the British had insisted on his removal, it was aboard a small British gunboat that he was taken away down the Danube. Around these two events has been spun a story accusing Horthy of ingratitude, but he could not have given way without exposing his nation to extinction, because the British-backed Little Entente, armed to the teeth and opposed to restoration of the Hapsburgs, would most certainly have invaded and occupied the whole country.

The hapless Charles, as he was depicted to me, must have been an utterly well-intentioned man who in peaceful times would have made an excellent constitutional ruler, but he was not a pilot for dangerous waters. To a man like Horthy or Bethlen, the king's actions appeared irresponsible and amateurish. As far as I could discern, the Regent bore no grudge against Charles or his family and viewed the aspirations of Otto, his son, with the sympathy natural in an old imperial and royal officer.

Faced with grave decisions, Horthy always asked himself and his advisers what would have been Franz Josef's attitude. I know of times when he had refused to do something but changed his mind on being shown that, in similar circumstances, Franz Josef had taken certain action. Franz Josef, once he had abandoned absolutism, ruled but did not govern. With smaller rights, Horthy served as a constitutional figurehead.

As such, was Horthy a good ruler? He was not brilliant, but it is questioned whether constitutional rulers should be brilliant. He had, however, an abundance of common sense, great patriotism, honesty and integrity. No one could truthfully deny that he did his best within the limits of his authority and according to his code.

It was a rule that Admiral Horthy could receive no one without the consent of the Foreign Office. On several occasions his aide came down to ask me to make a request for some American to see the Regent, because it was likewise a rule that the Foreign Office would not permit a citizen of any foreign country to see the Regent without the approval of the citizen's legation. Each time the Regent requested it, I made application, but seldom did the Foreign Office approve. The Regent had to forego seeing a lot of people whom he would have liked to meet, because the Foreign Office objected. They objected because they never knew what he was going to say. Being an old sea dog, he was outspoken. It never occurred to him to dissemble, and he would not have known how. If any correspondent asked him questions, he was liable to give answers which would involve Hungary in all kinds of trouble. On the occasions when permission was given for newspaper men to see the Regent, it was always with the provision that their copy would have to be submitted to the Foreign Office. On two or three occasions, I have seen newspaper or magazine men on their way from the Royal Palace beaming over the most wonderful interview they ever had—sensation after sensation. They could hardly wait to get to the telegraph office. But by the time the Foreign Office had finished, there was nothing left.

It can be seen from this that Horthy had little or nothing to do with the foreign policy of the country—in fact, little to do directly with the government itself. A very prominent Hungarian told me one day that the

Regent complained bitterly that he had a young fellow for whom he was anxious to get a position in one of the government departments, but could do nothing for him. Tibor Eckhardt told me that he went to the Regent because he thought things were happening that Horthy would not approve and should know about. When he informed the Regent of them, Horthy said, "It is much worse than you think—" so they sat down together and had a nice, antigovernment talk; but that is all that ever came of it. I myself have gone to him when I thought his government was doing things that it should not do, and he was always one hundred percent to my way of thinking, even when his foreign minister and prime minister were the ones of whom I complained.

He was greatly disturbed by Premier Imredy's introduction of anti-Jewish legislation in Hungary, and let this be known, but all he could do was to intrigue with a number of members of parliament, as a result of which Imredy, on November 23, 1938, was given a vote of no confidence and had to resign. However, when Teleki and others refused to take over the prime ministry and insisted that he reappoint Imredy, Horthy did so. Meanwhile, Imredy had obtained the support of some Catholic leaders and thus mustered a slight majority. From then on, whatever real power Horthy had was lost. But he did not stop intriguing against Imredy, and when some of Imredy's opponents went to Germany a few months later and brought back proof that his great grandfather had been born a Jew and baptized at the age of seven, the Regent was jubilant. He afterward told me the story with great exuberance, and said, "I wouldn't care if he were a whole Jew, but I pretended to be shocked." Imredy was so astonished, either because he had not known it or did not want it found out, that he fainted during the interview. He at once resigned, and this time Teleki took over.

Horthy and his wife, who would have made a perfect queen, were not to be spared personal tragedy. In August 1942, their oldest son Stephen was killed in an air accident over Russia. Their son-in-law also met his death in an air accident, and it is said, though as far as I know, it was never proved, that the Germans had a hand in it because Stephen Horthy had been elected vice-regent and after he was killed, it was pretty certain that Horthy's son-in-law would take that position. In ordinary times such a succession would not have happened because it smacked of a dynasty, but when Horthy announced that he wanted to retire and nominated his son as deputy regent in February 1942, parliament acquiesced in order to forestall the election of a Nazi, which might have happened under German pressure if the Regent had died without an automatic successor. Both the son and the son-in-law were very fine, capable men. The last time I saw Stephen was when he came to see us off when we returned to America in 1941.

Madame Horthy worried considerably about the future for, even as far back as April 19, 1940, my wife has in her diary:

Mme. Horthy came to see me. Looked very attractive and chic in trotteur with furs. Regretted instability of the times, especially not being able to insure the future of one's children. 'That is really what every man works for in every walk of life. For myself I should not mind and for my husband. I should be willing to live in one room. I could do my own cooking if necessary. But not to leave a solid future for one's children—that is too sad.'

How well she knew that she would not spend her old days in the royal castle! She played the part of the country's first lady with simple dignity. Her friends knew that she was primarily a loving mother and still the modest wife of an Austro-Hungarian naval officer whose dutifulness in service had not been stimulated by material rewards.

The sea, as is well known, creates a kind of solidarity and professional brotherhood among navy men of all nations, vestiges of which are felt even in wartime.

President Roosevelt always had a great interest in the Admiral. It began in the first World War. He told me he had never heard of Horthy until President Wilson sent him on a mission to Rome, when he was assistant secretary of the navy. The object of this mission was to induce the Italians to make more active use of their navy. He said it was his first mission and he was very anxious to make good. He was invited to a meeting of the Italian cabinet where he vigorously exhorted them, as instructed by President Wilson. Thaon de Revel, Italy's bearded and dignified minister of the navy, admitted that the Austro-Hungarian navy was much weaker than his own, but, he said, the enemy had excellent hiding places in the Dalmatian Islands. "Apart from that," he added, "they have a daredevil commander, Admiral Horthy, who will swoop out and attack on the most unexpected occasions. No, we cannot expose our fleet to that risk." When Roosevelt told me this story, he concluded, "That was my first diplomatic defeat, and I owed it to Admiral Horthy."

The President played cleverly on Horthy's leanings by addressing him as from sailor to sailor, and the Admiral was very responsive. In 1940, after Roosevelt's re-election, he asked me to inform the President by cable of his delight. Thinking that this might be made public in America and cause the Regent some embarrassment, I told him it would be rather risky because the Germans might be decoding our messages. He said he did not care if they did: He would like to have me send it; and I did.

Of the bond between men of the sea, Horthy gave me at another time a most enlightening example. The British brought a retired admiral to Budapest to keep the Regent informed and to get information from him. The Germans thereupon sent an admiral of their own who had been in the first war as their liaison officer with Admiral Horthy, then in command of the Austro-Hungarian navy. Horthy was staying in a hunting lodge at Godollo, a rural estate of the Hapsburgs, and when the German arrived invited him there for some shooting. This was in 1940, after the French surrender, when many expected the invasion of the British Isles. The Regent told me that he avoided any mention of the war because he did not want his old acquaintance to think he had invited him for the purpose of pumping him. He knew him as a tight-lipped man and was therefore doubly surprised when after the hunt, the German admiral burst into the following confession: "Admiral, I want you to know that we in the German navy have not changed under the national socialists. The other forces have to a certain extent, but the navy is what she was before. We are grateful to Hitler because he has done a lot for the navy, much of it in agreement with England, but we know that both he and Japan have made a fatal mistake by thinking that the air arm could take the place of the navy. The British navy is still intact and is a wonderful navy. We in the naval staff know that what was true in the last war is no less true this time, namely that sea power will win the war." The Regent added that he had not said anything, but was pleased to have his views confirmed from these quarters. Hitler obviously had not picked the right delegate.

4

THE SIGNIFICANCE OF REVISIONISM
IN HUNGARY

No one could be in Hungary very long without knowing that *"nem, nem, soha"* meant "no, no —never," and that it referred to the boundaries fixed by the Treaty of Trianon. If Japan had defeated us and made Canada and Mexico her satellites and given Texas to the latter and most of New England to the former, and had annexed California and Oregon, something similar to *nem, nem, soha* would probably have appeared in our flower beds, on our mountain slopes and would have burned in our hearts. It is very hard for one not intimately acquainted with the history of Hungary to understand what revision meant to Hungarians, but if we would think of it in terms of our own country, we could better appreciate the fanaticism with which Hungarians clung at the time of my arrival to the idea of some sort of revision of the Treaty of Trianon.

After being deprived by the treaty (June 1920) of two-thirds of her territory and one-half of her population, Hungary still retained 7,500,000 people who were almost homogeneously Magyar. Three and one-quarter million Magyars were allotted to Czechoslovakia, Rumania and Yugoslavia besides populations of other races. Of these three and a quarter million Magyars, about 1,600,000 could have remained with Hungary, being solidly settled along its periphery, without exposing any considerable number of non-Magyars to Hungarian domination. In other words, about one-third of the Magyar race was put under foreign rule and about one-half of this third had to suffer this fate needlessly— one of the errors which might have been avoided had the victors been willing to do anything else than dictate the peace. The Hungarians resented the iniquity imposed upon them all the more as the beneficiaries of the Trianon Peace Treaty (Slovaks, Croats, Transylvanians) had been brothers in arms, fighting the war to the bitter end. The Hungarians were well aware that the various national groups in Hungary had been offered a chance by the victorious Western powers to sit down at the peace conference as victors *if* they discarded loyalty and broke away from the Austro-Hungarian system. They especially resented the undue favors granted to Rumania who had betrayed her alliance with Austria-Hungary; had made a very bad show as an ally of the Western powers; had concluded after its rapid defeat a separate treaty with the Central powers, and in the end obtained more of Hungary's territory than was left to Hungary itself. To the Hungarian revisionist, this was adding insult to injury.

The peace treaties on the whole sanctioned the accomplished facts created by Hungary's neighbors during the period of armistice. Possession, as so often, was nine points of the law. The justification offered by the victors was that only by surgical separation could the declared war aim of national self-determination be achieved. It was assumed that, given a free choice, every ethnic group would want its own sovereign racial state. Where races were indissolubly intermixed, the proper method would have been to leave on both sides of a new frontier an approximately equal number of the heterogeneous nationality, but the victors solved every difficulty in favor of the Czechs, the Rumanians, and the Serbs. They did so even where no difficulty would have arisen in case of a more just decision.

It is a fact, though, that even the worst blunders committed at this time were morally and politically far less dreadful than the ruthless method adopted in the spirit of the Potsdam Conference in 1945, which disposed that populations should be adjusted to territories instead of frontiers being adjusted to the wishes of the populations concerned.

The Hungarians did not feel that the peace of Trianon was the final word of history and their revisionism was encouraged by the Covenant of the League of Nations, Article 19, which ran as follows:

The Assembly may from time to time advise the reconsideration by members of the League of treaties

which have become inapplicable and the consideration of international conditions whose continuance
might endanger the peace of the world.

This article was apparently adopted as a compromise
between the realists at the peace conference and the
idealists, who had wanted to do something more than
facilitate peaceful change. Professor G. M. Gathorne-
Hardy said in a Chatham House discussion that it was
"little more than a harmless concession to the feelings
of the vanquished party (meaning Woodrow Wilson
and Lord Robert Cecil) which softened the bitterness
of defeat by allowing them to voice their opinion as
to the desirability of some provisions for peaceful
change." This was not the view of President Wilson,
who sincerely believed that the League of Nations
would repair unjust decisions. Nor could it be the view
of the vanquished nations to whom Article 19 was presented as a silver lining of otherwise black clouds. The
Hungarians especially received encouragement and
comfort by its presence in the covenant.

On May 6, 1920, M. Millerand, President of the
French Republic, delivered the peace terms to the
Hungarian delegation with a letter according to which

> should an enquiry on the spot perhaps reveal the
> necessity of altering certain parts of the frontier line
> provided for in the Treaty, and should the Bound-
> ary Commissions consider that the provisions of the
> Treaty involve an injustice at any point which it
> would be to the general interest to remove, they may
> submit a report on this matter to the Council of the
> League of Nations. In that case, the Allied and As-
> sociated Powers agree that the Council of the League
> of Nations, if requested to do so by one of the parties

concerned, may, under the same conditions, offer its services to obtain by a friendly settlement the rectification of the original tracing in places where the alteration of the frontier is considered desirable by the Boundary Commissions. The Allied and Associated Powers feel confident that this procedure constitutes an appropriate method for removing any injustice in the tracing of the frontier line which may give rise to well-founded objections.

This letter apparently referred to the possibility of slight corrections, but, even so, nothing came of it. It was not even communicated to the boundary commissions.

Concerning the principle of revision, I think the opinion expressed by the English historian, Professor C. K. Webster, is irrefutable: "No territorial settlement in Europe has ever been permanent for very long. Clearly, then, if war is to be averted, something must be devised to do in the future what war has done in the past." It is apparent that the making of wise and durable peace treaties is absolutely necessary if this is to be accomplished.

Looking back, it is easy to understand that for political reasons no attempt was made by the League of Nations to put Article 19 into effect. We can also understand that those who considered themselves wronged could not look upon the League's failure to give them consideration with equanimity. They felt cheated and tricked. On March 30, 1920, Lord Newton in the British House of Lords said of Hungary:

Their crime is that they fought against us. That is perfectly true. But the Czecho-Slovaks and the Poles and the Yugo-Slavs and all these other people whom we now greet as friends and brothers fought against us too. Hungary really is in the position of a man who has had a paralytic stroke and is being constantly kicked and cuffed by his former associates and dependents.

Hungary never forgot that, when on August 29, 1921, the United States concluded peace, all mention of new frontiers was omitted. That omission was a strong gesture in favor of territorial revision and was so considered by Hungarians. In 1927, Mr. Lloyd George, former British premier and one of the big four at the peace conference, confessed in a letter to Mr. George Foeldiak, a Hungarian banker, that the authors of the peace treaties "never claimed for them such a degree of perfection that they held them to be immutable." Certainly, therefore, revisionism cannot be considered identical with aggressiveness as we have been taught to believe.

The revisionism I found in Hungary was a curious myth rather than a clear program. National disasters are just as conducive to psychological derangements as national triumphs. The main symptom, in both cases, is the growth of legends. In Hungary, people spoke with religious fervor of the restoration of the thousand-year-old realm, quite oblivious of the fact that in King Stephen's time, Hungary did not have the frontier which she lost in 1919. As I became better acquainted, I found that the camp of revisionism was somewhat divided against itself. Some people wanted restitution of the borders of 1914, others claimed all regions inhabited by Magyars, even if it meant the reincorporation of other elements. Others, very modestly, wanted but the inclusion of all Magyar regions directly adjacent to the new frontiers. Almost all the revisionists had two things in common: a desire for a common frontier with Poland and the return of Transylvania to Hungary.

A common frontier with Poland meant the taking over of Ruthenia. Eastern Hungary around the Tisza River area suffered greatly from droughts because all the water conservation projects, etc., were in Ruthenia and Transylvania. When these provinces were taken away, the whole flood protection system was destroyed and great hardship was caused in the eastern part of Hungary. As a result, when I was there this section was more inclined to Nazism than any other.

Hungary also wanted a common frontier with Poland because the Poles and Magyars had much in common and she longed for friendly neighbors. Hungary felt herself completely encircled by enemy countries, with the exception of Austria, which was weak politically and economically. Further, the Polish-Hungarian frontier had always been like the Canadian-American border: there had never been a war between Poland and Hungary, and each had confidence in the good intentions of the other.

Transylvania had played a great part in the turmoil of the first World War. In Transylvania were the largest compact settlements of Magyars which had been "lost" by the Treaty of Trianon. The trouble was that most of them were in territory separated from their fellow-Magyars in Hungary by Rumanian areas. For this reason it was frequently proposed to overcome Hungarian and Rumanian antagonism by compromise which would have established Transylvania as an autonomous state. These proposals came from Hungarians, not Rumanians, and I think they were prompted by the thought that an independent Transylvania would ultimately reunite with Hungary.

Hungary's preoccupation with this special part of the revisionist program was caused by historical precedent. Every Magyar had inherited the subconscious conviction that the Carpathian Mountains were the God-given wall against the East, against barbarism, against Asia, Europe's eternal menace. Even today, in spite of airplanes and atom bombs, people still cling to the idea of maintaining natural frontiers.

As time went on and I gained the confidence of my Magyar friends, I discovered that many responsible Magyars were by no means in favor of a revisionist policy. On the contrary, they considered it a serious handicap, because it had become a national obsession. The sober and intelligent administrators of Hungary's foreign policy knew that the Slovaks, though on very bad terms with their Czech cousins, did not want to return to the Hungarian fold. They also knew that revisionism was a dangerous toy and that Hungary was utterly unprepared for war. They realized that it was even questionable whether all the separated Magyars, if given a choice, would want to rejoin the old country. Most of them were farmers, and agricultural prices were higher in industrialized Czechoslovakia than in Hungary. The Hungarian Foreign Office was not fond of discussing revisionism and was always eager to emphasize that it was identical, in their concept, with peaceful change.

Foreign Minister de Kanya told me quite frankly that he considered revisionism insanity, but that there was nothing he could do about it since the Hungarian

people were not quite sane on that subject and foreign
policy could not be divorced entirely from home politics. He sought to keep it as subdued as possible since
he realized that the League of Nations never had any
idea of giving consideration to Hungarian claims.

To the politicians, revisionism was a godsend, but
more responsible men thought it dangerous. Therefore
the volume of the official clamor depended upon the
character of the prime minister. With General
Gombos, the noise was shrill, with Count Teleki it
was subdued, but it could never be entirely ignored.

Revisionism was the great obstacle to co-operation
with Hungary's neighbors. The Little Entente demanded that Hungary abjure revisionism and accept
the status quo, which was asking for the impossible. I
am certain that there never was a time while I was
there that the Little Entente, by making some slight
territorial concessions to Hungary, could not have
cleared the whole situation.

After World War I, as now after World War II,
newly established frontiers were soon considered
sacred and inviolate. With the same speed, they lost
this quality as soon as the tide turned. Although it took
longer to go from Prague to Ruthenia than it did to
go from Prague to London, and the Czechs had very
little need for Ruthenia, they considered the Hungarian claims to this territory outrageous. But when the
Soviet Union in 1945 claimed the same region, en-
larged by a slice of Slovakia, the sacredness and invio-
lability of the 1919 frontiers vanished. The Czechs,
somewhat shamefacedly, described their yielding as an
example of peaceful change.

After World War I, France, the dominating power

in Europe and the protector of the Little Entente, pursued a shortsighted, vindictive and narrow-minded policy, apparently confused by fear. In the Danubian Basin, her policy was purely militaristic, dominated by the idea that Hungary and Austria, being non-Slavic and therefore perhaps amenable to German allurements, should be kept down by the Little Entente. To be sure, some Frenchmen, for instance Prime Minister André Tardieu, advocated Danubian collaboration and solidarity, but these blessings could never materialize without a foundation of equality. Neither England nor France seemed to realize that to fill the vacuum created by the dissection of old Austria-Hungary and to set up a counterpoise to both Germany and Russia, it was imperative that the little countries, formerly part of Austria-Hungary, should co-operate closely and form a united front.

France seemed to have an unchangeable policy which took nothing into consideration that happened after the Treaty of Trianon. England did not seem to care one way or the other what happened. Neither apparently foresaw the danger to central and southeastern Europe of a defenseless Austria and Hungary, and Hitler later must have wondered at their stupidity.

Hitler would not have been Hitler if he had not used Hungary's territorial grievances for his devilish game. He played one nation against the other. He promised Rumania that her frontiers would be safe and at the same time dangled revision before Hungary's eyes as a reward if she would behave as he wished. Watching the rise of Nazism and realizing its dangers, responsible Hungarians foresaw that after the fall of Austria and Czechoslovakia, it would soon be

Hungary's turn. Admiral Horthy had the backing of his nation when, in August 1938, he rejected Hitler's proposal of a military alliance against the Czechs. However, the Hungarians could not help thinking that if Hitler destroyed Czechoslovakia or Yugoslavia and Rumania, it would be much better for them to get back as much territory as they could rather than let Germany have it, which was the alternative. For example, Kassa, which the Czechs called Kosice, the capital of Prince Rakoczy during his fight for Hungarian independence: Since the Czechs were going to lose it, why should it become German rather than Hungarian? Or Ruthenia, which was so important to Hungarian economy? Hitler had given Hungarians, Foreign Minister de Kanya told me, his solemn word of honor that after the dissolution of Czechoslovakia, Ruthenia and Kassa, with its hinterland, would be given to Hungary. According to Mr. de Kanya, this was not in response to any request, but a voluntary statement made by Hitler. However, when Count Teleki was unwilling to join in Germany's attack on Yugoslavia, in April 1941, Hitler made it know that he would invite Rumania to seize the territory in the Banat which had formerly been a part of Hungary.

At the time of the Munich conference, I happened to be in Washington. Mr. George Creel, the eminent writer, who had charge of the Bureau of Information under President Woodrow Wilson and had been more or less one of his right-hand men, Homer Cummings and William Gibbs McAdoo, Wilson's son-in-law, had dinner with me. We discussed the symptoms that seemed to presage another war. Both Mr. McAdoo and Mr. Creel confirmed the fact that President Wilson had strongly relied upon the League of Nations' ability and willingness to change boundaries. For that reason he had consented to many boundaries that did not seem proper.

For example, Hungary: the French had told Wilson that Hungary was going communist and it was necessary to make the frontiers conform to the ideas of the French general staff in order to protect European civilization. President Wilson was incredulous and sent George Creel to investigate. He spent a week with Count Michael Karolyi, the premier, and observed the latter's feebleness and conditions as they then existed, returning with the correct forecast that the communists would take over within a week. This induced Wilson to agree to the French proposal with the idea of determining the frontiers on a different basis when the communist interlude was over. However, once fixed, they remained fixed.

I have said before that responsible men in the Hungarian Foreign Office regarded revisionism as a serious handicap that diminished their freedom of movement. Not only Hitler but Mussolini played on this instrument. The Duce was, of course, not interested in improving Hungary's lot, but originally Hungary's discontent offered him the possibility of strengthening Italy's bargaining position toward Yugoslavia and France, against whom Italian revisionism was generally directed.

Mussolini took up the Hungarian cause and elaborated on Italian revisionism or expansionism in the Balkans, which involved placing Yugoslavia in a pair of Italian-Hungarian pincers. Later, when the Duce became afraid of Hitler, he supported Hungary, just

as he had assisted Austria, in order to buttress her resistance against German pressure. He competed with Hitler and posed as a greater champion of Hungarian revisionism than the Hungarians themselves. Men like Foreign Minister de Kanya and Baron Gabriel Apor, undersecretary of state, one of the best informed and cleverest of European diplomats, watched it with disquiet, as it is always risky to be on the thin edge of a wedge.

Sometimes Italy's ardor became embarrassing, as when Dino Alfieri, Mussolini's minister for public enlightenment, made a violent and unexpected revisionist speech at the opening of an Italian art exhibition in Budapest, to which the diplomatic corps had been invited. Basil Grigorcea, the Rumanian minister, attended out of politeness, being dean of the diplomatic corps. Don Ascanio Colonna, the Italian minister, and his staff were very much embarrassed. Baron Apor—and this was very characteristic of his kind of diplomacy—told me afterward that Prince Colonna should have warned Grigorcea in advance, just as he himself had done as minister to Vienna, when he kept the Rumanian envoy away from a revisionistic address delivered by a Hungarian politician. The probabilities are, though, that the Italian minister and his staff were just as much surprised as the Rumanian minister.

When Italy grew too interested in Hungarian revisionism, responsible Magyars, as I have said, felt uneasy. When Germany talked revision, they became thoroughly alarmed. On such an occasion, in May 1938, Mr. de Kanya said to me that any territorial gain obtained by agreement with Germany alone would be a mistake. To accept favors from any govern-

ment over the protests of other governments would make Hungary, he said, a partner of the former. Previously, in December 1936, Baron Apor had told me that Hungary would be very nervous if Germany began to back her revisionism because "it would indicate that Germany was getting too friendly for comfort." These two conversations occurred, as can be seen, before the war, when Hungarians were still hoping that they could avoid strangling entanglements.

Part Two

An Oasis in Hitler's Desert

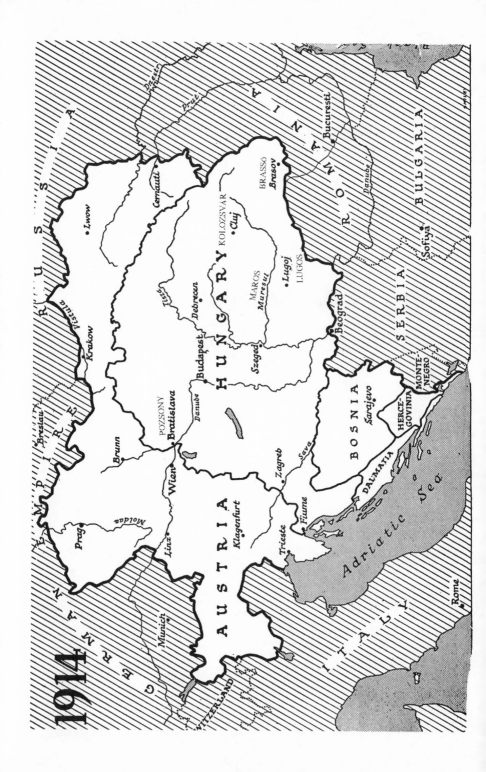

1

THE MURDERS OF DOLLFUSS
AND KING ALEXANDER

I T WAS not long after my arrival in Budapest that
the first glare of lightning broke from the clouds
which had gathered around Hungary when Adolf
Hitler had seized the helm in Germany. On July 25,
1934, Engelbert Dollfuss, the federal chancellor of
Austria, was assassinated, and the tremor emanating
from that political earthquake was felt distinctly in the
Hungarian capital, where everybody realized what it
would mean if the German army appeared on the
Hungarian frontiers.

There had already been considerable alarm, in
February 1934, when the Dollfuss government fought
its street battles with the party militia of the social
democrats. For a while no one seemed to know just
what was happening. For that reason I went to Vienna,
but I had a hard time finding the scene of action, as it
was out in the suburbs. It was quite interesting later
to read dispatches in the American papers describing
the fighting in "downtown Vienna" and attributing
it to anti-Semitism—dispatches which resulted in an
Austrian trade delegation which was about to land in
New York having to be landed in New Jersey. Actually, these reports were made out of whole cloth. There
was no anti-Semitism connected with the affair, and the
material damage was insignificant. Later I read an
article in *Collier's Weekly* which pictured Prince Star-

hemberg, leader of the Heimwehren, as standing in the ruins of an apartment house which he had just leveled with his artillery.

The facts were that the previous socialist regime had built apartment houses at strategic positions covering every bridge across the Danube. These apartment houses were well stocked with guns and ammunition. Therefore, when the revolution—for that is what it was—started in the suburbs, the police reinforcements attempting to cross the bridges were shot down. Prince Schoenburg-Hartenstein, Dollfuss' minister of war, took charge. He ordered the fuses removed from the shells and, using only the smallest caliber at his disposal, opened up with the artillery. Since the revolutionists believed it to be a real bombardment, they surrendered almost at once. I did not see any apartment house that was damaged to such an extent that the tenants could not return to their homes.

Dollfuss was a striking personality, carrying in a dwarfish body a giant's energy. He has been accused of being responsible for the episode of February 1934, because in March 1933, he had suspended parliament and had taken democracy into "protective custody." He did this, apparently, to avoid Nazi-Germany's "legal" conquest of Austria, through interference by blackmail, intimidation and bribery in her elections. Even among those who approved of Dollfuss' decision, some asserted that the suspension of parliament would have been excusable only if he, as leader of the Catholic Party, had chosen as his partners in government the social democrats instead of the Heimwehren, who were supported by Italy. This was a strong argument; but those who could look at that complex situation from every angle remember that the social democrats themselves were far from being angelic. Their armed party guard was dependent on Czech funds and military supplies. They had available a man born to be a leader, the genuine statesman Dr. Karl Renner—at this writing president of the re-established republic. But after the short period from 1918 to 1920 when he acted as chancellor, he had been permanently pushed against the wall by radicals like Otto Bauer and Julius Deutsch. These two never ceased flirting with the Soviets, with the idea of ruling the country from outside parliament by strong-arm methods. It would have been difficult for Dollfuss to find a common platform with people of this kind. As a matter of fact, the events of February 1934 showed that these men were completely discredited by their own followers. The workers simply disregarded their order to stage a general strike. Deserted by the left wing socialists, among whom Bauer and Deutsch fled to Czechoslovakia, the party guard could not be a match for the regular forces.

Hitler's forecast that, because of these February events the Austrian workers would join the National Socialist Party was a mistake; but one of the results was that the socialist workers watched as neutral onlookers the ensuing struggle between Dollfuss and the national socialists. This aggravated considerably the hard task of the Austrian police and facilitated the conspiracy that resulted in the cruel death of Dollfuss on that July day in 1934. Hungarians held their breath as they watched the dramatic development which followed. Hitler was just about to order his troops into Austria, under pretext of having to quell a civil war, when Mussolini ordered a troop concentration on the

Brenner Pass and declared that he would not tolerate any infringement of Austria's independence. At that moment, certainly, no one enjoyed greater popularity in Hungary than the Italian *capo del governo*.

There was also another event which captured Hungarian attention. In some Austrian provinces, national socialist storm troopers, equipped and trained by Germany, attempted an armed upheaval upon learning of Dollfuss' death. The Austrian army, although very weak as a result of the peace treaty of 1919, found it easy to subdue them in a few days. One strong group, however, succeeded in retreating to the Yugoslav frontier. The storm troopers entrenched themselves so close to the border that Austrian bullets would have fallen on Yugoslav territory, if the army had kept on firing. Across the frontier, Yugoslav army detachments held a solid watch and by doing so protected the national socialists. Finally the Yugoslavs declared their willingness to accept the storm troopers as guests and to send them by ship to Germany. The Brown Shirts were feted in Yugoslavia as if they were friends and visitors. In Budapest this was interpreted as a gesture which meant that Yugoslavia, threatened by Italian revisionism, was prepared to throw in her lot with Hitler. Mussolini's bold action in defiance of Hitler had thoroughly alarmed the Yugoslavs and this episode, I think, is worth remembering.

In November 1934, King Alexander, the royal dictator of Yugoslavia, together with M. Barthou, foreign minister of France, was assassinated at Marseille by Croatian terrorists. On November 22nd, Yugoslavia, Czechoslovakia and Rumania charged Hungary with complicity in that crime in notes to the League of Nations. They spoke of a "crime perpetrated by members of a terrorist gang settled in Hungary" and of the "responsibility of the Hungarian authorities for the aid and support granted to Yugoslav subjects." "Professional criminals," they alleged, "were trained in the territory of a foreign state."

A Yugoslav memorandum on November 28th pointed to the existence of camps of Yugoslav emigrants in Hungary, particularly at Yanka Puszta, where it was charged that the Croatian terrorists who assassinated King Alexander had been trained. The memorandum charged the Hungarian government with "criminal negligence" and practically accused the government of having inspired terrorist activities against Yugoslavia, and specifically with having trained the assassin of Alexander. Two days later, a Hungarian note to the League requested that the Council of the League of Nations deal without delay with Yugoslavia's accusations, calling them fantastic.

Great Britain was represented in Belgrade by Neville Henderson, afterward her last ambassador to national socialist Germany. In Yugoslavia he was just as fond of dictatorship as he later proved to be in Berlin. The Croats always maintained that he had encouraged King Alexander to set up a dictatorship instead of granting autonomy to Croatia, which had been promised her by the Serbs during the first World War. Mr. Henderson had reported to his government that Belgrade was much disturbed by the existence of the farm near the frontier in Yanka Puszta which was owned by a Croatian exile and used as a shelter for Croats who were hostile to the regime. Sir Patrick Ramsay, the gifted and colorful minister of His Britannic Majesty to Budapest, on reading copies of Henderson's dispatches, decided to investigate. He discovered nothing suspicious. In order to get Mr. de Kanya's reaction, I asked if he would have any objection to my sending someone down to Yanka Puszta. I thought he would try to keep me from doing so, but he said at once that he was perfectly willing. The Hungarian police, he added, kept an eye on the farm and had reported that the Croatian owner had received visitors there, but none of them had stayed with him and there was not the slightest sign of terrorist preparations.

Premier Gombos chose Dr. Tibor Eckhardt, a member of parliament and leader of the Smallholders Party, to defend Hungary at Geneva. I know Dr. Eckhardt very well and have always found him a competent authority on foreign and domestic affairs. He is interesting and thought provoking because he has the rare gift of seeing things realistically and of shedding light on them from the most unexpected angles.

While Mr. de Kanya and Dr. Eckhardt were in Geneva, the Foreign Office was taken over by the undersecretary for foreign affairs, Mr. de Hory, who proved to be the Hungarian version of Mr. Caspar Milquetoast. We were having a concert at the legation when the Greek minister came in and said there was a rumor that the Yugoslav authorities had put a lot of Hungarian men, women and children on a train and dumped them over the border. This was very interesting. I at once tried to check on it, but could not get in touch with anybody who would confirm it, or who seemed to know anything about it. The Foreign Office worked until late into the night and I saw several people there, but they knew nothing of it, so it seemed to be just a rumor. The next day was St. Nicholas Day, the Regent's name day, and the Foreign Office was closed. Although we tried all day long, since there were many rumors, we couldn't find any official who seemed to know anything about it. That night I attended the gala opera performance and ran into Mr. de Hory. He denied emphatically that Hungarians were being dumped into Hungary from Yugoslavia. The situation was puzzling. If the Yugoslavs *were* conducting a mass deportation of Hungarians, it certainly would not help them in the League of Nations trial. Therefore, it seemed certain that the Hungarian authorities would not deny it, but would rather proclaim it. I discussed the matter with my secretaries and we came to the conclusion that it must be a hoax.

In the meantime, a lot of wild stories were being sent to America. One correspondent in Vienna, whose point of view was his favorite café there, gave a very realistic description of Yugoslav troops invading Hungary. He described the death's-head on their uniforms and told all the "details." This story occupied the first column of the front page of the New York *Times*. Naturally the State Department was much exercised and telegraphed for information.

Actually, as I found out later, there were a thousand or more deportees, men, women and children. Their expulsion during the crisis was a result of internal strife brewing in Yugoslavia. The militarist group tried to exploit the death of the king for its factional purposes. Prime Minister Jeftic was following a moderate course of policy, but was fiercely opposed by General Zifkovic, who besides being the commander of the Royal Guards was also chief of the Serb secret military organization which in many instances imposed its will on Yugoslav policies.

Together with his militarist clique, General Zifkovic hoped that by provoking border incidents and eventual military clashes with Hungary, he would be able to increase the political influence of the militarists, eventually oust Jeftic and become himself prime minister and possibly dictator of Yugoslavia. The mass expulsion of Hungarians by Chetniks (irregular Serbian troops) of whom some forty thousand were mobilized at the orders of Zifkovic in the vicinity of the Hungarian border, was aimed at provoking incidents which might upset Jeftic's more moderate policy.

The Hungarian government forestalled this new danger by withdrawing all its frontier guards and troops about ten miles deep into Hungary, leaving the borderline completely unprotected rather than risk frontier clashes which might have set the spark to the keg of powder. Dr. Eckhardt informed Mr. Eden verbally of these portentous happenings. Mr. Eden took a serious view of the question, and fortunately, having been a schoolmate of Prince Paul of Yugoslavia at Eton, could make use of his private contact with him to advise moderation and avoidance of violence.

The entire Marseille case gradually developed into a dangerous game of power politics where the minor powers were simply used as pawns by the great powers. Dr. Eckhardt told me that when Mr. Laval arrived in Geneva, he presented himself, not having met him previously. Mr. Laval at first assured him that he felt no animosity toward Hungary, and then said: "I have not read your paper on the Marseille case; nevertheless, I can assure you that France will remain true to her alliances."

This simply meant that whatever the merits of the case might be, Mr. Laval would give full support to the Little Entente.

In 1934, the relations between Hungary and the Little Entente were tense. Yugoslavia appeared to be the weakest link of the chain, with King Alexander unable to reconcile the Croats and the equally suppressed political parties of Serbia. If anyone had told me that Hungarians were conspiring with the Yugoslav opposition in order to break out one of the fangs of the Little Entente, I should not have put it beyond them. The temptation *was* great. However, everybody, including the Yugoslav government, knew that the murder of King Alexander and French Foreign Minister Barthou was carried out by the "Ustashi" organization of the Croat leader Pavelich (later the Croat quisling), under the auspices of Mussolini.

Tibor Eckhardt told me afterward that the Yugoslavs had produced photographs at Geneva to "prove" Hungary's guilt. Among them was a picture which purported to show Croatian terrorists training with hand grenades at Yanka Puszta. This farm actually lay in a vast plain, but Eckhardt discovered in the background of the photograph the range of the Alps as they appear to those who look at them from northern Italy. Yugoslavia was showing the world that while the big powers were calling the tune, she knew, and thus slyly acknowledged, the facts.

The background of the Marseille case was most revealing of the state of European affairs and the "wisdom" with which they were conducted at a time when Hitler had already risen to power and had started his clandestine rearmament. Mr. Laval had made up his mind that he would come to terms with Mussolini— which in itself was not a bad idea; if his plan had worked, he might have prevented the formation of the Axis. But, in order to win Mussolini's favor and to avoid antagonizing him, the accusations in the Marseille murder case could not be directed against the real culprits, Mussolini and Pavelich. Italy had to be left out of the case completely, and Hungary, where nobody was implicated and where only small irregularities had been committed in connection with issuance of passports and control of Croat refugees, was slated for the role of the defendant instead of Mussolini.

The League of Nations was at its best in baring the explosive affair. The Council chose Mr. Anthony Eden as its *rapporteur*. M. Jeftic made his accusations: Hungary had not collaborated in the investigation after having recognized the presence of terrorists within her boundaries. Eckhardt, who in his defense of Hungary showed his mettle as a skilled diplomat, stated that Hungary's treatment of those Yugoslav exiles had not gone beyond the legitimate toleration due political refugees as long as their conduct did not surpass legal limits. He had already called the Yugoslav memorandum a calculated misrepresentation, and proved that the murderer of King Alexander had never been in Hungary. But this exchange was followed on December 10, 1934, by a resolution of the Council of the League: "Certain Hungarian authorities, at least by neglect, have assumed responsibilities and Hungary is expected to carry out an inquiry and to report to the Council in proper time the penalties imposed on guilty officials."

This did not mean very much. Belgrade had the day before contributed to a peaceful solution by revoking the expulsion of Hungarians, three thousand of whom had been put over the border by this time and were in a desolate condition. Five months later, in May 1935, Mr. Eden reported to the Council of the League of Nations that Yugoslavia had agreed to regard the question as closed and in the meantime, all of the Hungarians deported from Yugoslavia had been permitted to return.

In Appendix IV to this book, I am publishing an excerpt of a file, the possession of which I owe to an Italian whom I met in Belgrade and with whom I afterward became very intimate. So far as I know, he is no longer among the living. After Alexander's death he told me that he had been carrying messages between Alexander and Mussolini. He said that he had put everything down in writing and he would be glad to show it to me. Later in the day he brought it over.

He explained that his father had been a great friend of King, then Prince, Alexander's tutor and that he himself had become friendly with Alexander and the friendship had continued. Once, before making one of his business trips to Belgrade, he had been invited to Rome to see Mussolini, who apparently knew all about him and who asked him to probe into King Alexander's feelings toward Italy. After that, he had acted as a frequent and regular go-between, in most cases with the knowledge of the Italian minister to Belgrade.

The documents show King Alexander extremely

keen on concluding an over-all agreement with Italy and they show Mussolini extremely reluctant. It is possible that the Duce did not want to make promises which would have hampered his expansionist designs in the Balkans, but since he was not a scrupulous observer of pledges, I am rather inclined to think that he hoped for the Yugoslavs' early disintegration and did not want to strengthen the regime of a man who must have appeared to him as endowed with unusual energy and skill. Probably the fact that Alexander was so insistent gave additional force to Mussolini's expectation that Yugoslavia's days were numbered.

Judging from these documents Alexander was much cleverer than Mussolini. If the latter did connive in the assassination of Alexander, it would seem to have been one of the most stupid moves possible. Mussolini's Albanian policy and his Greek adventure revealed that it was his aim to make Italy the paramount power in the Balkans. It would be interesting to find out when he began to be more afraid of Germany in the Balkans than of France. It seems to be established that he defied Hitler when attacking the Greeks. I do not think he was farsighted enough to visualize a Yugoslav-Bulgarian bloc ruled by Soviet agents, rendering the Balkans a real threat to Italy's vital interest. It is certain, however, that Italian predominance in the Balkans today would be better for Britain—and for the world—than Russian domination.

The fact that Yugoslavia survived Alexander's death apparently made the Duce a little more amenable. Also, he wanted to organize resistance to Hitler's Austrian plans by the co-operation of his country with England and France, and this necessitated the improvement of his relations with Yugoslavia. Not before March 1937 did Count Ciano sign a nonaggression and friendship pact at Belgrade, but as early as March 1935, Count Viola de Campo Alto, the Italian minister to the Yugoslav capital, made a friendly speech and went so far as to emphasize Italy's sympathy for Yugoslavia's territorial integrity. This was a heavy blow to Hungarian revisionists. Mussolini exerted a twofold pressure upon Yugoslavia: On the one hand, he could fan the fires of separatist ambitions—for since the Serbian race represented only 34 percent of the population there was constant agitation on the part of the other nationalities represented in the remaining 66 percent, particularly Croatia, for independence. On the other hand, he could put pressure upon Yugoslavia by favoring Hungary's claim on territories handed over to Yugoslavia by the Treaty of Trianon. Had the Italian minister spoken of Yugoslav "unity," the revisionists would have felt better: for then it could have been inferred that Mussolini was relying upon revision rather than separatism for pressure upon Yugoslavia.

2

THE TRUE MEANING OF THE
ROME-BERLIN AXIS PACT

IT IS said that Mussolini wished Italy to stay neutral in the second World War. This may be true because neutrality would have served her well. Why, after the breakdown of the French army, which he had certainly not expected, Mussolini hastened to enter the war is not yet sufficiently clarified. Most people think that he considered Hitler's triumph final and wanted to secure his share of the great redistribution of the world. Others think he could no longer dare to resist the orders of Hitler, who had wanted Italy's military collaboration from the beginning. This view seems to be refuted by reports according to which Hitler considered Italy a liability rather than an asset and, therefore, wanted her to remain neutral. It is probable that Hitler did not trust Mussolini and that, victory seemingly assured, he did not leave Italy a free choice. In short, I believe that Hitler would have tolerated neutrality on the part of Italy only under a material guarantee which would not have been to Mussolini's liking, as, for example, German control of her naval ports. If this is correct, the Duce was no longer a free agent when he decided to enter the war.

For Hungary, it was a portentous event. After Hitler had seized power, what had been left of Hungary's freedom had hinged on the fact that two powers, Germany and Italy, wanted to influence her decisions. Now the two merged into one. Italy, as Germany's military ally and entirely dependent on German supplies, could no longer proffer even the little backing against German demands which she had given Hungary in the past. June 10, 1940 was a black day for Budapest. When I saw Mr. de Kanya, no longer foreign minister but still a power in Hungary, he took comfort in the thought that Hitler would now give more heed to the wishes of Mussolini. This did not sound convincing and I don't think de Kanya believed it himself, but he needed some comfort. In this same conversation, de Kanya with some bitterness accused Britain of having given encouraging pledges to Poland and Rumania without being prepared to come to their assistance.

He wondered if America would be drawn in, and I told him we would. It was hard for him to believe this, or that if we were, we would join in time to influence the final decision. At this moment, the prestige of the so-called democracies was at a low ebb. The French catastrophe and the evacuation of Dunkirk were disheartening. From a Hungarian point of view, Mr. de Kanya could see nothing but disaster. He felt, quite rightly, that whosoever won, Hungary would lose. His position vis-à-vis the English and French can be exemplified by what he had previously told me, that he thought very highly of the Germans and Austrians because he had lived with them most of his life and he had found them good, hardworking, decent people. He had not had a great deal to do with the English, but enough to see that they were a lazy people with a superiority complex, and he did not particularly like them. However, he said he would not mind living under British hegemony, but he would rather be dead than to live under German. The British would allow one to live one's own life, whereas the Germans would regulate every minute detail.

The man who coined the phrase "Rome-Berlin Axis" was in his grave when the Axis became a military reality. General Gombos had died in October, 1936. His death seemed to cause no regret. In fact, it seemed that every competent person from the Regent down was very much relieved. He had been prime minister when I arrived and for about three years thereafter. He was a professional soldier, but that did not prevent him from being a very keen politician. As a professional soldier, he was deeply impressed by the rebirth of the German army and air force, while as a politician, the man who had captured his imagination and admiration was Benito Mussolini.

De Kanya, backed by the Regent, was supreme in foreign affairs, but this did not handicap Gombos when he spoke, and de Kanya was often obliged to mend the china smashed by the premier's irresponsible utterances. De Kanya was often annoyed at Gombos' indiscretions, as were his colleagues in the Foreign Office. I remember Apor, one day when I mentioned something Gombos had said, breaking out with the statement: "That man is the biggest ass that ever lived!" I laughed heartily, and he looked surprised. He said, "But he is!" De Kanya never used this exact expression, but he said repeatedly that nothing Gombos said about foreign affairs was of any interest because it meant nothing.

In military affairs Gombos seemed to have more to say and he recommended for promotion to the general staff young officers who seemed to share his respect for the German army. This had serious consequences. Admiral Horthy, owing to his own tradition of an imperial and royal officer, stood above politics and did not interfere. By his acquiescence, the general staff was packed with Gombos' confidants who undermined the Regent's own policy of resistance to German demands.

There is little doubt that Gombos sabotaged Mussolini's efforts to develop a solid Italian-Austrian-Hungarian bloc, but history has proved him right because

Italy was not strong enough to keep up her opposition to Hitler's expansion. If Hungary had become involved with Austria, Germany would have crushed her long before 1944. After all, Czechoslovakia, the only country in the Danubian Basin able to boast of a strong military organization, did not lift a finger to prevent the disappearance of Austria in March 1938.

Hitler's generals must have been afraid of a Czech move, otherwise Goering would not have concentrated upon giving solemn assurances to Dr. Benes during the invasion of Austria. If Prague trembled, how could Hungary, entirely defenseless, act as Italy's vanguard?

On March 17, 1934, when Mussolini, Dollfuss and Gombos gathered in Rome to sign a Three Power Pact, providing for consultation and preferential trade agreements, everybody scented a far-reaching secret agreement. This became the occasion of a diplomatic stroke of luck. The Department of State was on tenterhooks because much depended on how far Mussolini would go in resisting Hitler. Thinking over the situation, I concluded that the Germans would be the ones most apt to have information as to what had happened at Rome, since they were the most interested party. The German minister at that time was Hans von Mackensen, a son of the great soldier who died in 1945. He was married to a young lady who was the daughter of Constantin von Neurath, and we knew them fairly well. He was very much more a soldier than a diplomat, and I didn't think that I would get much out of him. When I arrived at the legation, I was shown into the waiting room and had the feeling that someone had been spirited away with some haste. After a few minutes, he received me and answered my straight question directly. "The Rome Agreement doesn't mean anything; Gombos and de Kanya have just been here and in fact, were here when you arrived; they told me there was a secret reservation to the Rome Protocol to the effect that Hungary would not be a party to any, even defensive, alliance."

That seemed like interesting news, so I telegraphed it to the Department. Later in the day I received a telegram from the Department asking me to go to the Foreign Office to see if I could get this confirmed. I called upon Baron Apor, then head of the political section, and had quite a session with him. I didn't want to say that von Mackensen had told me anything, so I didn't mention his name, but I did tell him that I understood there had been some secret agreement. Baron Apor at once said there had been no secret agreement of any kind. For a minute I didn't know what to do. I felt sure there had been an agreement and that von Mackensen had told me the truth; but on the other hand, I didn't think that Apor would lie about it. I kept insisting that there must be something of the kind, but Apor continued to assure me that there was not. Finally I had a happy thought and asked, "Well, what did you agree?" He said again, "Only to consult." I said, "So you agreed to consult. Did you tell them that even if you consulted, you would not do anything?" He said, "Well, yes." Of course, this meant that the consultation amounted to nothing, since all parties knew that it meant nothing. I wired this to the Department. Later I heard that Rome and Vienna had insisted to the contrary, but three months afterward, the information Apor had given me was admitted to be true. Neither Apor nor de Kanya ever gave me any false information, as far as I know. But they were very adroit in not saying what they did not want to say.

Being prodded by the Duce to buttress Austria's resistance to German pressure, the Hungarians saw clearly the deep-seated antagonism between Mussolini and Hitler. Hence, they realized the folly of the British policy in connection with Ethiopia. They did not like Mussolini's African ventures. De Kanya said several times that Mussolini was very foolish, but the Hungarians felt that halfway measures would not accomplish anything except to force Mussolini and Hitler together.

Hungary and Austria incurred Mr. Eden's displeasure by refusing to join in the sanctions imposed on Italy in 1935, but it is an open secret that other states which pledged their co-operation kept on trading with Italy as before, surreptitiously. Mr. Eden seemed to care little for what was done privately as long as you followed his bidding publicly. The same lack of consistency prevailed during the whole Hitler period when small nations were permanently exhorted to display more pluck than the big powers could themselves muster.

Hungary did conclude a military understanding with Italy which, under certain circumstances, provided for military support by Italy in case of attack. Presumably this was in connection with the Little Entente, since the Treaty of Trianon left Hungary more or less unarmed. This plan provided that if Hungary were attacked, her army would retreat to a designated spot near Klagenfurth in the Austrian Carinthia. Here they would meet the Italians, who would come over the mountains with guns and enough military strength to protect the Hungarian army while it was in training. It was in effect a military alliance which at the time seemed impressive.

Its most interesting aspect was the apparent fear of German-Yugoslav collaboration, a fear which was by no means unfounded. Mr. Milan Stoyadinovitch, the prime minister under Prince Paul's regency, though loudly professing his loyalty to his Czech and Rumanian allies, was distinctly pro-German and a great friend of Goering, whom he pleased very much by treating Fraulein Sonnemann, with whom Goering traveled, as though she had already become his wife. This was something Regent Horthy refused to do, much to the annoyance of Mr. Goering, who, after that, was always very friendly with the Yugoslavs and correspondingly unfriendly with Hungarians.

The Serbs, afraid of Italian support for the Croats, found it advisable to play ball with the Germans after the latter had occupied Austria and become Yugoslavia's neighbor. Stoyadinovitch was not misled by Czech assurances as he knew too well the weakness of the artificial state and could not have been surprised at Czechoslovakia's swift surrender. Hostility to Hungary had always been the sole tie of the Little Entente, but now that Germany had become a restless giant, Hungary's position as number one enemy had changed.

During the sanctions against Italy (1935), a curious situation developed within the diplomatic corps in Budapest. The Italians did not want to meet the British, French or anyone else who was backing the sanctions, but they did not want to say this in so many words, In fact, the Italian legation in Budapest did not know quite what to do and, therefore, did nothing for fear of party watchdogs. Entertaining became very complicated. The diplomatic corps did not want to slight the Italians and made it a point to continue inviting them. Invariably the Italians did not answer their invitations. They did not like to refuse and they did not like to accept. The German diplomats were either much less timid or had better instructions. As far as I know, they went where they were invited, and this included many places where their host would have been much better pleased if they had declined. I think their attitude in this respect was correct. I feel that a diplomat's duty is to get information. He cannot do his full job if he avoids going out because of fear of embarrassing encounters. Naturally, after war is declared, the situation is entirely different, but up to that moment, it is the diplomat's duty to keep on the job. I never could understand calling home ministers and ambassadors because the country to which they were accredited had fallen into disfavor. It seems to me that that is the very time when we should have as much representation as we can get. Calling home the chief of a mission under such circumstances would seem to do most harm to the home nation.

Eden's sanctions brought Mussolini and Hitler together as the Hungarians had foreseen, and accomplished nothing otherwise. From where I sat, the sanctions seemed intended only as an idle gesture—and a very costly one. The situation that developed took away what liberty of action Hungary had possessed. She could no longer balance between the two powers, because Italy, instead of urging her to keep away from Germany, began to urge her to do what Germany wanted. From the signing of the Axis Pact in October 1936, Mussolini seemed to have lost interest both in Hungary and in Austria.

Early in 1937, Great Britain tried to repair some of the damage done by Mr. Eden. The result was the British-Italian agreement called the Mediterranean Pact. But things had gone too far. Italy between England and Germany was in exactly the same position in which Hungary had been between Italy and Germany. Mussolini was afraid of annoying Hitler by going too much toward Britain and at the same time afraid of being misused and deserted by the British; just as Gombos had been afraid of enraging Hitler by going with Italy and then being sold down the river by Italy. (This sentence ought to be read twice because it is the key to an understanding of that period. It also sheds light on the present. By appeasing the mightiest tyrant, we spread fear everywhere.)

Concerning Italy's military power, the Hungarians had no illusions. In May 1937, the Regent made an official visit to Italy; on his return he told me that the Italian fleet was antiquated and consisted partly of ships he had commanded in the first World War.

The return call of Italy's little king and his tall wife is in my memory like a grand theatrical event. The Hungarians as host were at their best. Some five hundred or more people attended the dinner in the grand ballroom of Franz Josef's palace under a ceiling of heavy silver, and a larger number attended the dance given the following night in the same room. Strict formality was observed at both events. The Hungarians wore their traditional uniforms to the dance, so it was extremely colorful.

After dinner, the party left the ballroom and went up into the old palace which looked out on the Danube and Pest. Budapest had a very fine system of illuminating public buildings and bridges. As we looked out, we saw not only the city as it normally was, but all of the illumination, even up on the hills. It was extraordinary. The old palace itself was lit by candles, thousands of them in a long row of rooms, possibly a dozen, opening one on the other so that it made a long vista.

When we were finally seated, the men were taken up and introduced to the king and the women to the queen. Apparently there had been much pressure put on the king by Italians living in Budapest—and there were quite a few—to give them some sort of decoration, because when I talked to him, the first thing he asked me was whether we had a large American colony. I told him no. He said, "Well, you are very lucky. We have a large Italian colony here and they are driving me crazy!" When he talked his mustache bobbed up and down and it was all I could do to keep from laughing. But he seemed to be a very nice man; we would call him democratic, since he put on no airs. I did not suspect at that moment that he would be capable of the heroism he showed in 1943. German troops had surrounded his house when he took Italy out of the war, and his courage should command our respect.

During the Eucharistic Congress held some time later in Budapest, I had the privilege of making the acquaintance of His Holiness Pope Pius XII, when, as Cardinal Secretary of State Eugenio Pacelli, he attended the Eucharistic Congress as the representative of the Pope. Foreign Minister de Kanya gave Cardinal Pacelli a luncheon and it so happened that I found

myself seated next to him. I do not remember ever
having received such a tremendous impression of anyone. When I came home, I said to my wife: "Today I
met a really great man."

I had two or three conversations with him during
his stay in Budapest and each time had the same reaction. I am, by nature and upbringing, not given to
a feeling of awe in the presence of high priests, but seeing and hearing this man, whose features and bearing
were more truly aristocratic than those of any noble-
man I had encountered, I felt instinctively that in
him there was burning a fire which did not devour,
but purified.

When Italy, having given two years' notice, withdrew from the League of Nations in December 1937,
Washington thought that Hungary, the "satellite,"
would follow suit. Despite the Axis, which was no
longer called Rome-Berlin, but Berlin-Rome, the Hungarians did not think of following Italy out of the
League. Afterward the Regent quoted to me the old
fable of the two frogs in the milk pail, one of whom
was drowned in despair whereas the other bustled
until the milk turned into butter. The British way of
life had always fascinated the higher strata of Hungarian society. There, England was the most popular
nation, whereas Germany was considered with a mix-
ture of respect and fear which is not conducive to love.
Among the lower classes, the most popular country
was the United States. There were then, and are now,
a large number of Hungarians in this country—about
one million—most of whom have relatives in Hungary
with whom they correspond.

Hungary remained in the League of Nations not

only because she had economic ties with the League which would have made it inconvenient for her to follow Italy, but also because she felt that it might displease England. The Anglo-Italian agreement of April 16, 1938, after Anthony Eden's resignation, was very pleasing to the Hungarians. Mussolini cabled to Neville Chamberlain that "to have settled in so frank and full a fashion questions outstanding between us places the relations between England and Italy on a solid and durable basis." How the Hungarians would have liked to believe it! Baron Apor, not usually given to undue optimism, expressed the view that the Axis was no longer what it had been, that Mussolini, like all Italians, was furious because of Hitler's entry into Austria and that the British-Italian agreement might prove stronger than the Axis pact. It has been said that Mussolini, in concluding the Axis pact, abandoned Austria. In spite of what later happened, I think this is not correct. All I know, and I think it will be borne out by documents, is that, on the contrary, the basis of the Axis pact was an understanding between Hitler and Mussolini not to change the status quo of Austria. Hence, by invading Austria, Hitler violated the pledge he had given the Duce, although before carrying out the invasion, he had forced Mussolini to agree to it.

AUSTRIA: PIVOT OF EUROPEAN STABILITY

E XPANSION OF Germany in central Europe was the main threat to the balance of power in Europe and thus to European peace. In this respect Austria's independence was the pivot: As long as it was maintained Germany could not expand in central Europe and in the Balkans; on the other hand, if Hitler were master of Vienna the road to Constantinople would be thrown open. This is the reason why the independence of Austria became the number one question for the Allied powers the minute Hitler rose to power.

The basis of the Axis pact of October 20, 1936, was, as I have said, Hitler's and Mussolini's mutual pledge not to change the status quo of and in Austria. Hitler promised to refrain from undermining and destroying Austria's independence—which of course was a fraud on his part; but what was Italy to do or, rather, not to do? Certainly she did not want to annex Austria. There was, however, one thing that worried Hitler: that was Mussolini's apparent inclination to flirt with the possibility of a monarchist restoration in Vienna as a means of bolstering Austria's self-assurance.

The restoration of the Hapsburgs in either Budapest or Vienna was very much feared by Hitler. It is odd that we in America consider the Hapsburgs decadent and think it would make no particular difference whether Hungary or Austria had a Hapsburg king.

The truth is that Franz Josef was a much better king and emperor than we credited him with being. To Hungarians and others in central Europe, restoration would have been a magnet that would have attracted millions of other former subjects, jeopardizing Hitler's power, as well as the Little Entente. Mussolini had that in mind when he favored a monarchy for Austria, but this went by the board when he and Hitler were pushed together. There was another reason why Hitler opposed the monarchy: It was of the utmost importance for him to achieve his first and decisive territorial conquest without resort to arms. It is an open question whether a monarchy in Vienna would have succeeded better than the chancellors Dollfuss and Schuschnigg in stemming the rising tide of national socialism in that German-speaking country. But Hitler must have realized that a crowned ruler was much more unlikely than Schuschnigg to surrender without firing a shot—he knew that the small Austrian army would be bound by stronger ties to a monarch than to a colorless president in a country without a republican tradition. In his early days as a violent nationalist, Hitler had a deep contempt for what he and his like called the boneless, decrepit, supranational dynasty, but the undisguised violence of his aversion to Hapsburg restoration had still another and more important cause.

Leftist propaganda, largely fed and financed from the outside, has convinced many Americans that Hitlerism was the child of a conspiracy of German aristocrats who needed a modernized type of their old militarism. "Nazis and Junkers" was the slogan. In reality, Hitlerism was mobocracy, it was national socialism, or the German brand of Stalinism. Hitler's natural enemies

were the Junkers and the other aristocrats, first of all
the monarchists. Among them, especially, were those
whom he had cheated into believing that he was the
pioneer of a monarchist restoration. They felt the
whole weight of Himmler's cruelty. The monarchists,
by no means the communists, were the only opposition
of which Hitler was really and permanently afraid. It
was, in fact, the only opposition which almost succeeded in killing him. Hitler objected to the restoration of the throne in Austria because he feared the
repercussions on Germany. Finally he invaded Austria
because he could not tolerate a plebiscite which would
have shown that the majority of a German-speaking
country was anti-Nazi. In that case, too, he feared the
repercussions. A successful restoration in Austria
would have encouraged the opposition in Germany.

No simple formula could ever do justice to the com-
plexity of the situation in the Danubian Basin in the
Hitler period. On the surface, as we have seen, it appeared as if there were two camps, one for and one
against revision of the peace-settlements of 1919. Hence
Germany, Italy and Hungary stood against France and
the Little Entente, though this grouping was not rigid,
because Italy and Hungary felt jeopardized by Hitler.
Now we have another element of division: Hitler's
anti-Hapsburg attitude was very much to the liking of
the Little Entente, for, Czechs, Serbs and Rumanians
were afraid of the effect a restoration in Vienna and
perhaps in Budapest would have on the peoples in
their countries who favored restoration of Danubian
unity. England's policy in maintaining a balance of
power, in the face of the growing power of Germany
and the Austro-Hungarian Empire, hinged, before the

first World War, upon encouragement of all pan-Slavic movements. She was instrumental in dissolving the Austro-Hungarian Empire and strengthening Slavs through backing the Little Entente—in which Mr. Benes was her obedient instrument. France had been persuaded to do likewise because of her constant fear of Germany.

Mr. Benes, during the twenty years which elapsed between the two world wars, had established a policy in central Europe aimed at the permanent disruption of Danubian unity. He had obtained power and independence for his nation by means of the slogan: destroy Austria-Hungary; he continued to pursue that policy when it was very much outmoded and even dangerous to Czechoslovakia herself.

Relying on French and British support, and later on collaboration with Soviet Russia, Benes created and obstinately maintained the Little Entente system aimed at the permanent subjection of Austria and Hungary. He was the standard bearer of the enemies of Hapsburg restoration, a symbol of Danubian unity which, in most parts of the former Austro-Hungarian Empire, might have been accepted by the majority of the people. Even after Hitler's ascension to power, Benes continued his "bad neighbor policy," and at the same time antagonized all the national minorities within Czechoslovakia, where, if the Slovaks are included, the non-Czechs amounted to one half of the population of the state.

Thus, in spite of democratic appearances, Mr. Benes' regime was resented as oppressive and hostile to the basic interest of the Danubian peoples, which is unity. He practically played into the hands of Hitler, whose

menace for a long time he did not recognize. Preceding
the Assembly meeting of the League of Nations, in
September 1934, the semiofficial newspaper of the
French Foreign Office, *Le Temps,* seemed to show
sympathy for the restoration of Danubian unity under
Hapsburg leadership in order to stop Nazi expansion.
So, on their way to Geneva, the foreign ministers of the
Little Entente held a meeting in Ljubljana (Yugoslavia) where they decided to protest with the French
government against such a change of French policy and
to warn the government of France that should they
continue this trend, the Little Entente would break
away from France and join hands with Hitler. On
several occasions, Mr. Benes had stated publicly that
he would always get along with the Germans, and his
policy betrayed that he considered restoration of the
Hapsburg monarchy and Danubian unity a graver
danger than the annexation of Austria by the Nazis. In
March 1938, when Hitler prepared to invade Austria,
Mr. Benes did not move a finger to bolster up Austrian
resistance. On the contrary, he had helped to under-
mine the internal order of Austria by rearming the
Austrian social democrats and inciting them to revolt
against Dollfuss and also by aiding subversive leftist
tendencies against Chancellor Schuschnigg while the
latter was desperately trying to stave off Nazi aggression
from the right. All this had considerably contributed to
a weakening and disintegration of Austrian resistance
against Hitler.

Thus, Mr. Benes paved the way for Hitler's blood-
less victory at Munich, in September 1938, and for his
triumphant march into Prague in March 1939.

Had the old Austro-Hungarian monarchy, which we

helped to destroy, been in existence during Hitler's rise, what a different situation there might have been! The Austria and Hungary which followed World War I had no military strength, nor had they any war potential because Austria had lost her best industrial region, the Sudetenland, and Hungary was chiefly agricultural. How could the appearance of a prince in Vienna or Budapest have affected the Little Entente, if all the different nationalities in these countries were as well satisfied as we were led to believe? The truth is that the Czechs had never really granted equality to Sudetenlanders, Slovaks, Magyars, Ruthenians and Poles, and the Serbs had to resort to a dictatorship to prevent the secession of the Croats and maybe Slovenes. The Rumanians were not any too kind to their Magyar subjects and had not done too well in administering the large territory which they had received from the victors. They were afraid of what they disparaged as "the ghost of a dead past." The Serbs, led by Stoyadinovitch, had an open ear to Goering's promptings. "Look," he whispered, "we Germans are not really interested in acquiring Slavic areas, but the Hapsburg tradition is very much alive among your Catholic Croats, and there is Mussolini and the Vatican."

Hitler exaggerated the chances of the Hapsburgs, but it was effective. In reality, the monarchist movement in Austria was rather weak. The socialists had successfully spread the notion that monarchy was identical with political and economic reaction. The nationalists were opposed to that supranational family. They spread the legend that Empress Zita had betrayed the army to Italy during the armistice negotiations in 1918. The Catholic Party, which dominated the scene, was not inclined to share its power with the champions of the pretender, still less to cede it to him. Dollfuss' and even Schuschnigg's bows to the idea of restoration were little more than empty gestures. Altogether, the strength of monarchism could not be gauged. There was an undercurrent nourished by the vague and in-articulate feeling that monarchism meant stability, be-cause it had given stability in a better past. Prince Starhemberg, the leader of the Heimwehren, said that Austrians would not mount the barricades for Otto, nor would they do it against him. Possibly if Otto had returned, the nation might have rallied around him, if only for the reason that Dollfuss and Schuschnigg were unable to bridge the abyss that separated them from the socialists.

In Hungary the prospects for restoration were no better than in Austria, largely on account of the inter-national situation. Hungarians liked the idea of having a monarchy but the throne had to be kept vacant to placate the Little Entente. Later, when German pres-sure grew, it became apparent that even greater risks were caused by the absence of a monarch. If Horthy had died, Germany would have redoubled her efforts to give him a quisling successor and it would have been very embarrassing to refuse. But there also was in Hungary a very strong anti-Hapsburg tradition. Even after centuries of Hapsburg rule, Magyar nationalists considered them a foreign dynasty. The fact that one-third of the Magyars in Hungary are Protestants has a strong political effect. The Turks, while they governed the major part of Hungary until 1698, favored Protes-tantism against the Catholic Hapsburgs. This estab-lished a tradition that was still noticeable when I was in Hungary. Restoration seemed to find a better ear among Catholics than among Protestants. Hungarian nationalists never forgave Franz Josef for calling on Russians to help put down the Magyar Revolution in 1849. All through the nineteenth century, Hungarian nationalists were afraid lest the Hapsburg ruler ally himself with the national claims of Croats and Slovaks against Magyar control. The most serious opposition to a Hapsburg restoration between the two wars were the so-called Free Electors who stood for monarchy as against a republic, but did not recognize Otto's claims as legitimate. They wanted a national king, probably unconnected with Austria. While I could speculate as to what would happen in Austria if Otto had returned, there was no doubt about Hungary's attitude. Otto would not have been well received at that time. Official Budapest was not at all enamored with the idea of restoration in Vienna, because it thought it would increase factionalism in Hungary, and that it would expose Austria to risks without corresponding benefits. The Foreign Office always made it clear, however, that it was not Hungary's province to interfere in Austria's affairs.

This was not the attitude of the Little Entente. Titulescu, the pro-Russian foreign minister of Rumania, for many years could never forego the pleasure of telling Hungary and Austria that a Hapsburg restoration would mean war with the Little Entente. As I have mentioned, Benes echoed it with Yugoslav leaders. Since this was considered an effrontery, even by antimonarchists, it contributed greatly to keeping the Hapsburg idea alive. I was startled when on February 22, 1937, Foreign Minister de Kanya gave me the remarkable information that according to the Czech minister, Mr. Kobr, Prague had decided to favor restoration in Vienna as an antidote to *Anschluss.* This must have been a passing mood, perhaps a trial balloon for some unknown purpose in Czech relations with Germany. Mr. de Kanya also explained to me that on the other hand the Yugoslavs were most afraid of restoration in either Budapest or Vienna, since it might look like a revival of the old dual monarchy. Most probably a non-Hapsburg candidate would have met with less resistance. However, the value of a monarchy without legitimacy is questionable. Mussolini undoubtedly toyed with the idea of putting an Italian prince on the Hungarian throne. A number of times this was mentioned, but received no favor in Hungary.

In November 1937, Tibor Eckhardt created a sensation by making a speech which was interpreted as monarchistic. His explanation was that he sought to free the problem from its evil atmosphere of underground conspiracy. Monarchism, he told me, legitimate or not, had to be the object of popular discussion. As a result of his speech, there was a great deal of discussion of Dr. Eckhardt, but practically none of restoration. People seemed quite annoyed that he brought the matter up in such a way. Temporarily he lost a great deal of his popularity as a result—especially with the pro-Nazi elements. But Dr. Eckhardt told me that in his conversations with legitimists he had advised them not to think of a *coup-de-main,* or any other interference with Hungary's constitutional and legal institutions.

When President Roosevelt received Otto in 1940 under the auspices of Mr. Bullitt, who was at that time ambassador to France, this was interpreted by many in Budapest as a symptom of a French plot aimed at forcing Otto on the Hungarians. Count Teleki was much upset about it. This was before Hitler's attack on France, when the latter was still regarded as the decisive power in Europe. Teleki told me that Hungary wanted to stay absolutely independent and not be connected with or dominated by either Germans or the French. He said there was no movement in Hungary for restoration; and the question of whether Hungary would have a king was something that the Hungarian people were capable of deciding for themselves at the appropriate time. Little Entente spokesmen could not have been more excited than Teleki and de Kanya on this occasion.

I met Otto a number of times while he was in America. I found him keen-witted and alert, although somewhat too reliant on his undeniable personal charm. It must be hard for a man to face the life he is facing after having been brought up from his childhood as His Majesty. I attended a large dinner in Washington one night and sat at the same table with Otto. It amused me very much to hear someone at the table address him as "Archie." I don't know what he thought of it, but he acted as though it were his name.

I am of the opinion that Otto's stay in America did not further his cause, as far as this country was concerned. Advised by an unworldly entourage, he attached too much importance to the friendly remarks of President Roosevelt. Czech propaganda, of course, held him under concentrated fire which did not allow an unbiased judgment. Completely disregarding organized teamwork, he exposed himself unnecessarily and seemed to be animated by the conviction that he bore an historical mission which was more important than his personal welfare.

The Hapsburg problem in Hungary and Austria has been blamed for the failure of all attempts to form a republican Danubian confederation. Hungary and Austria, however, could not be expected to renounce their freedom of decision, and at that time the economic problems involved seemed insoluble. Though American tourists were very much interested in the subject, Hungarians seemed to have very little interest in Otto and seldom voluntarily mentioned him. Whatever concerted movement there was toward restoration, it was negligible. No one, however, would admit that anyone but a legitimate Hapsburg heir could be crowned. I never did know whether this was due as much to loyalty for the Hapsburg family as to the fact that the Little Entente said that a Hapsburg would not be tolerated. The only person who ever mentioned a republic to me was Baron Apor, who said that he thought Hungary would some day be considered a republic, should the existing situation become stabilized, and he called my attention to the fact that it was in effect a republic on the French model at that time.

4

A REFUGE FOR ONE MILLION JEWS

U P TO March 1944, Hungary was the only European country east of the Pyrenees where the lives of Jews could be considered as secure. Besides the Hungarian Jews then numbering almost one million, sixty to seventy thousand Jewish refugees from foreign countries had fled to Hungary and lived there in safety until Hitler's armies occupied the country and ordered their systematic extermination. Hitler's wrath against Hungary had been largely provoked by the protection granted to the Jews, a large percentage of whom survived the Nazi period in Hungary; for by the time the German armies actually took over, Hitler was near the end of his tether.

The safety of the Jews in Hungary was largely due to the type of restrictive laws passed. Through them Hungary seemed to be falling in line with the demands of the tyrant; but was able to maintain an oasis of refuge. Had she refused to pass *any* such laws, no doubt the period of real security for the Jews would have ended much more abruptly than it did.

The first Hungarian Jewish restriction law was in reality a challenge to Hitler. When it was announced, I went to see Philip Weiss, a member of the Upper House and president of the Commercial Bank of Pest, Hungary's biggest financial institution, which controlled much of the country's industry and agriculture and indirectly the treasury. Philip Weiss was a good banker, conservative, cautious, vigilant, and his bank had survived the great crisis of the early thirties with an untarnished reputation. I wanted to hear the authoritative opinion of one who had always referred to himself as a Jew.

"Well," he said, "I thought I was a Jew, but now it seems I am a Christian." The law provided that anyone who had been baptized before a certain date was not to be considered a Jew. This stipulation was in direct opposition to Hitler's Nuremberg laws which made Jews of Christians, if they had certain Jewish ancestors.

Hungary's solution of the problem is only a small part of the story in central European countries. To understand what happened, we have to remember that anti-Jewish measures were one of the cardinal ingredients of the German foreign policy under Hitler. Compliance in this matter was the touchstone of friendliness toward Germany—and tyrants insist on being loved. Love of deity always has to be expressed by the observation of ceremonial and ritual; foremost of the religious rites prescribed by the national socialists was Jew-baiting. By refusing it, one was unmasked as a heretic; and heretics have to burn. I do not know whether Hitler really believed in Jews being vermin. Perhaps he was a cynic also in this respect, but it did not change the fact that he exacted anti-Semitism as proof of allegiance and affection. There was no reason whatsoever why Jews should have been more hostile to national socialism than non-Jews. They had often played leading parts in European socialist movements;

but by outlawing them Hitler made Jews his enemies. This enabled him to accuse other governments which did not outlaw them of tolerating anti-German tendencies in their countries. Thus he used anti-Semitism as a lever of intervention and aggression.

The reaction of governments who had reason to fear him can easily be imagined. They had to face a whole set of German demands, among them the call for anti-Jewish measures. This request—or to put it more truthfully, this order—was often linked with measures, fulfillment of which would violate vital interests. If you imagine yourself approached in the darkness of night by a husky robber who at pistol point informs you that he wants your money or your life, you will understand the position of small countries like Hungary. You know that if you refuse to give up your possessions, you may lose both your money and your life, and you do not have much time to decide the matter. Germany had a way of making a number of demands, most of which she apparently did not expect to be granted, but she never forgot them and it became more embarrassing to refuse as time went on. So these small nations, finding that Germany was set on anti-Jewish measures, felt that it was better to yield on that point than to endanger the whole nation. This explains, though it certainly does not justify, Mussolini's transition from freely expressed philo-Semitism to anti-Jewish laws. It explains, again without justification, the anti-Jewish measures of the Vichy regime which created a rift between Marshal Pétain and the Church. These are but two examples of a long series. If we compare the degrees of Jew-baiting as practiced in the countries which were under German pressure, we obtain a scale showing, first, the varying length of that pressure and, second, the varying moral strength of the resistance. It is a fact confirmed by Jewish refugees from central Europe that, despite Mussolini's anti-Jewish laws, they were infinitely better treated in Italy than in "liberal" France. Not many Italian Jews left their country; those who did were driven by fear of the Germans, not of their own government, and certainly not of their non-Jewish compatriots. The small Austrian republic resisted admirably, because both Dollfuss and Schuschnigg were faithful sons of the Catholic Church. Most submissive to German demands were, as in every other respect, Czechs and Slovaks. Even under Dr. Benes, one year before Hitler marched into Prague, Austrian Jews were turned back by Czech constables and handed over to the Gestapo—among them Robert Danneberg, the moderate leader of the Viennese socialists, who died after four years of agony in concentration camps. When Hitler occupied the Sudetenland six months later, fleeing Jews were again driven back by Dr. Benes' police; in 1939, the new regime under President Hacha as well as the Tiso government of Slovakia introduced and applied the Nuremberg laws lock, stock and barrel.

The plight of Jews in Rumania was even worse, but of that I shall speak later. Switzerland, the foreign nation for which I have the greatest respect and admiration, had to be cautious, acting on the theory that "we have to play anti-Semite in order not to be obliged to be anti-Semite." Not many Jews found a haven there, and those who did were ousted as quickly as possible.

The real exception was Hungary. Discussing Jew-baiting, Admiral Horthy once gave me the key to his attitude. "As a boy," he said, "I have received a good education. I shall not forget it." Jews to him were human beings as they had been to his idol, the Emperor-King Franz Josef, under whom children of Jewish parents had been members of the general staff, generals and admirals. The Regent's opposition to anti-Semitism was strongly backed by the Hungarian prince-primate, Cardinal Seredi and by both churches. In parliament the Regent's views on this matter were vigorously voiced by leading aristocrats who in their exclusive club, the National Casino, liked to chant a song of which the refrain was "No, we are not Aryans, we are not Aryans, no!" This referred to the Magyars' Turanian descent.

Anti-Semitism would have been good politics for anyone looking for cheap popularity. Anti-Jewish feelings were but slumbering. They had been very much awake in the early twenties, for two reasons. First, the general misery after the war had made people look for scapegoats, and in the Old World Jews have been the traditional scapegoats. Second, the communist interlude of 1919 was chiefly the work of Jews, according to Professor Jaszi, a leftist writer, who stated that Jewry had supplied ninety-five percent of the active figures of the revolution. I do not mean this to be construed as indicating that more Jews in Hungary favored communism than Gentiles. I have no way of knowing anything about it, since communism at the time I was there was underground.

It is obvious, and proved by history, that conservative regimes offer Jews the best opportunities, and of this Hungary was an outstanding example. Conservative Magyars were, as a rule, loyal to the Christian faith, and all churches in Hungary condemned anti-Semitism. Conservatives, especially people of title, are generally immune to racial nationalism. Kings and other aristocrats have an old tradition of tolerance toward Jewry. Ballin, the great Hamburg shipowner, who committed suicide because William II lost his throne, was a Jew whom the Emperor had treated as a friend. In old Austria-Hungary, anti-Semitic journalists had to be careful to avoid prosecution for insulting a religious community. Altogether, Jews had to be vitally interested in social and political stability because only in a well-established order did they have a safe position. Every disorder was certain to rebound upon them.

In Hungary every citizen had to pay tithes to some church, and the government made no distinction between Jews and Gentiles. The Hungary of my day was in religious and racial matters much more liberal than any other country with which I am familiar. People were very tolerant about religion, and I seldom knew to which church anybody belonged. It is also a curious fact that the men who occupied the highest positions in Hungary were very often Protestants, despite the fact that the country was two-thirds Catholic. Regent Horthy was a Protestant, as were Count Bethlen, Premier Gombos and Daranyi. Although I was a very close friend of de Kanya, I don't remember what his religion was, but I think he was a Protestant. As I think back, it would be difficult to say to which church most of my friends belonged.

Shortly after I arrived in Hungary, I attended a mass in the Coronation Church in honor of St. Stephen with the rest of the diplomatic corps. We sat on one side up near the altar. On the other side were dignitaries of the Hungarian government, and in front near the altar was a chair reserved for the Regent. Being a Protestant, I thought that I had better watch the Regent so I would know the right thing to do. I watched him a while and I saw he did nothing. Then it occurred to me that he must be a Protestant, so I concentrated on the prime minister, who did nothing either. So I decided to do nothing—and nobody paid any attention.

A special trait in the Hungarian character worked in favor of the Jews. I have already mentioned that to a Hungarian the only function of money is to be spent. The male members of the upper classes were seldom interested in business, even though they badly needed money. Most of them considered that money-making was really undignified. This created a general atmosphere similar to that of medieval times when rulers turned their business affairs over to Jews. A Magyar gentleman with empty pockets did not consider himself inferior to the richest Jewish merchant. "The poor devil," he thought, "has no greater pleasure than business." He did not begrudge him this pleasure. As a result, Jewry wielded immense influence as a necessary element of the Hungarian community. Von Erdmannsdorff, the German minister, understood perfectly when, commenting on the anti-Jewish laws, he said that Hungary was unable to act toward Jews as Germany did because there was no one to take their place. But at the same time that he was telling me this privately, Hitler was compelling him to put pressure on the government to do what he told me could not be done. It can easily be seen that this situation offered excellent opportunities to anti-Semitic demagogues. Financed by Germany, they appeared here and there. Recalling the cruelty of the communist regime of Bela Kun, they pointed out that there were too many Jews in Hungary; indeed about one-tenth of the population was Jewish.

Under the circumstances, it was heroic on the part of the regime to permit a strong influx of foreign Jews, chiefly Polish, Slovakian and Austrian. It would have been sufficient proof of courage if the government, defying German pressure, had protected its own Jews, at the same time keeping the borders closed. Hungary did more than she was morally obliged to do, by offering shelter to foreign Jews in addition to her own. She was not allowed to remain an oasis of compassion in a desert of oppression. But even when she yielded, Hungary did so more slowly and with more dignity than her neighbors.

Mrs. Anne O'Hare McCormick wrote in the New York *Times* of July 15, 1944:

> It must count in the score of Hungary that until the Germans took control it was the last refuge in Central Europe for the Jews able to escape from Germany, Austria, Poland and Rumania. Now these hapless people are exposed to the same ruthless policy of deportation and extermination that was carried out in Poland. But as long as they exercised any authority in their own house, the Hungarians tried to protect the Jews.

This was acknowledged by an American leftist, Mr. Jonathan Stout, who, in March 1944, wrote in the *New Leader:*

The clamping of the Nazi vise on Hungary is a greater tragedy than the American people realize. The fact is that Hungary for many months has willingly provided the route by which untold hundreds of Jewish and other refugees of the Nazi terror have been rescued.

These facts must be kept on record. I am pleased to say that the American Jewish Year Book observed through these perilous times a fair and levelheaded attitude toward Hungary. The Year Book reported truthfully that Hungarian concessions to Germany's anti-Jewish demands were meant to take the wind out of the Nazi sails. To do this is always risky because concessions are apt to entail further concessions, but Hungary was always playing for time. She did what a tree does in a storm—it bends in order to survive unbroken. For instance, when banks were ordered to reduce the proportion of Jewish employees to a certain percentage within five years, the unspoken idea was that in five years the storm would have subsided. Furthermore, all restrictions were strongly interlarded with exemptions. This was chiefly done in parliament, where Horthy's aristocratic friends and the prelates instructed by the Cardinal made their weight felt. I have mentioned that the aristocrats, despite their economic and political status, set the fashion as leaders of society and were copied by the middle classes. If national socialist demagogues were successful with the mob, more representative people remained decent. General Count Joseph Takach-Tolvay, one of those "detestable feudal lords," resigned as chairman of the Veterans Association when, after the German occupation of March 1944, the puppet government excluded

Jews from his organization. Count Stephen Bethlen, another "feudal lord," retired from political life long before the German invasion, protesting against the anti-Jewish laws, comparatively mild as they were. When Hitler offered a larger slice of Transylvania as a bribe, Count Paul Teleki refused to secure it by anti-Jewish concessions. "It was really surprising," wrote the American Jewish Year Book, "to note his resistance at this point, certainly a minor issue for Hungary after all the fundamental sacrifices extorted from her."

Before Hitler took matters into his own hands, the situation of the Jews as described by the Year Book was that

> considerable numbers of those who lost their original occupations found some devious but tolerated ways to earn at least some irregular income. The Jewish community was permitted to organize large-scale self-help. It was able to do so because, with the exception of land, no Jewish property right was violated until the fateful Spring of 1944. Jews dwelt safely in their original homes; there were no restrictions on their liberty of movement, travel or recreation, and no discrimination against them in the distribution of food. They were protected also from the malignity of the local Nazi groups.

Shortly before the German invasion, when Hitler's military fortunes had begun to wane, there was loud agitation for abrogation of the restriction laws, led by Andrew Bajcsy-Zsilinsky, member of the Smallholders Party in parliament. The Year Book states that: "One of the official German pretexts for the occupation was 'the unrestricted presence of some one million Jews as a concrete menace to the safety of German arms on the Balkan peninsula.' " So strong was the solidarity of the non-Jewish Magyars with their Jewish compatriots, that not even the puppet regime which the Germans set up in 1944 dared to follow openly the German method of deportation and extermination. When the German Gestapo took it upon itself to start the deportation of Jews, "tens of thousands of Christian Hungarians," according to the Year Book,

> are known to have rushed to the aid of Jews in distress, trying to shield and hide them, to take over their homes and valuables for safekeeping, and to help them in their futile attempts to escape. Both Catholic and Protestant clergymen issued thousands of spurious birth certificates, in the vain hope of saving their bearers from persecution. Young Christian girls have frequently been seen parading the streets of cities and towns arm in arm with young Jews wearing the Star of David.

It seems that not all that help was in vain. On November 26, 1945, Mrs. Anne O'Hare McCormick reported from Budapest:

> The Jews did not suffer so much as Jews in neighboring countries because the worst persecution did not begin until the Nazis gained full control in 1944. Jewish firms were 'Aryanized' before that, but many who took over were friends of the dispossessed and held their property in trust. Only a small minority of Hungarian Jews are Zionists. The majority are loyal Hungarians who desire to remain in their country and help reconstruct it. It is estimated that about 60 per cent are back.

In connection with the position of Jews in Hungary, Dr. Bela Imredy, minister of finance at the time I went to Hungary, is an interesting psychological case. He had risen to his important position through his own ability. During the time I was there he left the finance ministry to become president of the National Bank, with which he had formerly been connected. He was known to be very pro-English, and was highly thought of by both English and American bankers, as well as by the economic section of the League of Nations. Just why I do not know, but he acquired a reputation which induced many people to believe that he would make an ideal premier. As a banker he was close to the influential leaders of the Jewish community and he therefore seemed a perfectly safe person to entrust with the task of stealing German thunder and placating the Nazis by mock persecution of the Jews, which would allow them to survive with minor scratches.

In March 1938, he was made cabinet minister without portfolio so that he could devise his Jewish bill. It was introduced in April by Premier Daranyi, and generally fixed the *numerus clausus* at twenty percent for Jewish employment, giving business five to ten years to adapt themselves to it. People who had been baptized before 1919 and all those who had been in the armed forces during the first World War were not considered Jews. Daranyi declared that this was the limit of anti-Jewish measures that he was willing to advocate.

About a week before Imredy was made prime minister, in May 1938, he came in to see me in connection with the New York World's Fair. On all sides, everybody was talking about Imredy for the premiership, so I mentioned it to him. He seemed a little modest about it, but he told me his theories of combating Nazi penetration. They sounded dangerous to me. He believed it was much better to forestall the Nazis by passing the anti-Jewish law he had devised than to wait and be forced to pass much more severe laws. I did not believe it could be done, but he was sure that he could handle the situation and satisfy everybody without doing any real harm.

A rather colorless civil servant, the then Prime Minister Daranyi had also proved very weak. Everybody felt that the country needed a strong man in view of the occupation of Austria which had brought the German army to the border. Imredy seemed to be the answer to Hungary's prayer. I never knew anything to cause so much satisfaction all around as when he became Daranyi's successor.

Imredy began to be quite a big man, and his success went to his head. In December 1938 he introduced a new Jewish restriction bill. It went far beyond the first one, which had been in effect only three months. It reduced the *numerus clausus* from twenty percent to six. It excluded Jews from many professions, but above all, it adopted the criterion of race by declaring that a Christian was a Jew if his parents had been Jewish. Grandparents were still neglected. Jews, the bill provided, should keep the franchise, but only be allowed to elect a special Jewish representation.

When I heard about this bill, I got in touch with Imredy and asked him if he would let me see it before it was made public. He agreed to this and I went up one morning by appointment for that purpose. The only other person present was Richard Quandt of the National Bank. I did not know why he was there unless it was because he had been associated with Imredy in the bank. He was anything but anti-Jewish and was a very decided anti-Nazi. As Imredy read the bill aloud, Quandt and I looked at each other repeatedly. It was much worse than we had anticipated. I tried to argue with Imredy about it. I said I could not see why, if the Christians were being discriminated against as he claimed, a bill could not be passed to prevent such discrimination and to see that Christians who wanted to work had just as good a chance as did the Jews. I argued that each case should be considered separately instead of by an arbitrary rule which might do incalculable harm to the economy of the country. He would not listen to me, though we had quite an argument about it. That he was more interested in politics than in economics was very plain.

As soon as the bill was made public, opposition supported by the Regent and the churches became so strong that the ministry of justice a few weeks later announced the government was prepared to accept several changes in the restriction bill. One week later, on February 14, 1939, as I have recounted earlier, it became known through Regent Horthy that one of Imredy's great-grandparents had been the son of a rabbi and a Jew until his seventh year. Although this fact, even under the Nuremberg laws, would not have affected Imredy, he fell as a victim of general laughter, and Count Teleki became his successor.

Imredy soon began breeding mischief and revenge. His hatred against the Regent was intense and he bided his time, his soul now completely sold to Hitler. In October 1940, he thought that, owing to the fall of France and Italy's apparent weakness, German pres-

sure was strong enough to allow for his comeback. He
arranged a secession from the Government Party and
founded the party of Hungarian Renaissance. The new
party demanded adjustment of the "obsolete" govern-
mental system to national socialist principles; and the
Arrow Cross Party expressed its sympathy. Count
Teleki fought back, declaring that a million people
could not be deprived of their livelihood. When, in
April 1941, Teleki committed suicide, Imredy's hope
of using his corpse as a ladder to another premiership
was disappointed. Horthy nominated Ladislaus de Bardossy, a professional diplomat. In March 1942, he was
followed by Nicholas de Kallay, a great personal friend
of the Regent, who became a thorn in Hitler's side.
Imredy did not get another opportunity before the
Germans invaded the country in March 1944, and even
then, disgust for the traitor was so general that he
failed to form a quisling government, and the Germans
chose General Sztojay, who had been minister in Berlin. Imredy was one of his ministers, but a few months
later he was dismissed at Horthy's demand.

Otto von Bismarck once said that everybody is worth
the sum of his virtues minus his vanity. In the case of
Imredy, despite his ability, the balance was negative.
He used the confidence of political and business cir-
cles as his stepladder, but having reached the heights,
kicked it away, intent on reaching even greater heights,
perhaps the regency, by personal schemes which were
founded on the expectation of Hitler's unlimited victory. Thus he became not a tragic but a despicable
figure. It was very hard for those who had known him
through the years to understand what had happened to
him. One of his associates in the National Bank said

that he could not understand it and as far as he could see, when Imredy walked out of the National Bank to become premier, he lost every bit of reason he ever had.

Up to March 1944 Imredy was the only Hungarian premier who had made concessions to Hitler voluntarily, not only concerning Jews, but also in other respects. What weakened Hungary's resistance was that she was constantly being played against the Little Entente. Time and again, Hungarians were told by the Nazis that their neighbors were much more friendly to Germany than they were. This was a little alarming because territorial adjustments were to be made, and Hungarian leaders were always compelled to ask themselves whether by refusing Jew-baiting they did not endanger the fate of Hungarians under alien domination to the advantage of their masters. Of course, the Czechs, Slovaks and Rumanians were being told at the same time just the reverse; thus one was played against the other. Czechs and Slovaks had introduced the Nuremberg laws before World War II started, but in Rumania the development was even more turbulent. Prime Minister Goga, in December 1937, had suppressed Jewish-owned newspapers, excluded Jews from the civil service, and declared that the state would no longer deal with Jewish business. In January 1938, Rumania deprived them of their franchise. Goga's premiership ended after forty-five days, but in the summer of 1940, when Gigurtu, Goering's friend, became prime minister, Goga's decrees were revived. All Jews were dismissed from public services, newspapers and liberal professions; the Nuremberg laws concerning mixed marriages, the employment of non-Jewish servants, and so on, were introduced. A few months later, these examples were followed by Yugoslavia and Bulgaria, although there were but seventy thousand Jews among fifteen million Yugoslavs and only fifty thousand among six million Bulgarians—tiny numbers compared with Hungary's Jews. In November 1940, the Rumanian Iron Guard carried out mass assassinations among opponents and Jews. It was estimated that 2,160 non-Jews and 680 Jews were murdered. The government of General Ion Antonescu threatened penalties "in case of a repetition." In December he decreed that all Jewish-owned shops must be marked as such. In July 1941, when Rumania had declared war on the Soviet, all Jews were forcefully evacuated from the frontier provinces of Rumanian Moldavia. At the same time, the Bulgarians herded their Jews into ghettos. The same thing happened in October to Rumanian Jews, who were driven out from the provinces of Bukovina and Bessarabia, where they had been a numerous minority. In August 1942, the Bulgarian Jews were ordered to wear the Star of David and were expelled from the capital.

These facts have to be remembered if one wants to evaluate Hungary's record. It is senseless to compare her with England or Holland or Sweden. She must be likened to her neighbors: Rumania, Yugoslavia, and the two halves of the former Czechoslovakia: Bohemia and Slavakia. Then it becomes obvious that she maintained a considerable standard of decency as long as she could determine her policy in surroundings of moral decay.

5

THE BREAKING UP OF CZECHOSLOVAKIA

THIS BOOK is not meant to prolong the series of publications which either boast of successful diplomatic missions or make apologies for their failures. It can be said that my years in Budapest did not prevent Hungary from being drawn step by step into Hitler's net until she fought on the side of her enemies. My task, however, could be at best only to retard that development, and for that task a representative of the United States had very little to back him up. America was far, far away from eastern Europe. She was unarmed, she was a neutral, even after the outbreak of war. True, we did not hide our aversion to the Hitler regime. President Roosevelt and members of his cabinet used strong language to castigate it. While privately most Hungarians agreed with us, they were not in a position to say so publicly. It takes more courage on the part of small nations to speak plainly when a tyrant is on the threshold than it does on the part of a great power overseas.

I was asked many times if we would help Hungary if she followed our policy, and how, but I was compelled to say that we would not and I did not know how we could. Hungarians knew this very well. If they had thought that we would and could help them, the situation might have been quite different.

An American envoy could be little more than an observer. He could protect the interests of his country and of his compatriots and convey to the Hungarian leaders—and to a certain extent also to the public—the views of his government; and that is about all. Of course, we did everything possible against the spread of Nazism, and at times I departed considerably from the strict line of neutrality. We worked as closely as we could with the British and other Allied nations and helped where we could to bolster up the courage of the Hungarian government and to counteract German pressure as much as possible.

My counterpressure, alas, was restricted to persuasion. When France went down and England was assailed, I had to maintain a show of serenity and confidence. When Hungary was asked to yield to German military demands, I warned her of the bad impression in America. When she yielded, I had to investigate the facts and was again confined to the role of observer. Diplomacy unbacked by force is not entirely helpless, but it is not any too potent against the near threat of an enemy's army.

Hungary's inclination was to side with the Allies, but circumstances made it not so much a question of what the people would like to do but what they knew they had to do. Hungarians may feel now that their leaders made mistakes, and they certainly did, but in my opinion, no matter what policy had been adopted at any particular time, the result would have been exactly the same. I am glad that we did not make any promises to Hungary, as we did privately to the Poles and Serbs. We may be perfectly justified in refraining from making commitments, especially in minor affairs. But once we have pledged ourselves, we must live up to our obligations. It is unfortunate that in the service of our policy of appeasement, we have uselessly deviated in recent years from this course.

I have been told that Hungary's present plight is the well-earned reward of her sharing in Germany's temporary booty. It is said that the Hungarians should have acted like the Poles; but unlike the Poles, they were not attacked in 1939, and they had no army worthy of the name. However, unlike the Russians, they not only did not attack the Poles as Germany tried to get them to do, but they would not even allow the German army to go through Hungarian territory for that purpose. There was plenty of inducement for Hungary to join Germany, just as Russia did, and none to refuse, much less join with the Allies. Should they have rushed in voluntarily at a time when the French watched the Eastern tragedy from behind the Maginot Line, when Britain had but a handful of divisions, when we were neutral, when Russia was Germany's accomplice? If Hungary had not compromised with Hitler—if she had provoked him more than she actually did—what would have been the result? Her country would have been occupied in 1939 or 1940, instead of 1944. Hungarians would have been treated like the Poles—and another million Jews would have been murdered. Are we Americans, a world power who have been so ever-considerate of Stalin, entitled to condemn a small, defenseless people because they feared Hitler's wrath and met him halfway?

The full truth about Hungary's sharing of Hitler's booty is as follows: In March 1938, Austria was occupied by the Germans. Now Czechoslovakia was practically surrounded by greater Germany; and Hungary, as well as Italy and Yugoslavia, became Germany's neighbor. A few months later, Hitler sowed the seeds of secession among the Sudetenlanders, who, until then, had only demanded economic and political equality with the Czechs within the Czechoslovakian state. In July, the British government, with the consent of Paris and Prague, sent Lord Runciman on an unofficial mission to act as an impartial adviser to the Czech government in its dealings with the Sudetenlanders. The result was four plans, the last of which, published on September 9, announced that the language laws would be modified to establish equality of the German, Hungarian, Polish, Ruthenian and Russian languages with the "Czechoslovak" language, and that the principle of national self-government would be applied in the form of a system of cantons. So far, Hitler's and England's combined pressure had been beneficial, because all that should have been conceded twenty years before, when the new state was founded. But Hitler, who did not want peace, ordered his henchmen among the Sudetenlanders to reject the plan as coming too late. Then followed the war scare of the so-called Munich crisis. On September 21, 1938 the Czechs accepted the amputation of the Austro-German regions from Czechoslovakia, and Dr. Benes' minister of propaganda, M. Vavretchka, set the pattern of the ensuing collaboration by proclaiming that "often more courage is needed to live than to commit suicide," which was more true than heroic.

The plan which should have applied to all the minorities of Czechoslovakia had been wrecked. The Sudetenlanders had found another solution. Other nationalities began to clamor for the same right of secession. On October 1, the Czechs were deprived of

Teschen by Poland. On October 2, the Hungarian government announced that a mixed Hungarian-Czech commission would discuss the right of national self-determination of the Hungarians in Slovakia, in accordance with the decisions of Munich. On October 5, Dr. Benes resigned as president of Czechoslovakia, having nominated as foreign minister, Dr. Frantishek Chvalkovsky, an old pleader for co-operation with Hitler. In his farewell broadcast, Dr. Benes said: "Now it is particularly necessary for the Czechs to reach unity with the Slovaks. We must hasten to grant everything necessary." On October 9, the Ruthenians of the Carpatho-Ukraine decided on autonomy within the framework of the Czechoslovak state. The decomposition was in full swing. On the same day, negotiations began, with the approval of the Czechoslovak government, between Hungarians and Father Tiso, the leader of Slovakia. Two days later, in agreement with the Czechoslovak government, the Hungarian army carried out the token occupation of two Hungarian towns in Slovakia. Chvalkovsky hastened to Hitler and Ribbentrop, giving them assurances of Czech loyalty. On October 13, de Kanya declared that the conference with Tiso was deadlocked. He demanded 5,000 square miles, 79% Magyar, which would have left 150,000 Magyars in Slovakia and Ruthenia, but would have transferred 145,000 Slovaks and 30,000 Ruthenians to Hungary. Tiso offered but a small frontier strip.

This was followed by a crisis. Hungary called up five classes of conscripts. The Slovak radio warned that "the Czechoslovak army was ready." Negotiations were resumed. Hungary had insisted upon direct negotiations with Czechoslovakia, but since they had failed proposed a decision by plebiscite. On October 26, the Czechs, instigated by Hitler, accepted German-Italian arbitration, and rejected a plebiscite. Hitler thus forwarded an ambitious scheme to make both Czechoslovakia and Hungary subservient to his political aim, which at that time was the encirclement of Poland and the opening of a road toward Russia. After the acceptance of Hitler's proposal by Czechoslovakia, Hungary was no longer in a position to refuse, as refusal would only have led to Hitler's giving preference to submissive Czechoslovakia over recalcitrant Hungary—who thus would have lost the only remaining chance for the solution of her territorial dispute with Czechoslovakia.

On November 6 Horthy, riding on a white horse, led Hungarian troops into Komarom, a purely Hungarian town. On November 11, Horthy rode into the town of Kassa, completing the peaceful occupations granted by the Vienna Award. On November 20, the Czechoslovak parliament voted autonomous statutes for Slovakia and Carpatho-Ruthenia. Slovak was declared the official language of Slovakia, which put an end to the fiction of the Czechoslovak tongue. Actually, the two tongues, Czech and Slovak, are close relatives but not identical.

The participation of Hungary in reducing Czechoslovakia has been called her first open sin. Hungarians point to the fact that their action was in keeping with the Munich decisions; that Czechoslovakia had been compelled to disgorge what never should have become hers, and that Hungary, in these circumstances, could not refrain from taking back property previously stolen from her.

De Kanya, although not a revisionist, said that he approved of getting everything they could obtain peacefully to forestall Germany. He foresaw the German occupation of Czechoslovakia.

The Slovaks, not content with their autonomy within the reduced Czechoslovak state, pursued their ultimate goal of independence. For this, their leaders at that time were afterward accused of high treason, and I doubt whether this was justified. They certainly accepted German support to secure independence and later showed their gratitude by fighting against Russia, but Bolshevism appeared to that strongly Catholic people as a natural enemy; and one must not forget that they had been a part of Czechoslovakia for twenty years and had disliked it.

To combat Slovak separatism, President Hacha, Benes' freely and legally elected successor, dismissed Father Tiso as Slovakia's premier and ordered many arrests. Four days later, Slovakia proclaimed her independence. One day later, on March 15, 1939, Hitler did the most foolish thing of his career by sending his troops into what was left of Czechoslovakia. The damage he did himself by awakening the sleeping British was enormous. His profit was less than nil. It would be difficult to find in world history anything equally foolish—except, perhaps, Hitler's decision to counterattack in France instead of in the east, in December 1944. These two happenings reveal his small stature as a statesman and as a war lord.

With Slovakia independent and Bohemia a German protectorate, Carpatho-Ruthenia was a derelict. Hitler had promised it repeatedly to Hungary, but apparently had no intention of keeping his promise. Not only were the Czech garrisons kept there, but when they were withdrawn as a result of a Hungarian ultimatum to the Czechs, it became a no-man's-land, full of German and Hungarian agents, until the Hungarian army went in and took possession.

The occupation of Ruthenia, now a part of the Soviet Union, was carried out without the knowledge and council of Germany and very much against her wishes. It was Poland which urged the establishment of a common Hungarian-Polish frontier, in order to prevent the German army, which had entered Slovakia, from moving far east into the back of endangered Poland and establishing direct contact across Ruthenia with Rumania. Somewhat belatedly, Rumania had also sent regular troops into Ruthenia to establish junction with the German army. This junction was disrupted by the Hungarian occupation though it did not extend westward up to the important Dukla Pass, as Poland desired, because of a German ultimatum on the third day of the occupation. Nevertheless the usefulness and importance of this Hungarian move was fully justified by subsequent events when, after the German attack against Poland, Hungary prevented the German troops from crossing this strategic territory and opened up the Ruthenian frontier to more than a hundred thousand soldiers of the Polish army. These men were well received in Hungary and all but some thirty thousand clandestinely joined the armies of the Western democracies. Polish flyers thus participated in comparatively large numbers in the famous Battle of Britain, in the autumn of 1940, which saved England from German invasion. The remaining group of Poles who were unable to join the Allied armies stayed on in Hungary. Polish schools, even colleges, were established for their

children, and Polish-Hungarian friendship was publicly demonstrated.

The end of Czechoslovakia sealed the fate of the
Little Entente. Yugoslavia hastened to adapt herself
to the new situation. She stressed the cordiality of her
relations with Germany, at the same time trying to improve those with Italy and Hungary. Fear of Hitler
had now begun to overshadow every other consideration, and resentments were temporarily forgotten. The
Russo-German pact of August 1939 shook the world
with its implications. The neighbors of the two dictators
had held the wild hope that the two would annihilate
each other. Now the small nations huddled together.
Hungary and Yugoslavia seemed to understand best
what further litigation would bring to both of them.
Secret negotiations were started after the collapse of
France between Regent Horthy and Prince Paul of
Yugoslavia. As a result, on December 12, 1940, Count
Csaky, the Hungarian foreign minister, and Cincar-
Markovitch, his Yugoslav colleague, signed at Belgrade
a pact of lasting peace and mutual friendship, providing for consultation on all questions of mutual interest. Although this was not to last very long, at the moment both sides were sincere as they did not want to
be played one against the other. But the German dictator was not impressed. On March 25, 1941, the Yugoslav premier, Mr. Tsvetkovitch, signed his country's
adherence to the Tripartite Axis Pact. Ribbentrop
promised that Germany would respect at all times the
sovereignty and territorial integrity of Yugoslavia and
would not ask her to permit the passage of Axis troops.
Two days later, the Yugoslav air general Simovitch,
staged his *coup-de-main* which caused the resignation

of Prince Paul and King Peter's assumption of full royal power. The Germans interpreted this change as a hostile act, which it was, and on April 6 began to invade Yugoslavia and Greece. A few hours before their attack, Moscow had announced the conclusion of a Soviet-Yugoslav friendship pact, which did not promise help but only continued friendship in case of aggression by a third state. It must be left to historians to decide what would have happened if Tsvetkovitch had not been overthrown. It is improbable that Yugoslavia would in the end have been spared, although she might have postponed the invasion by appeasement. The Germans could have entered Greece from Bulgaria and Albania without crossing Yugoslavia.

For Hungary, the rupture between Berlin and Belgrade was fraught with destiny. Hitler demanded in an ultimatum not only passage for his troops but active military co-operation. On April 3, Count Paul Teleki received a message from the Hungarian minister in London that Mr. Eden had threatened to break off diplomatic relations with Hungary, unless she resisted actively the passage of German troops across her territory. That evening in the cabinet council, Teleki discussed the desperate situation in a gloomy mood. After having retired to his study he received at midnight the authentic news that the German army had just started its march into Hungary. This was more than Teleki could bear and that same night he committed suicide. It is rumored that his cabinet had turned down his proposal to reject German demands and that he had not been able to bear the ignominy of attacking a country with whom his government had concluded a pact of friendship five months before. However, there is reliable information to the contrary. The cabinet did not desert the premier, but he had been shown proof of an understanding between the German and Hungarian general staffs, thus confronting him with a *fait accompli.*

I have already mentioned that General Gombos was an ardent admirer of the German army. When he was prime minister, he had packed the general staff with young officers of the same creed and Horthy, relying on the old traditions of absolute loyalty and discipline, had signed those nominations. These men, not familiar with the world abroad, could not understand Horthy's and the government's hesitation to join with Germany. This, they thought, was Hungary's great opportunity. Hungary's entry into the war against Yugoslavia was really the work of an officers' junta, something previously unheard of in the country's history. Count Teleki simply broke down when the disaster was revealed to him. This was no longer his world. He used a pistol, but it was the bitter realization that he had signally failed that killed him.

Count Teleki died a martyr. I should like to say that he was a great statesman, but I am sorry that I cannot. That he did not know what was going on in his general staff is sufficient proof of his weakness. He considered himself very clever. Often he mentioned his Greek grandmother, always saying, "You know, the Greeks are a clever people," and then recalled his ancestor who had been prime minister of Transylvania and had dealt cleverly with the Germans on one side and the Turks on the other. Count Teleki thought he could do the same, and this accounts for many of the things he did and said which were entirely contrary to his cherished beliefs. When he wired Hitler congratulations and spoke exultingly in parliament of the fact that German soldiers were guarding the grave of the Unknown Soldier in France; when he went to Gombos' grave and to that of the Unknown Soldier in Hungary and announced the great German conquest— he was acting in the way he thought his Transylvanian and Greek ancestors would approve. When I remonstrated with him, he said it was cheaper to give bouquets to Hitler than bread. As I knew his intense hatred of national socialism and all it represented, I said nothing further, although I considered then and I consider now that his overconfidence in his own cleverness had much to do with what happened later.

Faced with the situation which had confronted Teleki and the crisis created by his suicide, the Regent appointed Foreign Minister Bardossy as premier and tried to make the best of a desperate situation. Such leadership as he previously had was taken away from him now, for he faced accomplished facts. So he proclaimed that Hungary welcomed the liberation of Croatia, which had announced her independence on April 10, 1941, and that it was Hungary's "imperative duty to take into her hands the security of that part of Yugoslavia which was cut off from her in 1918 and where such great masses of Hungarians are living."

It was through the activities of General Werth, the chief of the Hungarian general staff, that Hungarian troops participated in the occupation of Bacska, a northern province of Yugoslavia. Hungary was deprived at Trianon of a general staff and of a school for officers. The result was that in order to maintain her army she had to get leadership from without her bor-

ders. General Werth, a good soldier, was however, not
a Hungarian. He was brought up in the German tradition, and he betrayed Hungary. Incidentally, we are
apparently doing the same thing in Japan today. When
the time comes for Japan to be our ally—as she might
well be in the East—she will have to call upon her old
militarists rather than a young modernly trained corps
of officers.

After the German attack on Yugoslavia the question
was who should occupy Bacska, formerly a valuable
province of Hungary, the German or Hungarian
army? Apart from the considerable Hungarian minority inhabiting that territory, the Serbs, themselves, preferred Hungarian occupation. Thus, except for one
incident, when Hungarian troops in Novi Sad (Ujvi-
dek) at the order of the German High Command committed cruel excesses against the population, that territory escaped the brutalities inflicted by German
troops of occupation in other parts of Yugoslavia. It
also must be noted that the Hungarian government
applied reprisals against the military commanders
guilty of the Novi Sad massacre. Four of the responsible
high officers were condemned to death but were abducted by the Germans before execution and given
full rank in the German SS—proving in whose behalf
they had acted.

Shortly after Teleki's suicide, General Werth was
dismissed and replaced by General Szombathelyi, an
able officer, who later succeeded in limiting considerably Hungarian co-operation with the German army.
The planned German occupation of Hungarian key
positions was restricted to the passage of German
troops; and Hungary merely took possession of part

of the area of which she had been deprived in 1919, from which Yugoslavia had already withdrawn her troops.

6

THE DOWNFALL OF RUMANIA

I N EUROPE each nation seems to feel it necessary to be superior to somebody. The British feel themselves superior to everybody. The French feel superior to the Germans, Italians and most of the rest of Europe. Germans feel superior to Poles, Austrians and the Balkan countries, but although they talk of being supermen, they have a great inferiority complex toward the English, the French and others. Poles look down upon Russians; and Bavarians feel themselves superior to Prussians. Czechs consider themselves above Slovaks and Poles; Croats above Serbs; Austrians above Hungarians, and Serbs above Bulgars. All this is surpassed by the Hungarian superiority complex toward Rumanians.

History has shown that Europe's greatest threat is in the East. The nearer to Asia, the stronger the instinctive fear. Politically speaking, only Rumania separated Hungary from Asia, and the easternmost part of Rumania was farther to the east than the westernmost part of Asia Minor. Compared with Rumania, Hungary was intensely occidental.

At the time King Stephen made his historical decision to turn to Rome (in the year 1000 A.D.), religion was a decisive, formative influence in the world. Thus Hungary came under Western influence while Rumania remained with the Orthodox Church, which was oriental. By King Stephen's decision, Hungary came under the cultural influence of the Holy Roman Empire and what we call Western civilization. Rumania, facing the East and under Turkish domination for centuries, was different in outlook and way of living, so Hungary became and remained the most eastern outpost of Western civilization. The standard of living, especially of the working class, was very much higher in Hungary than in Rumania, and it was considered a great humiliation by Hungarians that so many Magyars were put under Rumanian rule by the transfer of Transylvania to Rumania.

The question of religion, of course, played its part—the majority of Hungarians being Roman Catholics and the Rumanians Orthodox. Hungarians felt that the Orient had snatched a part of the Occident, and this was not conducive to reconciliation. Transylvania sentimentally was to every Hungarian what the New England States are to us.

I have already mentioned the psychological importance of the Carpathian Mountains. Magyars felt that when Rumania stepped across the Carpathians, it was as though the natural wall against Asia had crumbled. To complicate it still more, a slight majority of the population of Transylvania spoke Rumanian, and most of the Magyars lived in an ethnographic enclave, separated by Rumanian areas from their mother country. Rumania treated the Magyars as subjects with minor rights, paying back in kind, they said, what Hungary had done to Rumanians.

When I saw him late in 1939, Admiral Horthy very frankly said that a fair settlement among the small nations in that part of the world was almost impossible within the existing international order because of the universal hatreds engendered by centuries of warfare. "If God," he said, "appeared to the King of Rumania and told him that unless he returned Transylvania to Hungary, Rumania would be wiped out in two years, there would be nothing that the King could do because if he tried to obey, he would lose his throne in twenty-four hours." A similar fate would befall a Hungarian leader, who, upon heavenly advice, would renounce Hungarian claims to Transylvania. Therefore, the Regent said, any settlement would have to be enforced and maintained by the great powers. What was needed was a European League of Nations which would not be an adjunct of Downing Street, the Quai d'Orsay, the Wilhelmstrasse, or Moscow. Mr. Churchill put forth similar although perhaps more utopian ideas during the war, but he maintained the great and immutable truth that the smaller problems of Europe could only be mastered as part of an over-all settlement and not piecemeal. The Transylvanian question was well suited to prove this. Hungary's and Rumania's quarrel was soon submerged in the much larger issue of the relations between Germany and the Soviet Union. In the treaties of armistice it became one of the elements in the gigantic struggle between the two worlds, the free and the totalitarian. As long as Hitler and Stalin co-operated smoothly, Rumania appeared only

as a bone of contention between Germany and Great
Britain. Germany needed Rumanian oil, and the British made Rumania the questionable gift of a military
guarantee.

There was also the legendary British-French force
which Marshal Weygand was said to have assembled
in the Middle East in preparation for a thrust into the
Balkans. In Budapest people hoped that the German
general staff would first try to decide the war in the
west, and that their country would be spared. At the
same time, Hungarians realized that their geographical position between Germany and Rumania would
expose them to grave dangers if the Germans found it
necessary to defend Rumania, either against Britain
or Russia, or to enter Rumania as a springboard in a
wider oriental strategy. Dislike of Rumania could not
prevent the Hungarians from being concerned about
the fate of that neighbor. The Transylvanian question
was suddenly less important than whether Germany
would take over Hungary in order to get to Rumania.

Just as politics make strange bedfellows, so does a
situation of this kind; but the chasm was too wide and
the time too short for effective co-operation between
Budapest and Bucharest. In the spring of 1936, Foreign Minister de Kanya told me that in the three years
he had held this post, Mr. Grigorcea, the Rumanian
minister, had visited the Foreign Office only three times
and had never called on him personally. Mr. Grigorcea
was an excellent diplomat; despite the fact that he
represented Rumania, both he and his wife were great
favorites in Budapest with practically everyone, from
the Regent down. Therefore, it can only have been
under instructions that he called at the Foreign Office

as infrequently as Mr. de Kanya said. His failure to do so more often was very significant.

In February 1937, Mr. Bossy, Mr. Grigorcea's successor, told me that Rumania was very anxious to make peace with Hungary, but, he added with a sigh, Rumania was in the position of a girl in love with a man who had never proposed—so what could she do but wait? This statement was also significant in that it showed the first effect of the fear which Hitler had begun to spread all over Europe.

In March 1939, after the breaking up of Czechoslovakia, nobody knew what would happen next. When Hungary and Rumania began to threaten each other by troop movements, it looked as though an awkward situation was developing. It was certain that if Hungary received from Hitler a promise for the return of Transylvania, no government would be strong enough to reject it, even if it meant permitting Hungary to become a base for German military operations.

The Regent told me that it was relatively easy to refuse to let the Germans go through Hungary to attack Poland because great friendship had existed for centuries between the two countries; but if the Germans wanted to pass through Hungary to attack Rumania, it would be quite different. Much as he would oppose it himself, he would not be able to refuse. In this situation, Hitler fully realized that he was able to flaunt Transylvania in Hungary's eyes to keep her in a state of confusion and indecision.

The Rumanians have always been able in the past to be on all sides and to end up with the winner. They profited very handsomely in the first war by these tactics, and King Carol apparently decided to act accordingly when Hitler began to disturb the existing situation. King Carol has been considered so much of a playboy that his abilities have been underrated. He was a typical Balkan ruler, with his passions, tenacity, ruthlessness and indifference to Western opinion. He wanted to rule and to be obeyed, and clashed with political leaders who, while disguised as democrats, had virtually the same ambitions. Since he was a strong personality, it was always a temptation to march with him. He had adherents and opponents in every party.

To speak of racial purity was even more amusing in Rumania than in Germany; yet Hitler had his representation there in the Iron Guard, led by Cornelius Codreanu. Prime Minister Duca used the policy of the iron fist against the Iron Guard and as a result was assassinated on December 3, 1933, being the first of a series of premiers who lost their lives in the struggle against national socialism.

After Duca's death, the Iron Guard was at least temporarily dissolved, and in March 1934, Codreanu was arrested. In August 1936, King Carol, as a concession to Hitler, dismissed M. Titulescu who had been one of the leaders of the Little Entente and very prominent at Geneva in the League of Nations. In order to split the Iron Guard, which he had been holding at bay, the King made Goga, leader of its royalist wing, premier, but dismissed him after forty-five days, when he had been sufficiently compromised. On November 30, 1938, Codreanu with thirteen other leaders of the Iron Guard was killed. The official explanation was that they had tried to escape when being transported to another prison, but it seemed to be generally accepted that this was a planned liquidation, in an endeavor to check the rise of German-fostered racialism. This explains why Carol found it convenient to leave in September 1940, one month before the German troops entered his country.

To go back: In August 1939, King Carol, referring to Hungarian-Rumanian frontier incidents and to Hungarian press attacks against Rumania's minority policy in Transylvania, declared that the frontiers once fixed could not be changed without risking a world cataclysm. The cataclysm started within a fortnight. On September 1 Germany invaded Poland. Two days later Britain declared war on Germany. On September 17, Russian troops invaded Polish territory. The partition of Poland as devised by Ribbentrop and Molotov prevented the Germans from reaching the Rumanian frontier through Polish territory, but Rumania felt the repercussion just the same. On September 21, the Iron Guard murdered Premier Armand Calinescu. Carol fought back like an angry hornet. Without trial, three hundred members of the Iron Guard were put to death. He was the only ruler who gave the national socialists a dose of their own medicine.

In the midst of these events, Hungary remained neutral, and Yugoslavia formally proclaimed its neutrality; the former announced her willingness to conclude minority agreements with Rumania and Yugoslavia. On September 24, Soviet Russia agreed to resume diplomatic relations with Hungary which had been severed eight months before.

When Germany overran Luxembourg, Belgium, the Netherlands and northern France, the stoutest hearts trembled. In Rumania Carol replaced his excellent foreign minister, Gafencu, a man with a Scottish mother, by Jon Gigurtu. On July 1, 1940, ten days after the French armistice, Prime Minister Tatarescu, once high in Hitler's favor and just now high in Stalin's, formally renounced the British-French guarantee of April 1939 to his country and stated that Rumanian policy would now be aligned with the "new orientation in Europe." Then he resigned and Gigurtu included the Iron Guard and the national socialists of the German minority in the new government; he declared that he would pursue a policy of sincere integration in the Axis system.

Just three weeks before, the Hungarian parliament had expelled Kalman Hubay, a leader of the national socialist Arrowcross Party, because he had proposed self-government of the racial minorities, giving special privileges to German inhabitants and discriminating against the Jews.

Hitler's victories in the west had shattered the very foundation of the Rumanian state, but six days after the French surrender, an even greater menace was revealed. In the general turmoil, this has almost escaped the attention of the world and yet it was not only a classical example of unprovoked aggression but also, with the exception of the formal seizure of eastern Poland, in November 1939, was the first decisive move of Soviet imperialism—a move no longer directed against German imperialism but pointing to the Balkan peninsula and to the Dardanelles. This should never be forgotten.

On June 26, 1940, the Soviet Union delivered to Rumania an ultimatum demanding the cession of Bessarabia and northern Bukovina. The time limit was twenty-four hours. The Rumanians replied that they were willing to yield, but asked for negotiations. This was brusquely rejected by the Soviets, who demanded evacuation of the two provinces within four days. On June 28, Bucharest yielded. Russian land and air forces at once started the invasion without waiting for the expiration of the four days. Russia's claim to Bessarabia was based on revisionism, because it had been hers until 1917. The pretext with regard to Bukovina was national self-determination; they claimed a predominance of Ruthenians or Ukrainians among the Rumanians, Germans, Poles and Eastern Jews of northern Bukovina. As a matter of fact, Bukovina had never been a part of Russia. Until 1777, she had been Ottoman; then Austrian until 1918 when she was presented to Rumania. The Soviets were interested in Bukovina because by annexing her they crossed the Pruth and Sereth rivers and got a foothold in the Carpathian Mountains. I do not know whether the Soviets acted with Hitler's connivance, but I doubt it; in the case of Bessarabia they apparently did—since that province is defined as being within Russia's sphere of interest in the Secret Protocol to the Russo-German Pact of 1939; but there was nothing in that treaty about Bukovina.

Russia's action undermined Rumania's rigid stand against revision. Her spirit was broken and she began to negotiate with Hungary, who claimed two-thirds of Transylvania. Frontier incidents followed, and the two nations seemed about to jump at each other's throats. Hitler was forced to take some action. Crutzesco, the Rumanian minister in Budapest at that time, told me that Hitler had cautioned Hungary against an open conflict. No doubt Rumania received the same advice.

Leon Orlowski, the last Polish minister to Hungary, was certain that Hitler was trying to form a Hungarian-Rumanian-Bulgarian bloc as a bulwark against Russia. Count Csaky, Hungary's foreign minister, thought the Germans were much worried. He said that they could not attack England for fear that Russia might take advantage of the opportunity and seize parts of eastern Europe, including all of Rumania. One can be sure that Stalin was not inspired by love of Great Britain. Hitler had advertised his eastern plans so loudly that Stalin could have no doubt of Germany's intentions after the fall of England. The two conspirators had reached the end of their collaboration; each began tentative independent operations. That was the portentous meaning of Russia's attack on Rumania.

Before Stalin attacked Rumania he invited the Hungarian minister, Mr. Kristoffy, whom he had never seen before, to call upon him. In Stalin's studio the following conversation took place:

Stalin: Has Hungary given up her claim to Transylvania?

Kristoffy: No, she has not.

Stalin: Why then don't you attack Rumania? Now is the time.

Kristoffy: I shall inform my government.

Stalin: All right. Do.

Kristoffy was amazed, and so were his superiors in Budapest. They decided against giving Stalin the pretext he desired, but the story is worthwhile remembering, because it shows that Stalin's present methods are by no means new, and sheds valuable light on his change of policy at the end of the war in allotting

Transylvania to Rumania, which now has become in effect a Soviet province.

On August 28, 1940, an Axis conference was held at Berchtesgaden, attended by Count Ciano, Ribbentrop, and the German and Italian envoys to Rome, Berlin, Budapest and Bucharest. Two days later, prime ministers Teleki and Gigurtu were summoned to Vienna, where another Vienna Award awaited them, this time concerning Rumania. Hungary received somewhat less than half of Transylvania and the Rumanian foreign minister, Manoilescu, said afterward that there had been a German ultimatum; neither the Rumanian nor the Hungarian delegates had been allowed to say a word. The Rumanian minister to Budapest told me upon his return from Vienna that "the Germans were nice, but Count Ciano nasty."

The Germans were more concerned with Rumania than with Hungary, whereas Mussolini, not directly interested in either, could afford to play Santa Claus for the latter. My Rumanian informant thought that the Magyars had gotten more than they ever dreamed of getting. The Hungarians felt the opposite way.

In reality, opinions were strongly divided. Thoughtful Hungarians were alarmed by Hungary's acceptance of a gift from Hitler when he was an enemy of Great Britain, but no one knew what to do about it. No one seemed to consider the territory that Hungary had taken from Czechoslovakia a German present. Then Hungary had acted on her own; but the second Vienna Award was not sought by Hungary. It was King Carol who personally requested arbitration from Hitler in order thus to obtain Germany's guarantee of Rumania's new frontiers; Count Teleki had insisted that negotiations be conducted directly between Hungary and Rumania. He felt that in having to accept part of Transylvania from Hitler's hands Hungary had definitely lost all chances for future possession of that territory. But he had no choice: no Hungarian government could reject even part-fulfillment of the old revisionist claim.

Not daring to advocate openly the rejection of the award, many, like Count Bethlen, said that Hungary should have the whole of Transylvania or nothing. He told Teleki, according to Dr. Eckhardt, that the whole thing should have been put off until the final peace settlement. Bethlen was right. That Hitler was not interested in a permanent solution of the problem was obvious. The new frontier was drawn purely along ethnic lines, neglecting all geographical and economic considerations and, most of all, those of communication. By drafting an impossible new frontier, Germany wished permanently to divide and rule both Hungary and Rumania.

In Rumania the government of Gigurtu had to resign. Ion Antonescu was his successor. Carol abdicated in favor of his son and left the country. King Michael accepted Antonescu as leader, called sonorously Conducator. He was Hitler's man, even more so than the people of the Iron Guard, some of whom did not want to be a branch of the German-controlled "Nazintern." When jealousies developed between the Conducator and the Iron Guard, Hitler regularly sided with the former, because the Guard was riotous and undisciplined. What the Germans wished most in that granary and oil font was quiet work. Rumania achieved for itself in 1940 the subservience that was forced upon

Hungary only in 1944, after the German army took possession.

Shortly after the outbreak of the second World War, when Germany's strategy was everybody's guesswork and France was still considered invincible, I had a conversation with Premier Teleki in which we agreed that no small country was safe; but he found comfort in the fact that there were many other small countries in the same dangerous position as Hungary, each of which seemed to offer Germany greater strategic advantages. He said that Russia and Germany were in reality enemies, but reasoned that this would protect Hungary since Germany would not like to provoke Russia by threatening the Balkans. He thought that Italy, and possibly Yugoslavia, might give Hungary military support in case of a German attack. He said Hungary would never allow German troops to enter and cross her territory. I wondered at the time what he would do if the German army started for Budapest, but I knew that he was trying to believe what he wished to believe; it was the old, old story of "it can't happen to us."

Later, when Germany launched its attack on Denmark and Norway, Ullein-Reviczky at the Foreign Office told my first secretary, Howard Travers, that he felt greatly relieved. I remember Mr. Chamberlain in the British parliament expressed delight at the same thing. It was natural that Mr. Ullein-Reviczky should try to get some comfort out of it. His reasoning was that the Northern States and the Danubian Basin had been standing behind the same horse and no one had known with which leg it was going to kick. Now it had kicked with the right leg, and Hungary had stood behind the left one. Reviczky thought, too, that Hitler was much afraid of annoying Stalin.

By April 18, 1940, de Kanya had made up his mind that the Germans were not coming into Hungary at all—that is, unless the British tried to cut them off from Rumanian oil supplies. The British had told him that they would not invade Rumania unless the Germans did; this seemed to make everything all right, as far as Hungary was concerned. I could not blame de Kanya or any other Hungarian for trying to be optimistic. I did not try to discourage him, but I did call his attention to rumors of German troops in Hungary and Rumania, and he admitted that this was probably true as both countries were flooded with tourists who no doubt comprised an advance guard.

The Regent was not so optimistic when I talked to him on May 7th. He said that conditions had changed quite a bit since he had told me that Hungary would defend herself against the German or any other army to the last drop of blood. With the Western powers always on the defensive, Hungary's military position had become hopeless. The Hungarian army could retire behind the Tisza River, that is, to the east, and there make a desperate effort; but this would amount to abandoning Hungary and defending Rumania. He said that if the Germans demanded passage Hungary could do nothing but yield. His only hope then was that the Allies would not move in the Mediterranean region; for if they did, Germany would have to protect Rumanian oil.

Exactly five months later—and little more than a month after the nazification of Rumania—on October

7, 1940, the Rumanian legation in Berlin announced that German troops had been sent to Rumania with the latter's consent "to reorganize the Rumanian army with all equipment essential for modern warfare." A few days later, the German news agency stated that "in response to Rumania's request for assistance under the recent agreement" the Reich had dispatched a military mission with the necessary training formations and accompanying fighter squadrons as an additional precaution for the airfields. This announcement did not surprise anybody in Budapest. We knew that the German troops were passing, often in mufti, always secretly, and if possible, in the dark of the night. There had been all sorts of rumors. The British and French legations had made protests, but no one seemed to be able to say just how the troops were getting through. The French legation was on the Danube, and their staff were watching with field glasses while many German boats seemed to be going through. They saw all sorts of things that looked like guns, but actually could not spot any troops or say definitely what the boats were carrying. It seemed to be the general impression that troop trains would have to go through Budapest. All the military attachés were doing everything they could to find them.

About this time the Hungarian government forbade military attachés to leave Budapest without permission. Our military attaché, having heard that German troops were bypassing Budapest and going through Szolnok, asked for permission to visit an American doctor at Szolnok and received it. When he got near the Szolnok station, he cut across the fields toward the station and arrived about the same time as a German troop train.

He was promptly arrested, but released when his identity became known. When he returned to Budapest, he was informed by the Department of National Defense that they intended to ask for his recall on the grounds that he was a spy. When I told the Regent about it, he was greatly amused. "Spy?" he said. "Why, of course he is a spy! All military and naval attachés are spies. I was a spy myself when I was one—that is what these attachés are for." Later, the officer who had made the threat of expulsion came to the legation and apologized.

An interesting fact in connection with German troops passing through Hungary was that they were not permitted to travel by road. In February 1941, Premier Teleki told me that a few weeks before, when a German troop train had arrived at the frontier, the Hungarians had no engine available. The German commander, after a short wait, lost patience and ordered his men to alight, unload their equipment and proceed as a motorized column. The Hungarian officier in command of the frontier stopped it by ordering his frontier guard to load their rifles. It is really amazing how much the Germans took from the Hungarians during these years.

7

CENTRAL EUROPEAN DECLARATIONS
OF WAR

~~~~~~

THE COMPLEX which made European nations feel superior to their neighbors and particularly to their eastern ones made Hungary very sensitive about being called a Balkan nation. Croats and Transylvanians also seem to resent being considered members of the Balkan group. Indeed it would be necessary to give the term Balkan Peninsula a very wide interpretation in order to include Hungary, but she could not help being the European gateway into the Balkans and this determined her fate in the Hitler era.

It is difficult to determine exactly German strategy in the Balkans. It was certainly dominated by her desire to protect the right flank of the armies which were to launch the attack on Russia. If things had gone better in the war against the Soviets, the Germans might have attacked Turkey should they have found it necessary, but my impression is that they entered the Balkans really to protect their oil supplies first, and secondly to stake out strategic positions which they might find useful if occasion demanded. The negligence with which they treated the whole Mediterranean Basin is still unexplained. Perhaps they did not feel themselves strong enough. They certainly made poor use of their Greek bases.

The Magyars were bitterly hostile to Italy during

the Greek campaign, which had started in October 1940. There was great merriment everywhere because of Italy's humiliating defeat. Italy was Hungary's closest friend and had just helped her to obtain half of Transylvania. It would seem to be in line with Hungary's interest that the influence of Italy should grow in the Axis camp as a result of military triumphs. Yet every Hungarian was simply elated by her setbacks. Possibly they were influenced by memories of the first World War. In that war, Hungary as a part of the Hapsburg realm had fought against Italy. The war veterans were still influential and while they welcomed Italy's strategic support, they could not be expected to have much love for the Italian army.

Among those who displayed their delight at Italy's defeats was the Regent, not because of antipathy toward Italians but because he considered it a setback for the Axis.

Probably the chief reason for Hungary's sympathy toward the Greeks was chivalry. They were a small people defying what looked like a great power. We felt the same when Finland was attacked by Russia. The Hungarians allowed their feelings to run away with their political sobriety. For, Italy's difficulties in Greece augmented the danger of German intervention in the Balkans. Many Hungarians realized this, but they could not help but be pleased at the unexpected success of the Greek army.

Not only Rumania but Bulgaria, too, became Hitler's victim before he took Yugoslavia and Greece. Just as Hungary was his corridor to Rumania, so the latter was his deployment area for the invasion of Bulgaria;

and the more troops he needed for that new purpose, the more transports passed through Hungary.

On October 17, 1940, the Bulgarian government denied the presence of German troops in its country, but it was generally known that the number of husky German "tourists" had been increasing there rapidly. On December 3, M. Popoff, the Bulgarian foreign minister, declared that his government was making every effort to keep the nation out of war. He called Bulgaria's relations with Russia friendly. One month later, Professor Filoff, the Bulgarian premier, said he was determined to safeguard his country's neutrality and that neither communism nor national socialism were suitable systems for Bulgaria.

The British, giving vent to their displeasure, severed diplomatic relations with Rumania on February 10, 1941, stating that she had become a military base for Germany without protest. Sir Reginald Hoare, the minister, said at Istanbul, on his way home, that there were three hundred fifty thousand German troops in Rumania, most of them close to the border of Bulgaria. He also announced that the Bulgarian army stood on the frontier of Greece. This fact was stressed by Mr. Rendel, British minister to Sofia, who said on February 27 that the Bulgarian army had been virtually mobilized, but was not facing the Germans on the Danube.

It was obvious that Bulgaria had thrown in her lot with Germany. On March 1, 1941, in Vienna, Filoff signed Bulgaria's adherence to the Axis Pact, and German troops openly occupied Bulgaria. The German news agency intensified the war of nerves against Yugoslavia, which had not yet fallen in line, by announcing that the occupation was carried out "in agreement with the Bulgarian government in order to counteract British intentions of spreading the war into the Balkans." Prime Minister Filoff declared that the presence of German troops did not alter Bulgaria's policy of peace. But Britain broke off diplomatic relations, and Vyshinsky, deputy foreign commissar of the Soviet Union, declared that the Soviets did not share the opinion of the Bulgarian government that the presence of German troops in Bulgaria would facilitate the preservation of peace.

These events in Bulgaria must be considered as one of the last preparations for Hitler's attack on the Soviet Union.

Hungary's situation deteriorated rapidly. Three days before Hungary began to occupy Yugoslav territory, the British government had informed the Hungarian minister in London that the British legation in Budapest under Mr. (now Sir) Owen St. Clair O'Malley was being withdrawn because Hungary had become a base of military operations against the Allies. She was included in the Allied blockade. The Soviets had also rebuked Hungary. M. Vyshinsky told the Hungarian minister in Moscow that the USSR disapproved of Hungary's action against Yugoslavia. This was another straw in the wind. Soon the wind became a storm, and Hungary, like all her small neighbors, was a tiny skiff in the tossing sea. The great duel between pan-Germanism and pan-Slavism began, the life and death struggle between what amounts to two versions of the same totalitarian paganism—between Russian and German national socialism.

The outbreak of the war between the two tyrants rendered Hungary's situation much more serious than before. Hitler was obliged to take stern measures, and the Hungarians knew the penalty of disobedience. Unlike other nations, the Magyars could not find any comfort in Hitler's difficulties because Russia loomed up as an even greater danger.

Looking back, one can easily find fault with Hungary's participation in the campaign against Yugoslavia. Hungary's modest and very limited participation in the war against the Soviets presents itself in a very different light. Today we are better equipped to pass judgment. Our own position was simple. Germany was an enemy of our British friend and soon to be our own enemy. Russia involuntarily became an ally. We wanted quite naturally Germany's defeat and Russia's victory. Hungarians did not want either. To adopt this attitude is by no means as foolish as it may appear to some Americans who have become imbued with the slogan of "unconditional surrender." Many wars in history have ended without a clear-cut decision, and this was frequently a better solution than complete victory of one side. Often it was even a fairer solution, because almost never has one belligerent been completely right and the other completely wrong. Woodrow Wilson's postulate in 1917 that the war should lead to a peace "without victors and vanquished" was one of the wisest of his utterances. When Russia entered the war, that was the desire of most Europeans. Today Americans might well ask themselves whether our own country would not be safer now if our victory had been just sufficient to establish German democracy and reliable control of German and Japanese re-

search and production, without depriving twenty nations of the four freedoms for which we supposedly
fought the war. The catchwords "unconditional surrender" put Stalin on Hitler's throne and have prevented us from devoting constructive thought to the
future.

In the preface to this book, I have pointed out that
in a war of coalitions, where on each side several nations combine temporarily for specific ends without
giving up their distinctive principles, every belligerent
can find himself fighting on the right side and at the
same time on the wrong side. As Soviet imperialistic
designs are now revealed, it is apparent whether or not
we wish to admit it that, by sending a few troops against
Russia, Hungary fought on the wrong side as Hitler's
ally, but on the right side as an opponent of Soviet
Russia.

What happened in Hungary after the Soviet armies
liberated her fully justified anything Hungary did. As
a matter of fact, much as she hated communism, Hungary co-operated with the German army against Russia
slowly and reluctantly. According to reliable estimates,
Hungary's troop contingent in the east did not exceed
thirty thousand in 1941 and one hundred fifty thousand in 1942. After that, it went down rapidly because
when the tide of the war turned, Hungary could increase her resistance to German pressure in the hope
that the Western powers would occupy her by way of
the Mediterranean.

On June 21, 1941, when Hitler launched his attack
on Russia, General Antonescu, the Conductor of Rumania, hastened to proclaim a holy war for the recovery of Bessarabia lost to Russia the year before, and

said that Rumania was fighting at the side of the finest army in the world. On June 24, Slovakia, previously the eastern part of Czechoslovakia, declared that she was on Germany's side in the war against the Bolsheviks and that the Slovak army had joined the forces of Germany. On the same day Hungary severed diplomatic relations with Russia. Three days later, Premier Bardossy declared war on Russia without previous consent of parliament or Regent Horthy. Bardossy claimed Russian air attacks on Hungarian territory in violation of international law, but in this instance, as in his later declaration of war against the United States, Bardossy was influenced by Germany's use of the Transylvania problem as a means of pressure.

Rumania partook of the war against Russia with all her strength. Her losses were enormous, amounting to a quarter of a million in the first three months. Unlike Hungary, Rumania wished territorial conquest. Not content with the return of Bessarabia, General Antonescu on October 18, 1941, declared that Rumania was annexing what he called Transnistria, that is, the part of the Ukraine between the rivers Dniestr and Bug with the port of Odessa as capital. Many more Soviet soldiers died at the hands of Rumanians than as a result of Hungary's intervention, but when Stalin fixed the new boundaries after the war, Rumania was again the winner because imperialistic interests, not good or bad behavior during the conflict, influenced his decision. He was certain of Rumanian subservience, but knew that Hungary was a hard nut to crack.

The policy of Russia's allies was affected by the trend of her relations with these small nations. Britain and the United States acted upon the principle that Rus-

sia's enemies were also their enemies. The Soviets did
not reciprocate our loyalty. On December 6, 1941 the
British government declared that from the following
day Britain would be at war with Finland, Rumania
and Hungary because of their refusal to cease hostilities against Russia. The Soviets declared war on Bulgaria and Japan only when the fighting was over in
order to determine the conditions of peace.

It is interesting as well as important that neither the
United States nor Great Britain were ever officially
at war with Slovakia or Croatia, although both countries declared war on the two English-speaking powers
immediately after Pearl Harbor. Washington and London refused to acknowledge the existence of a state of
war with these two little nations because they were not
recognized as sovereign states: A declaration of war
coming from Hitler-made Slovakia or Croatia was like
a challenge from a gymnastic or choral society. This
procedure, however, should not be allowed to cloud
our political judgment and sense of justice. The Slovaks, according to the official Czech fiction, were part
and parcel of the Czechoslovak nation. I mention this
not because I am advocating that all Czechoslovaks
be blamed for the deeds of the Slovaks, or Yugoslavia
for the action of Croats. However, the fact that we were
not at war with Croatia and Slovakia while we were
with Hungary should not influence our attitude toward the latter. Actually, although Hungary declared
war on us, it was illegal since it was not approved by
parliament or the Regent.

I was not in Hungary on December 12, 1941, when
Prime Minister Bardossy announced that Hungary's

diplomatic relations with the United States were severed. Bardossy called up the legation and informed
them that a state of war existed, but he insisted it was
not a declaration of war. He was asked to put this
statement in writing, but was reluctant to do so. Upon
being informed that no attention would be paid a ver-
bal statement, he sent a letter of confirmation. In this
letter he reiterated that it was not to be regarded as a
declaration of war, but that the Hungarian government
considered a state of war existed between the two countries. Apparently Bardossy realized that he could not
get the consent either of parliament or the Regent to a
formal declaration of war. When the first secretary of
the legation, Mr. Travers, made his good-by call on the
Regent, the latter said to him: "Remember that this
so-called declaration of war is not legal; not approved
by parliament, not signed by me." Obviously, Hungary being forced by Hitler to declare war, Bardossy
took it upon himself to do so. Whether he was a pa-
triot or a scoundrel is a matter of opinion. He was
later executed for his usurpation of the rights of parliament and the Regent.

President Roosevelt evaluated the situation correctly.
He knew that war declarations coming from those small
countries were forced by Hitler and he was, therefore,
inclined to ignore them. On June 2, 1942, that is, after
six months of Soviet insistence, the President sent a
message to Congress stating that Rumania, Hungary
and Bulgaria had declared war on the United States,
but he added: "I realize that those three governments
took that action not upon their own initiative or in
response to the wishes of their own peoples, but as in-

struments of Hitler." Not before July 18, 1942, did
Congress declare that there was a state of war between
us and those nations.

Before our diplomats left Hungary, they were the
objects of stormy proofs of friendship. One of our secretaries was invited to dinner by a friend who belonged
to one of the leading families of Hungary. He told her
that his things were packed and that he could not dress,
and she told him that it made no difference. He
thought, therefore, that he was dining *en famille* and
was astonished when he arrived, to find a large number
of prominent people—members of parliament, members of the cabinet, and so forth—assembled. When
they sat down, he was seated on his hostess' right. During the course of the dinner, the hostess arose and said,
"I am not accustomed to making speeches, but since
our guest of honor tonight is an enemy, I feel that I
must explain this. I am not pro-German; I am not pro-
English; I am not pro-American; I am just pro-Hungarian and as a pro-Hungarian, I ask that you all rise
and drink a toast to a speedy American victory." The
guests arose, drank the toast and dashed their glasses,
according to the old Hungarian custom, to the floor.

We left Hungary in March 1941, about a year and a
half after the invasion of Poland. It was customary,
when diplomats left, for the members of the diplomatic
corps and friends to gather and bid them good-by. The
tremendous outburst of friendliness which accompanied our departure from Budapest was not, I hope,
altogether due to a desire to make a pro-Allied demonstration, but it amounted to that. My wife wrote in
her diary concerning our departure:

Nicholas Horthy, former Hungarian Regent, checks some of his papers in the witness cell block of the Nuremberg prison, Nuremberg, Germany, 1945.

THE WHITE HOUSE
WASHINGTON

December 31, 1937.

Dear John:-

        I am delighted to have your letter of December sixteenth, and when you see the Regent again please tell him from me that we sailors must stick together!

        I am glad you find that the Nazi movement does not seem to be making much progress. The other day we had word from Bucharest that seems disturbing. Perhaps you will let me know what you hear of the trend toward Nazi control in Rumania.

        With all good wishes for the New Year,

        As ever yours,

Franklin D. Roosevelt

Hon. John F. Montgomery,
American Legation,
Budapest,
Hungary.

Madame Horthy, the Regent's wife, played the part of her country's first lady with simple dignity.

Foreign Minister de Kanya felt that whoever won World War II, Hungary would lose.

Bela Imredy, pro-Nazi, who earned his countrymen's ridicule and contempt during his short term as premier of Hungary.

Count Paul Teleki's premiership ended in suicide over Hungary's junta-organized entry into Germany's war against Yugoslavia.

Admiral Nicholas Horthy, the man who tried to steer Hungary safely between the combating forces of pan-Slavism and pan-Germanism.

Left to right: Premier Teleki and the gossipy foreign minister, Count Csaky, on an official visit to Rome.

Premier Nicholas Kallay, whose plan for Hungary's surrender to the Anglo-American armies was defeated by the Teheran decision against invading through the Balkans.

When we arrived at the airport, we were greeted by members of the Foreign Office, and the Regent's aide-de-camp stepped up to present me with many good wishes from the Admiral and his wife, and an enormous bouquet of lavender and white orchids, trailing across from one arm to the other and far down over the side. After another five minutes I was so overwhelmed with flowers that I could not carry them, and an airways employee staggered away on several trips to transfer them to the plane. John and I were surrounded by our friends.   It was a bewildering, emotional moment. People kept on thrusting little parcels into my hands. The Archduchess Gabriella brought violets and cookies adorned with good-luck symbols. Suddenly we were hurried away and everyone swarmed out from the building to the terrace. While the engines were warming up, Stephen Horthy came with more orchids. Then the door was closed, and up we went while handkerchiefs fluttered below and hats were swung to and fro. John and I were quite spent after all the tears and emotion. Never have I had so much human kindness lavished upon me as during that last hour in Budapest.

And as we neared the end of the first lap of our journey westward:

The reddish soil, striking in color even from above, told us that we approached Spain. At Barcelona, the pilot set us down deftly despite the deep mud. We had the first bananas since leaving America. We put our watches back two hours and soon were in the air again towards Portugal. I shall never forget the vastness and beauty of the great Iberian plateau, with its stupendous white cloud-banks. We passed over hundreds of miles without a sign of human habitation. The surface seemed to be purely of stone, with deep canyons and crevices pitting it in every direction. It depressed me, and I remembered the white-haired Foreign Minister de Kanya's jesting and yet ominous remark that soon he would apply for an American immigration visa. What we left behind was a world of fear.

Part Three

An Island in the Soviet Sea

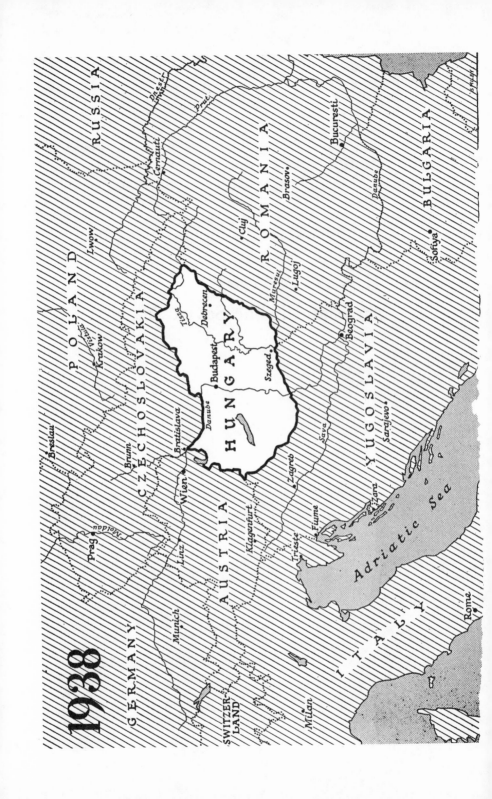

1

HUNGARIAN ATTEMPTS AT MAKING
SEPARATE PEACE

AFTER WE left Hungary I kept up a regular correspondence with members of the legation and with friends. Thus, I was quite familiar with the state of affairs up to the time our mission left Hungary. Upon their arrival in this country I met them out in the harbor, and we all dined together that night. I got full reports from them of Teleki's suicide and the events that followed so swiftly.

Tibor Eckhardt and Leon Orlowski had left Budapest before I did but, as they had to take a roundabout route through Africa, did not arrive until some months later. Eckhardt established himself in Washington and immediately made contact with Hungarian representatives in all parts of the world, and with various people in the State Department and embassies in Washington. In this way he has kept remarkably well informed. Orlowski established himself in New York and, through the Polish underground and acquaintances made during his diplomatic career, also has kept very well informed.

We three, having been friends in Budapest, naturally stayed in close contact after our arrival in America. I kept receiving letters from friends all over Europe. It is amazing that there were so many. The letters came in various ways—some were simply handed to soldiers after the arrival of the American mission. Letters were given to newspaper men, not necessarily in Hungary, but in Italy, Germany and elsewhere. A number of letters were merely posted in America or Switzerland and other countries where the mails were free, with no indication of the sender. There was a period during the siege of Budapest when none of us could get any information, but letters got through in a remarkably short time after it was over.

Many of these letters I did not dare answer and those that I did were very carefully worded. We had a letter from an American friend of ours who went back to Budapest early in 1947 and made inquiries concerning people with whom he had been on the most friendly terms, only to be told that it would be better not to go near these persons, as they were already under suspicion due to their friendship with the Allies. So my friends passed their friends up with very heavy hearts.

Liberated by American troops from the German concentration camp Dachau, along with Leon Blum, Schuschnigg and others, Mr. Nicholas de Kallay, the last prime minister of Hungary before Germany actually took over, has sent me some valuable material covering the sequence of events preceding and during his term in office from March 1942 until March 1944. Thus most of the events which took place from the time of my departure from Hungary to Mr. Kallay's arrest are described on firsthand evidence by the person most qualified to know the facts. His story of Hungary's unsuccessful attempts to withdraw from the war is of particular interest.

From the time that Mr. Kallay was appointed prime minister by the Regent in 1942, continuous attempts were made by Hungary to reduce the army fighting against Russia and to end belligerency. Mr. Kallay, in partnership with the minister of the interior, Mr. Keresztes-Fisher, and the Hungarian Foreign Office, initiated widespread anti-Nazi action in which leaders of the opposition also participated. These included the president of the National Bank, Mr. Baranyai, the leader of the Liberal Party, Mr. Rassay, the leader of the Social Democratic Party, Mr. Peyer, and the vice-president of the Smallholders Party, Mr. Bajcsy-Zsilinsky (who later was executed by the Nazis as leader of the Hungarian underground).

Kallay's policy was twofold: He wanted to extricate Hungary from the war, but at the same time avoid German military occupation, which was bound to lead to mass extermination of Jews and anti-Nazi Hungarians.

In the summer of 1943, Prime Minister Kallay sent his personal envoy to Istanbul to establish direct contact with the Western Allies with the purpose of offering them Hungary's unconditional surrender and military collaboration whenever military operations of the Allies would render it possible. The envoy in Istanbul at first contacted the American consul, Mr. Berry, and then having waited in vain for six weeks for an answer, established contact on September 9 with the British ambassador to Turkey, Sir Hugh Knatchbull-Hugessen. The ambassador reported to Mr. Eden that the Hungarian envoy had arrived to offer unconditional surrender and future military co-operation on the part of Hungary, and was authorized by cable from Mr. Eden to enter into conversations with the Hungarian representative. The British ambassador then arranged with the Hungarian representative to check on his authorization to conclude an arrangement with Great Britain for the Hungarian government. As agreed, the Hungarian minister to Portugal, Mr. Wodianer, visited the British representative in Lisbon, Mr. Standale-Benett, and gave him the asked assurance.

After these preliminaries, an agreement was concluded between the British and Hungarian authorized representatives containing the following points:

(a) Hungary offered unconditional surrender to the Allies.

(b) The time when this unconditional surrender should become effective was to be determined by the Allies, who meanwhile would conclude military agreements with Hungary.

(c) Great Britain undertook to inform her allies of the abovesaid facts. America was to be informed immediately and the Soviets after one month. Britain requested that no other contacts be made between Hungary and the Western Allies.

(d) The British representative advised Hungary not to provoke German military occupation of Hungary as it would impair or render impossible future military co-operation between Hungary and the Allies and might even lead to the immediate transfer of the Hungarian army to the Russian front by the Germans.

(e) The Hungarian Foreign Office was to establish permanent contact with the British Consulate in Istanbul.

This contact was established in the Foreign Office by Mr. Zsentmiklosy, undersecretary of the Foreign Office, who received a secret code from the British and a short-wave transmitter which functioned in the subsequent period until the military occupation of Hungary by Germany. Mr. Zsentmiklosy was executed in 1944 by the Germans for this service.

The Hungarian declaration of unconditional surrender was submitted at the Quebec Conference where Mr. Roosevelt and Mr. Churchill took notice of it and also informed the Soviet government. The agreement, although not put in writing, was adhered to by both sides. Military agreements had been prepared in all details to assure collaboration of the Hungarian army with Anglo-American armies whenever their strategic plans allowed for doing so. An exchange of general staff officers had also been prepared. The Western Allies at that time did not request Hungarian collaboration with the Russian army, and the Hungarian government at that time could never have undertaken any such obligation, as the army was willing to collaborate with Anglo-American armed forces, but not with the Russians.

This military plan was never carried out. At the Teheran Conference, in December 1943, proposed Allied invasion across the Balkans was dropped at the request of Stalin; thus there was no Anglo-American army near enough to accept the unconditional surrender of the Hungarian army or to develop military collaboration.

But whatever collaboration was possible was put into practice during the period when the Hungarian government was still free to act. It became a regular practice of Allied airplanes to fly over the western part of Hungary to attack German industries located in Austria. The Russian airmail to Tito' flew at regular intervals over Budapest. The Allies never bombed Hungarian territory, and orders were found with Allied flyers-who eventually made forced landings in Hungary, forbidding them to bomb Hungarian territory. These facts which could not be concealed from the Germans went beyond neutrality, as neutral states objected to Allied warplanes flying over their territory and even pro-Allied Turkey had shot down British and American planes flying unauthorized over its territory.

From January 1943, on, Hungary had not sent soldiers or war materiel to fight Russia. In fact, no Hungarian troops participated from that time on in any fighting against the Russians until March 1944. On the contrary, whatever troops and armaments could be withdrawn from the front were ordered back to Hungary. Nonbelligerency was also extended to the various partisan groups in neighboring countries. Their leaders were invited to Budapest and secret agreements were concluded not to fight each other, not to take prisoners, and even to exchange those who had been captured. In the case of the Yugoslav partisans, the Hungarian government had established friendly contacts with the Serbian partisans of Mihailovitch before Teheran. Then, in the autumn of 1943, Tito's partisans repeatedly crossed into Hungarian territory and provoked border incidents. Prime Minister Kallay ordered the Hungarian army to refrain from retaliation and immediately sent his representative to the Tito forces and agreed with them to refrain in the future from all armed incidents and hostile acts.

From September 1943 until the occupation of Hungary, the German minister to Budapest, Mr. Jagov, steadily avoided personal contact with the prime minister, as the latter previously had refused to receive him. German-Hungarian relations became even more strained when in February 1944 the Hungarian chief of staff, in a note which could be qualified as an ultimatum, requested from General Keitel, the chief of the German general staff, that a) all Hungarian troops be immediately brought to Hungary from Russia; and b) the Carpathian Mountains be defended exclusively by Hungarian troops; German military forces, even in case of further withdrawal, being kept from entering Hungarian territory.

Even in the first days of March 1944, when the Germans requested passage for three thousand German military trucks to carry troops and war materiel across Hungarian territory, Prime Minister Kallay flatly turned down the demand.

I was gratified during those years to find that the American press gave Hungary some credit for the efforts—so far as they were publicly known—of Premier Kallay's government.

On September 13, 1943, Mr. Russell Hill reported to the New York *Herald Tribune:*

The Rumanians have sent a larger contingent of troops to Russia than any of Germany's 'other allies' —the number has been variously estimated at between 300,000 and 700,000—and they have suffered by far the heaviest losses. It is in Hungary that opposition to the German war is best organized and most articulate. The Hungarians have prepared well for the day when Allied troops arrive . . . There are in Hungary today eleven anti-Nazi newspapers, of which the leading one is the liberal daily 'Magyar Nemzet' . . . But even the parties which support

Premier Kallay's government have given the Germans only minimum co-operation. There never have been more than four Hungarian divisions at the Russian front. The Germans have not been allowed to control Hungary militarily as they have Rumania and Bulgaria. They have been restricted to railroad stations and airfields, and German troops are not seen in Budapest or other Hungarian cities. Undoubtedly, the Germans could have forcibly denied the Hungarians their relatively free press, their parliamentary institutions and their independent national existence.

Undoubtedly, as Mr. Hill says, the Germans could have denied the Hungarians their relatively free press, but it would have necessitated German garrisons of at least three hundred thousand men.

On October 11, 1943, the London *Times* reported that a Swedish journalist, K. G. Bolander, after a visit to Hungary, had written in the *Svenska Dagbladet:*

The greatest surprise was to see how widespread and marked anti-German feeling was and how openly expressed. The Hungarians are well aware that they are in the wrong box, but also know that attempts to get disentangled from Germany may lead to German countermeasures resulting in complete annihilation, and the possibility of the Germans letting loose neighboring peoples on Hungary. The Slav menace in the case of a German breakdown is considered even greater, and the Hungarians' only hope seems to be a miraculous intervention by the Allies. . . .

Budapest has to say 'No' to German demands almost every day. No troops have been sent to the Balkans, and when Hungarian troops recently found

themselves fighting on the Russian front, it was because the German retreat had been so quick that the
Hungarians, though actually only supply line troops,
found themselves in the front line.

A prominent politician told me that the question
for Hungary was whether the Germans, the Russians
or the Anglo-Saxons would be first in the country.
'Of course, we wish it will be the Anglo-Saxons even
if we dare not believe in it,' he said.

When Hitler's patience was finally exhausted and on
March 19, 1944 he occupied Hungary, even Mr. Elmer
Davis, director of the U. S. Office of War Information,
in whose organization American and foreign communists and fellow-travelers seemed to be extraordinarily
well represented, wrote in the Washington *Post:*

Hungary was the only country in southeastern Europe which permitted many of its newspapers to
publish news from neutral and Allied sources. Until
the Nazis performed their latest act of cannibalism
and swallowed up their satellites the other day,
Hungary was the only country in southeastern Europe whose press had never been 'co-ordinated' to
serve the will of Hitler.

Some Hungarian newspapers in recent months
published at least as many items coming from neutral, British or American sources as from German
sources, and often Allied news received better play
than enemy items. I have seen Budapest newspapers
with the full text of speeches of President Roosevelt,
Vice-President Wallace and Wendell Willkie . . .
Hungarian publishers were permitted to publish
translations of current American books, which were
sold openly in Budapest book stores.

Indeed, it is possible that Hitler found it necessary to occupy Hungary by force, violence and fraud instead of by consent simply because the Hungarians knew so much about the coming Allied victory . . .

In other words, Hungary was not even willing to curb its free press in order to please Hitler. Hungary's resistance was outright provocative and it could not last.

The Germans had a large fifth column in the country; but the statement that the fifth column was identical with the German minority is not true. Germans should forever hate and despise Hitler for his destruction of what had always been the best element of the German race, namely, the German minorities in eastern Europe. These people, bearers of occidental civilization, were with few exceptions law-abiding citizens, and when national socialist agents began to bring them the gospel of the German master-race, the general reaction was one of reticence; they wanted to keep out of trouble. This attitude became very dangerous for every member of the German minority when the German armies approached, and when the various governments gave in to Hitler. His proclaimed doctrine was that he was not only head of Germany but Fuehrer of the whole German race, so that every German, wherever he dwelt, owed allegiance to him. Hence to be anti-national socialist was less risky for a Magyar or a Rumanian than for a Hungarian or Rumanian citizen of German origin. The latter exposed himself to being treated as a traitor to the German race. By these means, Hitler succeeded in terrorizing the German minorities for whom he claimed special privileges, a kind of extraterritorial rights within the countries whose subjects they were. This was the origin of a real tragedy. Afraid of Hitler's revenge, the German minorities accepted a new policy which, in case of Hitler's defeat, had to prove suicidal. Nations which had lived on good terms with their German minorities began to consider them a menace.

In Hungary, Hitler's attempt to use the German minorities as a Trojan horse was partly unsuccessful. The most numerous German element were Swabians; deliberate, levelheaded, hardworking people who never had political ambitions. German agents distributed money, even cows, which they presented as Hitler's personal gifts. The Hungarian government invented an amusing device to counteract this form of propaganda. Assessors were sent to the farms belonging to Germans, and they began to count the cattle and survey the fields. When the peasant asked what was the matter, he was told that the authorities, informed of his desire to move to Germany in accordance with the Fuehrer's wishes, wanted to fix the indemnity they would have to pay him. This was just about the time when Germans were being forcibly repatriated from the Baltic States. The trick was very effective since not one of them wanted to leave Hungary and go to Germany. All of a sudden, there was a large number of applications to Magyarize German names. Actually the national socialists in the end amounted to about one-third of the German minority.

Apart from Imredy after his conversion to Nazism, the prime ministers showed remarkable energy in fighting national socialism. Fortunately the Hungarian branch was mostly riffraff. In March 1937, Tibor Eckhardt, who was in the van of the fight against national socialism, estimated that not more than ten percent of the population supported that movement. Hitler's successes should have caused a national socialist boom, but Hungarians seemed to be horrified by his methods. At the height of his diplomatic successes in the spring of 1939, national socialists received sixteen percent of the vote, about the same proportion— and to a large extent representing the same people—as the communists received in the 1945 elections. On the whole, Hungarian national socialism would have been negligible if it had not fascinated a good number of professional soldiers who, quite erroneously, regarded Hitlerism as an attempt to rebuild the military strength of the German nation.

Hitler's crooked cross could not be displayed in Hungary because as early as May 1933, Mr. Keresztes-Fisher, minister of the interior, had decreed that no profanation of the Hungarian flag by any emblem, nor any use of emblems representing the symbol of a foreign nation would be tolerated. Some months later, he forbade the "wearing or exhibiting of the swastika in any form" and ordered the destruction of all badges showing it. Then Mesko, at that time leader of the Magyar national socialists, introduced the fashion of wearing green shirts with the Arrow Cross, a combination of four arrows which resembled the swastika. Later Count Alexander Festetics, another nincompoop, became head of the Arrow Cross and after the fusion of the different groups, claimed, at the end of 1937, in an interview with the *Daily Telegraph,* three hundred thousand members, which in my opinion was an enormous exaggeration.

The occupation of Austria by the Germans encouraged Major Szalasi, Festetics' successor, to resort to terroristic methods like those used before by the Austrian national socialists. For this he was arrested and given three years in jail. On February 24, 1939, the government disbanded his Hungarist Party, seized its funds and literature, and made many arrests. The straw that broke the camel's back was the explosion of hand grenades in front of the Budapest Great Synagogue. Then in August 1940, came the Vienna Award by which half of Transylvania was restored to Hungary, and a few weeks later Major Szalasi was released from prison under an amnesty. The Arrow Cross and the revived Hungarist National Socialist Party united under his leadership. There is little doubt that more tolerance toward the national socialists had been one of Hitler's conditions in Vienna. Peaceful relations, however, did not last long. In November, the government announced that a national socialist plot had been discovered. Its aim was to kill Keresztes-Fisher, and to kidnap the Regent in order to compel him to release national socialists from prison. The government arrested several hundred national socialists and stated that 236 hand grenades had been found in national socialist homes. It should be remembered that the government took these energetic steps when all Europe was already at Hitler's mercy. He must have been exasperated by Hungary's habit of withdrawing after a short time every concession made to the Hungarian national socialists. As a sequel to the discovery of the plot against the Regent, two national socialist members of parliament were sentenced to long terms of penal servitude at the end of 1941.

2

RUSSIA'S RESPONSIBILITY

IN WORLD WAR II

THERE WERE, of course, in Hungary as in other countries, people who without being national socialists advocated a policy of appeasement. Count Stephen Csaky, foreign minister in 1939 and 1940, was a member of this group. His political stature, however, was so insignificant that he had no real hand in Hungarian foreign policy. It would have been more to the point to have called him the prime minister's undersecretary for external relations. Imredy undoubtedly chose him because he wanted him. Teleki, I am sure, would have much preferred de Kanya, but did not want to make a change because he considered it would be very difficult to replace Csaky. He knew that if he dismissed him, he would have to replace him with someone acceptable to Germany and Italy, and de Kanya was distinctly not acceptable. Teleki preferred the devil he had to the devil he might have. He did not trust Csaky, however, so he set up his own foreign office at the prime ministry and privately sent emissaries to various countries. This created a very curious situation. Many diplomats started to bypass Csaky and call on Teleki, but they found they couldn't get anywhere at all. When asked a question, he replied with something irrelevant about the Boy Scouts and his experiences when he was young, and went on and on as though he had not heard the question. If you asked him again, he repeated his tactics. Soon we all gave up and stopped calling.

This was obviously Teleki's object, for when he wanted to talk, he talked quite freely. At various times he employed subterfuges for that purpose. On several occasions I was called by Countess Teleki and invited to tea. When I got there, I would find Countess Teleki and her sister or just the Countess, but in a few minutes the prime minister would come in and the ladies vanish. On these occasions he would talk at length and without reservation.

Count Csaky talked—he loved to talk. When you called on him, he never was in a hurry, and he told you all kinds of wonderful stories. The only trouble was that most of them were untrue; you never knew what to believe and what not to believe. On one occasion, he entertained me at length with accounts of his prowess as a fighter pilot in World War I. It did not occur to me to question him, as I didn't know how old he was, but when I happened to mention something about it, everybody laughed and I was told that he was in school in Paris during that war and had not participated in any fighting. On another occasion, when he was telling me about Hungary's refusal to let German troops go through to Poland, he embellished the story by saying that, to make it impossible, the Hungarian government had taken up the railroad tracks and blown up the tunnels. I was accordingly surprised to meet a man who that afternoon had come in to Budapest by train from near the Polish border where he lived. He laughed heartily at Csaky's story.

Shortly after Sumner Welles made his trip to Europe

as President Roosevelt's special envoy, Csaky told the secret committees of the upper and lower houses that he had met Welles in Italy, and that Welles had told him Germany would be the dominant power in Europe for the next five years and any nation would be foolish not to play along with her during that period. I doubted this statement very much. I wrote a personal letter to Mr. Welles and received a categorical denial by telegraph, with instructions to go to the highest possible authorities and inform them that the statement was untrue.

Csaky probably in his heart was pro-Ally, but he was very much flattered by any attention he received from the Axis leaders and particularly from Mussolini; he liked to feel that he was one of the big boys himself. Csaky, like Teleki, imagined himself a very smart fellow. He greatly overestimated himself by thinking that he could outsmart people like Hitler and Ribbentrop.

His idea of cleverness is exemplified by a letter which I received one day within half an hour after I had arrived home from the Foreign Office, where I had spent about three-quarters of an hour with him. In our conversation Csaky had said nothing to indicate that there was any deterioration in Hungary's relations with America. But the letter stated that relations between the two countries were bad and that he was sorry he had not had time to discuss it with me in our conversation. He said, further, that as far as he was concerned, they would not get any better and would probably get worse, unless he got satisfactory answers to some questions, which he then proceeded to put. The questions really accused our government of various unneutral acts—raising an army for the Czechs, raising money for the Czechs, and other things which he probably knew were not true. He apparently hoped that I would be foolish enough to reply, thus giving him something to take with him when he went up that week to the launching of a boat in Germany. He probably thought it would be very nice to hand this to Mr. Hitler and show what important work he was doing.

I did not even acknowledge the letter, but telegraphed the State Department and awaited instructions. Nearly a week went by, and I knew the Department was waiting for Csaky to get on the train. As I expected, a few hours after he was out of Hungary, I received instructions to go to the Foreign Office and, in effect, tell them our relations with the Czechs were none of their business.

Voernle, a strong pro-Nazi, afterward minister to Ankara, and in charge during Csaky's absence, was undersecretary. We called him "Fishface" and that was a good description. I saw him and carried out the instructions, which he received very solemnly. As I walked out, I said, "I presume in the event that you decide to declare war, you will give us the usual diplomatic courtesies?" and even he had to laugh at that.

It was customary to give the foreign minister a dinner once a year and it just so happened that prior to this, Csaky had accepted an invitation at our legation on a date which turned out to be the day on which he came back from Germany. I told my wife that I was quite certain the guest of honor would not be able to come. I felt sure he would be ill. I could not imagine anyone having the face to attend a dinner under the circumstances. But when the time came, lo and behold, Csaky was there just as suave as could be. He never mentioned the exchange of "compliments"—on the contrary, was full of information about Germany. He took me into another room and told me in great detail everything that he was supposed to have seen and heard, and ended up by saying that the Foreign Office had discovered a German spy in their own ministry.

Since the German minister, although he was a very nice fellow, was a hard man to entertain because so many people did not want to be entertained at the same time, I had invited him to the Csaky dinner. Many people considered the latter a Nazi and it seemed a good time to have all the Axis people. I wondered what he thought when Csaky and I left the party for so long. Csaky apparently was desperately anxious to fix things up, and I suppose he found a good lie to tell the German minister later.

Csaky and I broke later over an incident in connection with Imredy. The latter came to see me one day in great excitement. He said that Csaky had told him that I had said in a recent conversation that Imredy was intriguing against the Regent in various ways. Imredy said that this was not true, and he demanded an explanation.

Whenever I went to the Foreign Office or anywhere else for an important conversation, I had a stenographer meet me at home immediately thereafter and dictated the whole conversation while it was fresh in my mind. I knew I had made no such statement. I asked my secretary to bring in a draft of the conversation. Without looking at it, I handed it to Imredy, and he read it over. I said: "Is there any such reference?" and he replied that there was not. I said: "Well, that is the conversation." He seemed mollified and finally left.

If there is one thing that is supposed to be confidential, it is conversation between a diplomat and the foreign minister. Accordingly I wrote to ask Csaky for an explanation. Ignoring the falsity of his statement, Csaky attempted to justify his course by the fact that Imredy was on the foreign affairs committee of parliament. After consulting de Kanya, who was greatly astonished at Csaky's behavior, I presented the Regent's chief of staff with copies of the correspondence and also told him of Csaky's previous letter concerning American-Hungarian relations.

The Regent sent for me. I immediately explained that I felt myself in an extremely awkward position: I could no longer call on Csaky because I could not trust him, and therefore felt myself cut off from official information. The Regent said, "Well, come to me. I will get you any information you want." We arranged that I was to call his aide-de-camp as often as I wanted. This proved to be very useful. Later, while the Foreign Office were denying the presence of German troops on the way to Rumania, the Regent not only confirmed it but sent me daily the exact number that were passing through.

There was genuine relief when Csaky died in January 1941, of food poisoning which he had acquired during an official visit to Belgrade. After his death, appeasement was no longer tried and the Magyars, having learned that the Germans used every concession to extort more concessions, developed the abrogation of concessions to a high art. The Germans called it sabotage.

One story came up during Csaky's term as foreign minister which I was disposed to doubt at the time because of my previous experiences with him; but it has since been proven true for the most part at the Nuremberg trials.

In November 1937, when war was still a little way off, Tibor Eckhardt had told me that according to information he had, the German general staff would never agree to war as long as they had to fight on two fronts. The only solution the general staff considered feasible was to neutralize the Soviets or make them their allies first. This, as we know now, was an accurate forecast. In a conversation on October 4, 1939, Mr. de Kanya expressed the opinion that the German and Russian *rapprochement* had not been the consequence of Great Britain's military opposition to Hitler, but had been going on for some time. As far back as a year before, de Kanya said, he had reached the conclusion that Germany and Russia were coming to a general understanding. He had no doubt that Stalin had definitely committed himself to Germany well before he had started conversations with Britain and France in the summer of 1939 concerning an alliance against Germany.

German-Hungarian relations were not based on mutual trust but the Hungarians had their channels and German diplomats and officers, especially anti-national socialists, told their former comrades-in-arms more than they would have revealed to us or the British. Hence I was certain that something was behind de Kanya's vague allusions.

In 1940 Mr. Leon Orlowski, whom I have already mentioned as the last Polish minister to Budapest, told me the following story: In May of 1939—that is, between three or four months before the outbreak of

war—a Hungarian lawyer employed by the Polish legation told him that he had it from very high authority
that Stalin and Hitler had agreed on the division of
Poland. Orlowski was naturally distrustful, especially
since the lawyer was unwilling to reveal the source of
his information. Nevertheless, Orlowski reported this
to his government, as a rumor.

In the fall of 1939, when history had confirmed the
rumor, Orlowski asked the lawyer whether he felt authorized to name his informer. The lawyer stated that
he had been pledged not to do so, but now felt free to
say that it was Monsignor Alexander Ernszt, leader of
the Christian Socialist Party and minister of education in Count Teleki's government. Ernszt had his information from Count Teleki, who wished to give the
Poles a warning, but was too cautious to commit what
the Germans would have called an indiscretion. Mr.
Orlowski, at that moment the envoy of a defunct country, was still interested in worming out the truth. He
asked Tibor Eckhardt if he would not sound out Foreign Minister Csaky. According to Csaky, Hitler came
to the conclusion in March 1939, that time was
running against him, as Great Britain and other nations were rearming. Hence, he decided that he had to
advance his plans. He discussed the situation with the
general staff, but they, still enjoying a great measure of
independence, were firm against war. On one front,
they said, if sufficiently prepared—yes; but on two
fronts—no.

Baron von Neurath, former foreign minister and at
that time protector of Bohemia, was informed of the
general staff's hesitation. He called in General Sirovy,
prime minister of President Hacha's Czechoslovak

regime, and said to him: "We know you as a great
friend of the Russians. Naturally, you would like to
see Germans and Russians as friendly as possible because that would help your own people. With that in
mind, I suggest that you see Stalin and sound him out
as to the possibility of a pact with Hitler on the basis
of a partition of Poland."

General Sirovy, Count Csaky went on, visited Moscow and was told that they were interested in the idea,
and he so advised von Neurath. Baron von Neurath
then went to the Fuehrer with this information, but
Hitler was hesitant. He was afraid of Stalin. Nevertheless, he discussed it with the general staff, and they
liked the idea. The partition of Poland, the general
staff considered, would be sufficient safeguard against
Russian aggression. Accordingly, Hitler, addressing his
party chieftains in April 1939, told them that Russia
was not interested in defending Poland.

When the British and French, Count Csaky said,
came to Moscow in August, Stalin had already made,
in principle, a deal with Germany, knowing that the
latter could offer him more than the Western powers
were willing and able to tender; but neither Hitler nor
Stalin wanted to make this fact known before the invasion of Poland could be started.

As I have said, I doubted Csaky's story: To me it
smacked of his usual desire to add drama to the facts. It
was true that very soon after the Russo-German pact of
August 23, 1939, Poland was partitioned; but confirmation of any agreement on that partition by a formal
pact came out only in the Nuremberg trials.

Perhaps I should say "leaked out." The Russian

representatives insisted on keeping the text of the secret treaty out of the official Nuremberg records.

According to Richard L. Stokes, correspondent for the St. Louis *Post-Dispatch* at Nuremberg, the existence of the so-called "secret protocol" was first mentioned during the defense of Rudolf Hess, by Dr. Alfred Seidl, attorney for Hans Frank, Nazi governor general of Poland. "At the insistence of the Russian prosecution which has always shown itself acutely sensitive in this matter," Stokes reported in his article of May 22, 1946, in which the text of the protocol was published for the first time in America, "Seidl was stopped in his tracks."

Some weeks later, however, despite continued Russian protest, an account of the documents drafted from memory by Dr. Wilhelm Gauss, legal adviser of the Nazi Foreign Office, was placed in the evidence.

Still later, when Dr. Seidl again tried to bring up the secret protocol he was prevented from entering the text as evidence, but at the suggestion of Mr. Thomas L. Dodd, the American deputy prosecutor, the witness on the stand at the time, Ernst von Weizsaecker, was permitted to give the contents from memory. At Mr. Stokes' request, Mr. Dodd obtained a German copy of the agreements from Dr. Seidl and arranged for their translation into English.

Since the agreement is of such historic importance, and the account of this portion of the trial itself should be of considerable interest to the reader, I am including Mr. Stokes' article in full, along with the Gauss affidavit as published in the *New Leader* the following November, in Appendix I of this volume.

The secret protocol attached to the nonaggression pact signed in Moscow on August 23, 1939 by Molotov and Ribbentrop, demarcated the spheres of interest in the Baltic States, Poland and Bessarabia between the German Reich and the USSR. A second agreement made a month later in Moscow modified the spheres of interest in Lithuania and Poland.

One wonders why more publicity was not given the secret protocol when it was published in this country and why there was not more discussion in Congress concerning the documents.

In an article published in the *New Leader* for January 4, 1947 Julius Epstein, author and political analyst, quoted the Official Report of the English Parliamentary Debates (Hansard) of October 23, 1946, as follows:

> Mr. Thurtle asked the Secretary of State for Foreign Affairs if, in order that the British public may have an opportunity of reading it, he will arrange for the publication, in a convenient form, of the recently discovered text of the supplementary secret agreement concluded between Nazi Germany and the USSR just prior to the Nazi attack on Poland, which led to the world war.
>
> Mr. Bevin: The text of the secret protocol attached to the nonaggression pact of 23rd August, 1939, has been published in the British Press. No advantage is seen in making any official publication of the text.
>
> Mr. Thurtle: Does not my right Hon. Friend agree that in view of the importance of this as a factor in precipitating the world war, it would be as well to have an official record of it?

Mr. Bevin: I think it was published in a reputable newspaper, the *Manchester Guardian,* and may be taken as accurate.

Mr. Warbey: Can the Minister say how the Press got hold of a copy of a document under official control?

Mr. Bevin: I have not the slightest notion. I have been trying to find out that process for a long time.

It is known that the American State Department has copies of these documents, but although they were published a few times in the American press, no official statements have been made about them.

The testimony offered at the Nuremberg trials proves beyond doubt that when offered partnership both by Britain and Germany, Russia chose the latter whom she feared more, but with whom she could accomplish more quickly the conquest of border territories and acquisition of seaports; and signed a secret agreement with her for the partition of Poland. Stalin knew that if he took England for a partner, his country would lie at the mercy of Germany's armies. On the other hand, having been informed that Germany's general staff only awaited assurance that Germany would not be faced by enemies on two fronts— that she was ready for war—and realizing that with Germany his ally between him and England, the prospective enemy, he would be in a better position and have more booty as well, Stalin became the "trigger man" for World War II by signing the pact with Germany. Since it seems to be true that Hitler would not have attacked Poland without Russia's guarantee, Stalin bears a heavy responsibility for his role.

We owe it to ourselves to obtain clarification concerning the origin of the second World War. The fact that the Soviet Union later became our ally must not deter us.

Nobody can say what would have happened if Stalin and Hitler had not come to terms. What would be the situation today if Stalin, instead of becoming Germany's ally in 1939 had become the ally of England and France? I have already pointed out that in a war fought by coalitions, it is almost axiomatic that you fight on the right side and at the same time on the wrong side. We need not feel ashamed if Russia's early guilt comes to light, but we ought to be ashamed if we lend ourselves to abetting political fictions and historical forgery. We should insist tenaciously upon obtaining the whole truth. As Americans we share the responsibility for the world that has resulted from the war. We should not be kept in darkness.

During my stay in Budapest, two or three events in connection with the Soviet legation seem to be very typical of the real nature of the Red Empire. The first minister after I arrived was Mr. Beksadian, a fat man with a stout wife. He was an Armenian. They were quiet, rather shy and inoffensive. He showed me a picture of a palace in the Caucasus which he said was his home. Apparently he belonged to the new upper class in Russia, and he was supposed to be a great friend of Litvinov's. This was perhaps his undoing.

He went home with his wife on leave, apparently without misgivings, but he did not return to Budapest. His disappearance was quite a mystery. We all wrote eventually to our ambassadors in Moscow to find out what had happened to him, since all inquiries at the Soviet legation were fruitless. Even the secretaries who spoke English suddenly could not understand when you asked them about Beksadian. Eventually we learned that Mr. Beksadian, his wife and his son, who had been held as a hostage in Russia, had been "liquidated" during the great purge. When the news reached Budapest eventually, many people regretted that they had not shown him and his wife a little more personal kindness.

His successor, Mr. Sharonov, was young, lively, and a good linguist; he and his supposed wife threw grand parties in the best (or worst) Hollywood manner. Obviously they were allowed to spend money without stint. Their dinners lasted at least three hours. Two orchestras played at their receptions, and movie cameras followed everybody around. He had a strange habit, during the war, of inviting foreign diplomats, friend and foe, Germans, Englishmen, Frenchmen, Japanese—all indiscriminately. At one of his receptions, he insisted upon having the German minister and me appear in a movie with him. It appeared in all the picture houses of Budapest. I made no objection, but I said, as we were being posed, "I wonder which one of us will get fired first for this." The German minister turned as red as a beet.

The Russian legation's funds for entertainment seemed to be unlimited, but when the minister's wife needed a new pair of stockings, she had to send old ones to Moscow before she could get a replacement. Sharonov was a very agreeable fellow, but he was certainly ignorant of the world—or he pretended to be for his own reasons. He insisted that Soviet industrial production was many times that of the United States, and often said this in my presence. At first, I tried to argue about it, but I saw there was no use. Apparently he believed it to such an extent that nothing would change his opinion. Perhaps he didn't dare to say otherwise.

3

THE GERMAN INVASION OF HUNGARY

$\sim\sim\sim\sim\sim\sim\sim\sim\sim\sim\sim\sim\sim\sim\sim\sim\sim$

AFTER NICHOLAS DE KALLAY was appointed premier by Horthy, Hungary's resistance to Germany increased steadily. Not only was unconditional surrender to the Western Allies secretly attempted in the summer of 1943, but on April 5th of that year, Prime Minister Kallay visited Mussolini in Rome and proposed joint diplomatic steps to be taken in Berlin against German pressure, and a policy of friendship to be initiated in the Balkans in order to bring about, with the inclusion of Italy, a bloc of nations uniting Hungary, Rumania, Turkey, Greece and even Finland for resistance against German oppression. Mussolini promised an answer for the autumn of 1943, but it never came forth.

In the same month, Admiral Horthy visited Hitler's headquarters accompanied by General Szombathelyi, chief of the general staff, who had succeeded General Werth after the Yugoslav affair and had undertaken to purge the officers' corps of Hitler's admirers. During the Regent's homeward journey the Germans published the following communique:

The Fuehrer and the Regent expressed their firm determination to continue the war against Bolshevism and its British and American allies unerringly until final victory is won . . . The Hungarian nation will mobilize all its forces for this end, for the liberation of Europe and for the security of the life of the Hungarian people.

After Horthy's return to his capital, the Hungarian government issued its own communique stating only that the Regent had visited Hitler on the latter's invitation; at the same time the government made it known that the words "and its British and American allies" had been inserted by the Germans without Horthy's consent, a good example of Ribbentrop's statecraft.

Budapest kept on exasperating Hitler. On May 6, 1943, Premier Kallay adjourned parliament to prevent its being used for national socialist propaganda. When Hitler demanded that Hungary send three Hungarian divisions to the Balkans where, from south of Belgrade to the Bulgarian zone of occupation, he wished Hungarian armed forces to carry out the job of policing Yugoslavia for the Germans—promising to supply five Hungarian divisions with armaments if this request were granted—the Hungarian government refused. The government not only prevented Germany from penetrating Hungarian industry but was also successful in recouping a part of the Hungarian industrial shares which the Germans had seized in Austria when they occupied that country in 1938. Concrete results were obtained in this respect concerning the Danubian Steamship Company, its coal mines in Pecs and workshops in Obuda. The Hungarian government also refused to export more cattle to Germany than usual. The production of oil wells in Lispe was deliberately reduced by fifty percent. The government systematically reduced the production of the Hungarian airplane factories which were supposed to deliver two-thirds of their output to Germany.

The Germans used high-pressure methods to coerce Hungary to increase her economic assistance. In 1943 the German minister Clodius showed Hungarian negotiators statistics proving that Czech industrial deliveries to Germany amounted to twelve times those of Hungary, although Czech industrial capacity was in ordinary times only three times that of Hungary. Clodius openly threatened Hungarian independence if she did not help Germany. But he obtained no results.

Hungary was supplying the Vatican City with most of its food and all the wheat it needed. To help the starving population of Greece and also Belgian, Dutch and French children, entire gift trains carrying food were sent to those nations. The Hungarian government also deliberately diverted a considerable part of its foreign trade from Germany to neutral countries such as Turkey, Switzerland and Sweden, despite serious German displeasure.

Under Kallay's government several thousand French escaped war prisoners were allowed complete freedom in Hungary, including feedom to work; and those unable to work for a living were housed and kept in good hotels at Lake Balaton. British and American prisoners of war were courteously and humanely treated in Hungary. Of all of the Axis belligerents, Hungary alone fulfilled to the last letter the Geneva Convention concerning prisoners of war.

The democratic and leftist parties of Hungary, including the Social Democratic Party, the labor unions, the leftist newspapers, etc., still enjoyed comparative freedom, as was not granted to any similar organizations anywhere else in German-dominated countries of Europe at that time, with the exception of Finland. At that time, the only places besides Hungary in which the Social Democratic Party existed were Switzerland and Sweden.

On July 25th, 1943 Kallay nominated Mr. Ghyczy foreign minister. This must have taken considerable courage, as Ghyczy was generally known as outspokenly anti-Nazi in the Foreign Office. In September, Ghyczy sent to Sweden as minister Mr. Ullein-Reviczky, who had an English wife and was working definitely against the Nazis. By September 21, Germany had threatened to sever her diplomatic relations with Hungary if she continued to refuse further military and economic support.

Adolf Hitler was a great legalist. In Germany during his long struggle for the chancellorship one of his main slogans was: "Legal, until we are in power." He used and misused all of the facilities afforded to a demagogue by a democratic constitution. President von Hindenburg had nominated him chancellor when he became the leader of the largest party. Hitler remained a rigid legalist even after having seized power. Every murder, every thievery and cruelty was authorized by law or by decree. Only these were now national socialist laws and decrees.

Hitler was a great legalist even when he conquered foreign countries. He did not invade Austria before Seyss-Inquart had sent him an invitation. It did not make much difference that Seyss-Inquart was not entitled to send an invitation and that he did not even send it because it was written by Goering in Berlin. When Hitler marched into Prague, he had a legal authorization, namely, the consent of President Hacha, extorted by third-degree methods.

All this sounds rather odd, but Hitler had reasons for observing legality. He did not want his troops to enter chaotic countries. The administrative task of the conqueror is greatly facilitated by a pretense of legitimate continuity. The conqueror needs civil servants, police forces, courts, even soldiers under their own officers. He cannot make use of natives without their chieftains. Above all, he wants to collaborate with a legitimate government, since if he creates a vacuum, every group of escaped politicians can try to establish itself as the real government, as a government-in-exile, or in some corner of the country. Hitler saved Mussolini from Gran Sasso, not because he liked him, but because he needed a legitimate government in northern Italy to offset the only genuinely legitimate government of Marshal Badoglio in Rome. Otherwise Hitler would have needed an army to maintain order in that part of Italy which was still under German occupation.

In 1934, at the beginning of his career as a conqueror, Hitler had made the mistake of having Dollfuss murdered. In 1938 he was wiser. He could have sent to their deaths Chancellor Schuschnigg and President Miklas, but instead he invited Schuschnigg to Berchtesgaden and compelled him to accept traitors as members of his government. Then the traitors provided Hitler with his legality. In 1944, when he decided that

Hungary had exhausted his patience, he could certainly have had Regent Horthy, Premier Kallay, General Szombathelyi and Foreign Minister Ghyczy assassinated. Instead, he invited Horthy to Klessheim and presented him with an ultimatum. He needed legality.

The events that followed could not be reported to the world press. Though Hitler's iron curtain was less solid than the one used by Stalin, it was very dense. But the scant reports that came via Turkey and Scandinavia at the time have been supplemented by personal narratives from Kallay and others, and it is now possible to reconstruct the story.

Before Schuschnigg went to Berchtesgaden in 1938, he asked Dr. Richard Schmitz, Mayor of Vienna, to take over if he did not return. Before Horthy went to Hitler's headquarters in 1944, he sent telegrams to all Hungarian legations ordering them not to recognize any Hungarian government that would be the result of eventual German occupation. Horthy, summoned to Klessheim with his war minister, foreign minister and chief of general staff, left Budapest on March 17, 1944. The ultimatum he received upon his arrival demanded complete mobilization against Russia; nomination of a quisling government; unconditional inclusion of Hungary in Germany's war economy; German control of waterways and railways; strict application of the Nuremberg laws against one million Jews in Hungary; extradition of Axis deserters, refugees and Polish soldiers; and Hungarian workers for German factories. Hitler also demanded that German troops be allowed to enter Hungary to assure her external and internal security.

The Regent rejected the ultimatum outright. Hitler

had expected that; everything was prepared for a lightning blow. At midnight from March 18 to 19, powerful German forces numbering eleven divisions and including blinded trains, motorized guns and the heaviest "tiger" tanks crossed from Austria into Hungarian territory and reached Budapest at four o'clock in the morning. Simultaneously, Hungarian airfields were invaded by paratroopers, who met with only slight resistance since all the Hungarian forces were concentrated on the eastern and southeastern borders of Hungary. Fearing retaliation by these troops, the Germans, assisted by Rumanian troops, closed off the eastern half of Hungary on the line of the River Tisza to prevent their contact with Budapest and kept up this control for several weeks.

According to Kallay, news of these happenings was continuously transmitted in code by the secret Hungarian broadcasting station to the British in Istanbul, but no reply or advice was received. The government could not contact Regent Horthy, as his homeward bound train was halted on the Hungarian border and was only allowed to proceed to Budapest next day at eleven o'clock in the morning when the Germans had already seized all the strategic positions. All the government could do—since to organize armed resistance was impossible—was to destroy all secret documents in the various government offices and to advise Hungarian diplomatic representatives abroad, the Anglo-American military personnel which had clandestinely come to Hungary and anti-Nazi political leaders of the impending danger.

The Gestapo was already at work rounding up conservative elements, the legitimist nobility, priests,

trade union leaders, anglophiles, journalists, nationalists, and of course, Jews, hundreds of whom committed
suicide. Keresztes-Fisher, the minister of the interior
and his brother, Horthy's former aide, were among the
first people arrested. The SS agent, Ludvig Veehsenmayer, had arrived as Germany's new envoy and pleni-
potentiary, with, as the Germans announced, "special
authorities to intensify the common conduct of the
war."

Upon his arrival in Budapest, the Regent summoned Prime Minister Kallay and his government to a
conference. Mr. Kallay has personally sent me details
of this meeting. The Regent told them that as early as
autumn of 1943 Hitler and Ribbentrop had requested
the removal of Kallay from the Hungarian government, as they had evidence of his collaboration with
the Allies. Horthy had resisted but now, under violent
pressure, he said he feared he would have to appoint a
new government. However, he requested Mr. Kallay to
carry on the government business meanwhile.

Kallay refused. Stating that Hungary's sovereignty
for the time being had ceased to exist and that due to
German occupation all acts from now on would be unconstitutional and legally null and void, he asked the
Regent to assume the same attitude. But Horthy replied that the war was nearing its end; that maintenance of Hungary's resistance as far as it could go, and
the ability to fight against the German oppressors at
the appropriate time required his stay in office in order
to save whatever could be saved. He expressed his belief that the Allies would land in the Balkans within a
few months and that the Germans would meet swift
defeat. He believed it was in the interest of Hungary

that the army should not be disbanded or destroyed, as it was still needed to help the Allies prevent the destruction of the country and to maintain order in the Danubian Valley at the end of the war when anarchy would become inevitable.

On March 20, 1944, at dawn, German storm troops surrounded the prime minister's home and Gestapo agents forcibly entered his apartments. By then he had fled to the Turkish legation where he had been invited by the Turkish government to take refuge.

Meanwhile Horthy—the safety of whose family, including a three-year-old grandson, had been threatened if he did not co-operate—put off nominating a new government. He yielded only after Hitler had promised to restore Hungary's sovereignty if she received a "trustworthy regime."

On March 23rd the Germans announced that Horthy had appointed General Sztojay. The new premier by grace of Hitler and Veehsenmayer had been the Hungarian minister to Berlin. My Hungarian friends like to emphasize that he was a Serb and that his name had previously been Stojakovitch, but I am not fond of using that as a pro-Magyar argument. If we do not accept Hitler's race theories, everybody must be the sole judge of his own nationality. Many of our best generals and admirals have German names. If they had been defeated instead of being victorious it would not have been proper suddenly to discover that they were not really Americans.

Soon Hitler was to learn that the Hungarian cat had nine lives. Until the German occupation, Horthy had exercised his regency strictly within its narrow constitutional limits. But with the constitution no longer in existence, he resolved to do for the country everything within his power irrespective of formal limitations. There was no longer a parliament, many of its members having tendered their resignation in protest against the puppet government formed in April. The Regent was the last remnant of the constitution. He recognized that Hitler would have imprisoned or killed him if he had not needed him as a show of legality. This gave his position a certain strength, and the Admiral decided to use it to the limit.

Sztojay's case has not yet been sufficiently clarified, but it seems that he did not remain consistently a quisling, although under his regime Hungarian anti-Nazis were seized by the Gestapo, sixteen thousand businesses were confiscated without compensation, and in June the Gestapo deported a hundred thousand Jews from Hungary to Poland where they were slaughtered by the Germans. This aroused protests from the World Jewish Congress, King Gustav of Sweden and Mr. Eden. On the other hand, instead of being a mere tool in Veehsenmayer's hands, Sztojay carried out several of Horthy's orders. In August 1944, he relieved three ministers of their posts. They were Imredy, who had become minister of economic affairs after having tried and failed to form a quisling government of his own, and two members of Imredy's unsavory party of Hungarian rejuvenation: Antal Kunder, minister of trade, and Andor Jaros, minister of the interior, one of the worst persecutors of the Jews. Sztojay also rejected Germany's demand that Hungary break with Turkey and on August 25th dissolved all pro-German parties. Soon afterward two chiefs of departments in the ministry of the interior, Laszlo Endre and Laszlo

Baky, who belonged to Szalasi's national socialist party
and were Hitler's special spies in the Sztojay outfit,
tried to remove the premier by a *coup-de-main,* to
open the way for Szalasi. They concentrated *gendar-
merie* forces from the provinces around the capital.
The Regent got wind of it and ordered two divisions
under General Miklos to Budapest. Then he called
Sztojay and informed him of the conspiracy, ordering
him to remove the two traitors, which Sztojay did not
dare to carry out. So shortly afterward, the Regent dismissed the Sztojay government and nominated a new
one under General Lakatos. People called it Horthy's
"bridge party" because it consisted of his personal
friends, elderly gentlemen unable to cope with the
situation.

That Hitler accepted this rebuff can only be understood if one remembers that the summer of 1944 was
the time of Germany's greatest withdrawal from the
east, its so-called retreat into the inner fortress. Hitler's
teeth were no longer as sharp as they had been. On August 22nd, M. Draganoff, foreign minister of Bulgaria,
had dared to stress his country's friendly relations with
the Soviet Union and to announce that Bulgaria's
troops would be withdrawn from Yugoslavia. He also
said that Bulgaria was doing her utmost to make peace
with the United States and Great Britain. He would
not have made that speech if the Germans had still
been in a position to punish him. On August 23rd,
King Michael of Rumania had made his *coup d'état,*
replacing General Antonescu with General Sanatescu,
and issued the following proclamation in the old Rumanian tradition of flying to the victor's rescue:

The dictatorship has come to an end and with it all oppression . . . The United Nations have recognized the injustice of the dictate of Vienna under which Transylvania was torn from us. At the side and with the help of the Allied armies, and by mobilizing all the forces of the Fatherland, we shall cross the frontiers imposed on us by the Vienna Award and liberate Transylvania from foreign occupation. The new government marks the beginning of a great era in which the rights and liberties of all citizens will be respected.

On August 26th, Radio Sofia recognized Bulgaria's withdrawal from the war:

In accordance with its firm determination to pursue a policy of complete neutrality on the part of Bulgaria in the war between Russia and Germany, the Bulgarian government has given the order that all foreign troops crossing into Bulgarian territory shall be disarmed. In accordance with this order, the German troops who have so far crossed into Bulgarian territory have been completely disarmed. Bulgaria has approached Great Britain and the United States asking for information on the terms under which she could withdraw from the war.

A superficial observer might be inclined to say that all three, Rumania, Bulgaria and Hungary proclaimed their defection from Hitler almost simultaneously when a general German retreat allowed them to do so. In reality, there was an important difference. Rumania and Bulgaria did not risk anything when they began to defy Hitler, because his troops had already been ordered to withdraw from their territories. But Hungary was still firmly occupied by the Germans. The great and decisive difference was that Rumania and Bulgaria were outside of Germany's "inner fortress," whereas Hungary was considered part of it. Hitler abandoned Rumania and Bulgaria but clung to Hungary, hence Hungary was the only one to risk a terrible vengeance by challenging the Fuehrer, who had become a cornered thug and was therefore more vicious than ever.

This world would be a better, more decent place if the leaders of the English-speaking nations developed a tiny part of the courage shown at that time by Admiral Horthy. On October 15, 1944, he broadcast from Radio Budapest a proclamation, the text of which will be found in Appendix II of this volume, in which he reviewed Hungary's case against Germany in uncompromising terms.

The Germans acted with their usual speed and energy. Before Horthy had ended his broadcast, they attacked the radio station and killed most of the student guards, who had been summoned to defend the entrance. The Regent managed to reach his palace, which the Germans at once besieged. The fight cost considerable destruction, and all but fifty members of the palace guard lost their lives. These fifty later had their throats cut and were thrown into the Danube. Horthy, his wife, daughter-in-law and grandson were seized and deported to Germany. Now was the great hour for Major Szalasi, leader of the Arrow Cross. Backed by the Germans, he named himself Regent and broadcast to the nation in best national socialist style:

A selfish coalition of interests formerly led a parasitic existence on the life of our nation, and when the nation took up arms in the struggle for freedom, that coalition, which had nothing to do with our nation, did all it could to make us fail in this struggle. It did so to place its own vile and craven interests above the interests of the nation, even at the cost of the latter's destruction . . . The only guarantee of our survival and self-preservation is the throwing of all our might into the decisive struggle. . . .

The decisive struggle was soon ended. Seven weeks later, Szalasi fled to Vienna, shortly before the siege of Budapest began.

For some time no one knew what had happened to Admiral Horthy and his family. However, they were found and released from a German concentration camp by the American army. The Admiral spent some time thereafter in custody at Nuremberg, where he was held as a possible witness. So far as I know, no charges were ever made against him. Notwithstanding this fact, he was and still is under house arrest, at this writing, in a small home in Weilheim, Bavaria, where his family reside with him.

They obtained their food from UNRRA up to the first of December 1946, but from then on were left practically without sustenance for some time until they were put on DP rations.

Attempts of friends in America to send money to the Horthys were unavailing for a long time. C.A.R.E. packages reached other people, but not the Horthys. The Admiral spent some time in a hospital recovering from an operation said to have been due to malnutrition. No one seems to know why he should be held under house arrest. If he is actually a prisoner, then he is not being properly fed. No one knows when he will be free from all restraint. The only explanation seems to be that Tito has made several demands and that our government is holding him for that reason. No one seriously thinks that he will be turned over to Tito, but our government has been very responsive to communist clamorings so far as the Horthys are concerned.

Perhaps with the turn of events its attitude will change, but when, in the spring of 1947, the Horthy's son, Nicholas, Jr., who was found in a German concentration camp and had been given a clean bill of health after being released, made application for a visa to come to America on business, it was turned down. This despite the fact that he had been assured in advance that there would be no difficulty in getting one. It seems incredible, but within twenty-four hours of the time he filed his application, an Hungarian communist-inspired weekly paper, published in New York (with a circulation of hardly more than five hundred copies daily) came out in screaming headlines, demanding that he be excluded from this country—whereupon the higher-ups in the State Department ordered that the visa be refused.

Mr. Kallay wrote me:

> How can it be that Nicky Horthy was refused a visa in the United States? That young man who fought always against the Germans and the Hungarian Nazis, protecting the Jews and saving a lot of them? He was beaten and put into a sack after he was captured by the Germans—now he cannot even enter the United States on a visit because of communistic objection.

Mr. Kallay himself became a German prisoner on November 17, 1944, when he gave himself up to avoid further embarrassment being caused the Turkish government by German demands that he be turned over to them.

4

RUSSIAN TACTICS IN CENTRAL EUROPE

~~~~~~

THE SPECTACLE of former allies emphasizing their contributions to the common victory is never edifying, and I should not mention it were it not necessary to refute one assertion of our indefatigable "Russia firsters." Their favorite argument in defending the Soviets' conduct in eastern and central Europe is that it was, after all, only the Red army which pushed the Germans from the countries in question. Even if that were true, it would not justify the actions which followed; but it is not true. Germany withdrew from the Balkan regions because, pressed by the Allies from *all* directions, she had to shorten her lines of supply and of defense. Only after that great regrouping were the Russians able to advance. The same applies to the British advance in Greece. The Red army bagged Rumania, Bulgaria and Yugoslavia almost without firing a shot. In Hungary it encountered but rearguard actions of the Germans and of small Hungarian contingents. The fighting in Hungary was tenacious in spots, for instance around the capital where Germans were predominant, but the Russians were allowed to overrun mountain positions in the Carpathians which normally could have been held for months, even by inferior forces. For the spirit of the Hungarian army was by then divided and disrupted. Hence the historic truth is that all these countries, including Hungary, fell to the Russians like ripe fruit from a tree which had been shaken by all the Allies together. No one ally acquired a special monopoly of conquest.

As I mentioned in the preceding chapter, the announcement of Bulgaria's withdrawal from the war happened on August 26, 1944. With it was an appeal made to us and to Great Britain for armistice terms. There had been no war between Bulgaria and the Soviet Union. Bulgaria had been at war with England and the United States since December 13, 1941— almost three years—but this had not caused the Soviets to declare war upon her. On August 29, 1944, three days after Bulgaria had proclaimed her desire to return to neutrality, the Soviets became suddenly hostile. They announced that they did not recognize the neutrality declared by the Bulgarian government; they considered it "entirely insufficient in the light of the existing situation." This was explained as a reference to the continued presence of German troops in Bulgaria, but in reality there were but a few remnants left, and they could not resist being disarmed by the Bulgarians.

The next day, on August 30th, a Bulgarian armistice delegation headed by an aged and highly respected democrat, former Premier Mushanoff, arrived at Cairo, Egypt, to start armistice negotiations with the United States and Great Britain. The conversations began on September 1st. On September 2nd, to placate the Soviets, the Bagrianoff government resigned and was followed by a cabinet headed by Kosta Muravieff, another meritorious liberal. Mushanoff was a member of this cabinet. On September 3rd the Soviet Tass agency wrote that Bulgaria's neutrality was being used to cover the exodus of German troops. Russia concentrated troops along the Danube on Rumanian soil. On September 4th the Bulgarian armistice delegation was induced to depart from Cairo. The official pretext was that it had been dispatched by the Bagrianoff government and was therefore no longer authoritative, but the real cause was increasing Russian pressure. Muravieff no longer dared to provoke Stalin by talks with the United States and Great Britain. Even if every male and female Bulgarian had started sliding on his or her knees to Moscow, it would not have diverted the "Generalissimo of mankind" from his clear purpose. He did not want Bulgarian neutrality, he did not want Bulgarian collaboration, he did not want peace with Bulgaria—he wanted Bulgaria. On September 5th, Russia declared war on Bulgaria. Molotov's note charged that

> the Bulgarian government even now refuses to break with Germany and is carrying out a policy of so-called neutrality, on the strength of which it is continuing to give direct help to Germany against the Soviet Union by sheltering the retreating German forces from pursuit by the Red army. . . . The Soviet government cannot regard this policy of Bulgaria in any other way than as the actual waging of war in Germany's camp against the Soviet Union. . . .

The next day Bulgaria asked the Soviets for an armistice. Two days later the Red army invaded Bulgaria and again, after two days, on September 10th, Moscow announced that hostilities with Bulgaria had come to an end. All of the little country was occupied. On the preceding day, the Soviets had installed a new government. The genuine liberals and democrats, Muravieff and Mushanoff, were imprisoned as fascists, because where Stalin's arm reaches, friends of America and Great Britain have to perish. The new cabinet was headed by colonels Georgieff and Veltcheff, well known as the leaders of the "Zveno," which on May 21, 1934, had made a *coup-de-main* against king and parliament and had established for seven months a regime of fascist republicanism. As well-tried totalitarians, they were immune from "Western democracy." On September 13th, Colonel Georgieff sent an armistice delegation, not to Cairo but to Marshal Tolbukhin.

The above facts are not well known in this country. The story of how Stalin liberated, that is, pocketed, Hungary's next-door neighbor, Rumania, is, I think, better known and therefore I shall devote to it only a few words. In the case of Rumania, Russian military action was justified and necessary: the Red army had to pursue the Germans across Rumania. It is the political conquest that followed which is of special interest. An armistice is ordinarily arranged by soldiers. After the armistice the peace treaty, duly negotiated, settles political matters. Nowadays, armistices seem to be misused to create accomplished facts which anticipate the peace treaties and can hardly be changed by the peacemakers. Very typical was Point 19 of the armistice terms which Rumania received on September 13, 1944: "The Allied governments consider the decision of the Vienna Award as invalid and agree that Transylvania *or the greater part of it* should be returned to Rumania." This one sentence was the key to a whole set of political plans. It showed, first of all, that the Russians had made their choice. They had decided to treat Rumania better than Hungary, not because they liked Rumania but because they were resolved to keep her. If the peasant woman fattens a pig, the motive is not love. Apparently the Hungarian coup of June 1947, was not envisaged at that time. Stalin's appetite grew as he ate. Thus Hungary which in 1944 was still considered by him as remaining outside of the Soviet orbit was taken over by him in 1947 due to the weak resistance of the Western Allies.

America and Great Britain wanted to reserve the Transylvanian question for the final peace settlement, but as usual, Russia had her way; the result was the compromise expressed by the words "or the greater part of it." By inserting these words, the English-speaking governments thought that no final solution would be possible without their consent. Stalin accepted what looked like a compromise with delight because it offered him the opportunity to keep Rumanians in suspense.

On December 2, 1944 Premier General Sanatescu resigned and was followed by General Radescu, chief of the Rumanian general staff. In his government, the new "National Democratic Front" consisting of communists, left wing agrarians and socialists, was strongly represented. Peter Groza, a member of that front, was vice-premier; Visitanu, another member, foreign minister; and Patrascanu, a Moscow-trained communist, minister of justice. The popular old-party chiefs,

Maniu and Bratianu, were dropped. General Radescu enjoyed the confidence of Great Britain and the United States. He hoped to re-establish a decent, democratic and independent regime despite the presence of so many tools of Moscow in his cabinet. However, owing to that stipulation of the armistice concerning Transylvania, Stalin had the whiphand. His agents spread the notion that the final solution of that national problem depended solely on Stalin, whose troops were in occupation of the country; therefore Rumania must lean entirely on the Soviets. This propaganda prepared the ground for the bold and I hope well-remembered action of Vyshinsky, deputy foreign commissar of the Soviet Union, who on March 12, 1945, removed Radescu as a fascist beast and made Peter Groza premier, announcing at the same time that with this trustworthy man in the saddle, Stalin had decided to put the whole of Transylvania under Rumanian administration.

The United States and Great Britain were not asked for their advice. Had they protested, Moscow would have replied that the final settlement was still up to the peace conference. General Radescu was given sanctuary in the British legation.

While the Russians were ousting from the Rumanian government all the friends of democracy known to be friends of Great Britain and the United States, they were putting into key positions Rumanians who formerly had served the Nazi system very efficiently.

The London *Times* stated that Tatarescu, the new vice-premier and foreign minister, had been prime minister of the government which in July 1940 had renounced the Anglo-French guarantee and reorientated Rumanian policy to Hitler's "new order." The

Moscow *Red Star* stated that Rumania's historical parties had become "archeological parties." By the time the Paris Peace Conference convened, Russia was firmly entrenched in Rumania, whereas in Hungary she had suffered a major defeat at the elections in November 1945. To Rumania was awarded *all* of Transylvania and Hungary was punished for holding out against sovietization.

It is incredible that the United States and Great Britain were fooled by Stalin into accepting the veteran Soviet agent, Brozevitch, now called Marshal Tito, as the savior and leader of southern Slavic democracy. But when the Russians entered Belgrade on October 20, 1944, Churchill sent congratulations to Tito and Subasitch. And on January 18, 1945 he forced young King Peter to accept the so-called agreement with Tito which had been hatched by the Soviets.

Hitler's ship foundered on a rock named Winston Churchill, but the speech Churchill made that day is one of which he can hardly be proud:

> I am the earliest outside supporter of Marshal Tito. It is more than a year since I extolled his guerrilla virtues to the world. He is one of my best friends. I earnestly hope he may prove to be the savior and unifier of his country, as he is undoubtedly at this time its undisputed master. . . . In pursuance of our joint policy, we encouraged the making of an agreement between the Tito government, which with Russian assistance, has now installed itself in Belgrade, and the Royal Government of Yugoslavia which is seated in London . . . Marshal Stalin and His Majesty's Government consider that agreement on the whole to be wise. We believe that the arrange-

ments are the best that can be made for the immediate future of Yugoslavia . . . King Peter II agrees in principle with these arrangements, but makes certain reservations . . . It is a matter of days within which a decision must be reached upon this matter, and if we were so unfortunate as not to be able to obtain the consent of King Peter, the matter would have, in fact, to go ahead, his assent being assumed.

The last sentence was greeted with hilarity in the House of Commons.

Since we followed the lead and accepted the guidance of Great Britain in our dealings with Yugoslavia and also with Czechoslovakia, we might have some excuse, but no great power ever should allow itself to be led blindfolded. Close co-operation with Great Britain is necessary, but we should always know where we are being led.

Czechoslovakian affairs were as badly managed by the British Foreign Office as were Yugoslavian, and in both instances we were accomplices. By overthrowing the social order of 1919, Hitler offered the West the opportunity to correct mistakes committed at Versailles. If the British had kept in mind the truthful report of Lord Runciman when he offered plans for settlement of minority claims, they would have known that something had been basically wrong with Czechoslovakia. The British Foreign Office then might have formed a Czechoslovakian government-in-exile not under Benes but composed of men willing to fulfill the broken pledge of Thomas Masaryk, that is, to make Czechoslovakia a second Switzerland, a country of complete ethnic equality, a real home for its many nationalities—Czechs, Germans, Slovaks, Magyars, Poles and Ruthenians. This great opportunity was missed and the well-deserved reward is being reaped. History has repeated itself, in reverse. In the first World War the Czechs in exile—not at home, where they were loyal to Franz Josef—pinned all their hopes on czarism and pan-Slavism. When the czar distrusted deserters and when Russia went down, they became "Westerners" and embraced the fallacious concept of national self-determination, which when granted to them denied self-determination to any nationality but Czechs. In the second World War, Benes began as a Westerner but quickly became an Easterner, when he recognized that his burning desire to take vengeance on his Czech opponents—Sudetenlanders, Magyars and Slovak autonomists—could only find satisfaction with Stalin's permission and help. The price was submissiveness, even the cession of Carpatho-Ruthenia with parts of Slovakia to the Soviet Union.

Thus Hungary became an island in the Soviet sea after having been an oasis in Hitler's desert.

Russia's active role in Hungary began with the siege of Budapest on December 24, 1944. On the same day Moscow announced that an Hungarian national assembly had been set up at Debrecen. General Voeroes, who, in November had escaped to Russian lines and ordered the army to join the Russians, declaring Horthy's regime the legal one, appeared as defense minister and General Miklos as premier. During the siege a Hungarian armistice delegation arrived in Moscow, and on January 21st Premier Miklos signed an armistice with Russia, the United States and Great Britain. But it was not until February 12th that the Budapest siege ended and weary citizens of Hungary, who had been caught between the two fires of German and Russian armies, could leave their cellars.

Then came a period of calculated destruction. The Russian method of occupation follows a certain pattern necessitated by the differences between the East and West in standards of living. After a spearhead of disciplined troops which destroys any remaining opposition, propaganda shock troops arrive. Their job is to destroy all evidence of higher than Russian standards of living in enemy territory, before the ordinary soldiers appear upon the scene. A man who eats at a table and sleeps on a bed is considered a bourgeois. Boxes had to be substituted for tables and straw for beds.

In Hungary such a policy meant destruction of workers' and peasants' homes as well as those of the wealthy classes. The peasants, according to Dr. Eckhardt, who as a leader of the Smallholders Party had much contact with them, are the sturdiest element in Hungary. They are individualists; they refuse to be pushed around. In his opinion Bolshevism will find them a stubborn obstacle. I fully share his views.

The population at first looked to the Russians as liberators after the German occupation; but the Russians did not feel that they were liberating a people. They looked upon Hungary as an enemy country. With the troops came Mathias Rakossi and other collaborators of Bela Kun (whom the Russians purged in 1936 as a Trotskyite) in the Hungarian communist interlude of 1919. After more than twenty-five years' service with the Soviets they are again controlling the Hungarian people, and pretend to be Hungarian patriots.

An account of the Russian occupation of Hungary as seen through the eyes of members of the Swiss legation and consulate, who were ordered to leave Budapest in April 1945, appears as Appendix III of this volume. In it are details of the looting which took place; the wholesale rape of women from the ages of ten to seventy years; the theft of funds in bank and legation safes, including those belonging to other nationals than Hungarians; and of the destruction wrought in Budapest by the siege.

Colonel Dallas S. Townsend, who was second in command of the American military mission in Hungary returned here in the spring of 1946. He has told me a great deal about civic conditions in Hungary under Russian occupation.

In return for the Hungarian provisional government's promise to pay $300,000,000 in reparations and to furnish troops, etc., the Allies promised to set up a Hungarian civilian administration. This they did not do; though the Hungarian government kept its promises. The civilians were under the control of the Red army, and even the Allied Control officers have not been able to get into some parts of Hungary since the armistice without permission from the Russians; in many cases it has been refused.

The $300,000,000 reparations amount actually to about $1,100,000,000, for the dollar was specified as that of 1938, and a five percent a month penalty for delay in delivery was imposed. Due to Russian interference deliveries have been slow and penalties have been huge. In addition, the Russians seized practically all major factories in Hungary on the pretense that they were German property, although in every instance the factory had been taken by force or under duress from original Hungarian owners. None of this property was credited against the reparations figure; at the same time, their seizure made it more difficult for Hungary to make good on the reparation terms and gave Russia a stranglehold on Hungarian economy.

When the Russians felt that they could win an election, they decided to start in Budapest, having been assured by the local communists that the leftist bloc would carry Budapest by an overwhelming majority. The idea was that a big victory in Budapest would help them in subsequent elections in the provinces. Campaigns were conducted by the leftist bloc practically without opposition. The communists had plenty of money. The other parties had none. Further, the leftist bloc had transportation, whereas the other parties had none. To anyone not knowing conditions in Hungary this would not seem particularly important, but it is absolutely vital. Col. Townsend said he saw any number of funerals, where the coffin was in a pushcart and the mourners followed on foot behind. His office was often importuned by the families of people seriously ill for the loan of a jeep to get them to the hospital. Outside of the supporters of the communists it was impossible for anyone to get anywhere.

When the elections were held in Budapest, in November 1945, there were enormous parades, with thousands of people carrying red flags and shouting for the leftists. There was no parade and few meetings were held for the opposition. Communists promised that if they were elected they would see that everybody got plenty of food. They of course gave Russia credit for food allegedly sent into the country. They said: "We better have a communist government that is right in line with Russia, because the British and Americans are not going to do anything for you. Russia will take care of you if you have a communist government. If you don't, it won't be so good for you. If you want to eat, vote the communist ticket."

To those who watched all this, the predictions that the communist-dominated leftist bloc would not carry the election seemed fantastic. One member of the American mission remarked that he could not believe the opposition would poll ten percent of the vote. Yet the leftist bloc lost the election. The voters paraded, had a secret ballot, and voted as they pleased. The elections that followed in the provinces were similar defeats for the communists. The leftist bloc got only forty percent of the vote, of which the Communist Party proper got sixteen percent.

Nevertheless when the elections were over the Communist Party demanded control of the three most important ministries: the interior, and through that control of the police; commerce; and supplies. Three communists, all of whom were actually Russian citizens and who had spent most of their lives in Russia, were appointed to these posts. The communists insisted on naming as vice-premier, the Hungarian renegade Mathias Rakossi, whose position amounts to that of a dictator.

Then the communists began to work on parliament. First, they accused one member after another of various crimes, and uncovered imaginary conspiracies which enabled them to eliminate many important people in the dominant Smallholders Party, formerly friends of the Allies. On three occasions the majority was purged in an effort to reduce it to a minority. No one ever knew who would be next to fall under communist pressure. The more prominent and important you were the sooner your turn was apt to come. People were picked up all the time, on the streets and everywhere else. Families whose members disappeared often appealed to the American commission, which made attempts to find out what had actually happened, but were met with rebuffs. If members of a family bothered the police force, they were told they would be arrested themselves if they came around again.

Russians systematically brought about the worst inflation in world history in order to destroy capital, render the monied class impoverished and force people to subjection. This was the price the Hungarian people paid for having established by free elections a democratic government as requested by the Yalta Agreement.

Colonel Townsend said that after the elections were held and the communists still controlled public affairs, the people began to wonder. They began to think that maybe the English and the Americans could not do anything for them and maybe they better get in line with the Russians. The Colonel criticized our government for permitting Russia to get away with all this and said that we had lost so much prestige that by the time he left he might as well not have been there at all.

5

THE ISLAND SUBMERGED

PRESIDENT ROOSEVELT considered dissolution of the Austro-Hungarian monarchy one of the worst blunders of the peacemakers after the first World War. He planned a Danubian confederation with the idea of unifying the Danubian region. He was not interested in dynastic restoration, but certainly would not have objected to it if it had facilitated reconstruction. I have been told that both he and Mr. Churchill had agreed before Russia entered the war that American troops should occupy the Balkans, Hungary and Austria, but that Mr. Benes, when informed of it, hastened to negotiate a Czech-Polish customs union in order to strengthen his bargaining position toward the other prospective members of the Danubian confederation, and concluded as early as June 25, 1941, a secret agreement with the Soviets.

At the Moscow Conference (1943) Molotov immediately brought up the bogey of the *cordon sanitaire* and sabotaged the sound idea of a Danubian federation. The communique issued by the Moscow Conference contained a special declaration on Austria, and many people wondered why that little country had been singled out in this manner. Those who were familiar with the background were able to understand. There was, first, the wish

to open the way for the Austrian people themselves, as well as those *neighboring states* which will be

faced with similar problems, to find that political
and economic security which is the only basis for
lasting peace. (Italics mine)

The New York *Times,* probably on higher inspira-
tion, commented November 6, 1943, on that passage as
follows:

It is no doubt open to many interpretations, but its
implications seem to point in only one direction,
and that is co-operation for 'political and economic
security' between Austria and her neighbor states.
When Austria-Hungary was broken up into its com-
ponent parts, a great economic unit vanished from
the scene . . . but all the many schemes for closer
political and economic co-operation among the central European states launched before the war led to
nothing, and the one structure that did arise, the
Little Entente, was too narrow and exclusive and fell
apart at the first blow.

The declaration of the Moscow Conference is therefore a promise that renewed efforts in that direction
would find support from all the three powers, including Russia, which previously had opposed all
'federation' plans in eastern Europe.

In the same declaration there was a statement re-
minding Austria that she had "a heavy responsibility
for having participated in the war on the side of Hitler." This was Molotov's way of reintroducing the arbitrary discrimination which, applied by the peacemakers after the first World War, had rendered a
Danubian confederation impossible. Today we understand much better the ways of Moscow. It is not certain
that the Soviets are opposed to a Danubian confedera-

tion. It is, however, quite certain that they will only allow it to materialize under their own aegis and not as a creation of the West. I should not be surprised if the Soviets made, before long, great efforts to bring it about in order to chain Hungary and Austria to their system, of which a chief pillar is, of course, Czechoslovakia. On December 31, 1944, Jan Masaryk said quite frankly:

> We want a strong and democratic Poland, but only a Poland which will collaborate with the Soviet Union. We have neither time nor inclination for a different solution of the Polish question. We want a decent and democratic Hungary which will let us live in peace, but again only a Hungary which will collaborate with the Soviet Union. The same is true for Yugoslavia, Austria and Rumania.

I want to make clear that I am not concerned with the non-Slavic nations of central Europe alone. It would be a foolish policy to say: "Let the Slavic countries go where they belong." As long as it is not proved by genuine elections, held in an atmosphere of real freedom, I shall not believe that the majority of Slavic nations—Poles, Slovaks, Czechs, Serbs, Croats, Bulgarians and Slovenians—are in any way more pro-Soviet than the majority of Hungarians, Rumanians and Austrians. On the contrary, I think that the elections in Austria and Hungary, which simply crushed the communists, were typical of the entire region.

The Russian armies looted and took away everything; they transformed regions of agricultural abundance into deserts of famine and starvation. We and the British at the Potsdam Conference gave them a legal title for some of their looting by enabling them to call "German assets" everything in which Germans or Germany had acquired a share, or where they had taken a hand in developing production for their war economy. Wholesale pillaging, as we have shown, is an important tool in making these countries ready for the role they are destined to play within the expanded Soviet orbit. The Russian-occupied countries are being proletarianized and leveled down to Soviet standards.

One of the chief means of accomplishing this end is the so-called "land reform," which has been set up under Soviet supervision in Poland, east Germany, Rumania, Yugoslavia, Hungary and even in Bulgaria. I use the word "so-called" because genuine land reform consists of partitioning oversized estates into holdings which are capable of maintaining themselves. Genuine land reform does not permanently reduce production, but under Soviet land reform the holdings into which every large property is broken are too small for the proprietors to maintain themselves. The purpose is to enforce gradually collective farming, ultimately replacing the former owner by a bureaucrat.

Under the Potsdam formula as interpreted by Russia, practically everything is subject to seizure, since every larger business within Germany and German-occupied countries was taken over by the Nazis. Businesses belonging to Americans are subject to seizure because the Germans took them over during the war, and hence, to the Russians, they are German assets. The oil wells in Hungary belonging to the Standard Oil Company of New Jersey work under permanent threat of being taken over by the Russians; the Russians have kicked out a part of the American personnel in charge and insist on having oil pumped as fast as they can so that if ultimately the wells have to be returned, there won't be much left. The American personnel were barred for some time from the plant because they objected to Soviet exploitation of the wells, knowing that it would result in great damage and possible ruination.

As Colonel Townsend showed in the case of Hungary, the Soviets have a fine system of increasing reparations by levying penalties for actions that they control; thus the actual amounts are subject to almost unlimited expansion. The army lives off the country meanwhile; the Soviets make no effort to furnish food, clothing or anything for the subject peoples. Much of the supplies, medicines, clothing, etc., sent from the United States and other countries and distributed by communist officials, finds its way into the black market. Thus with what the Soviets take officially and what their army takes unofficially, there is little left.

The general plight of the Hungarian people was further aggravated by mass deportations started with consent of the three major powers. At Potsdam the Big Three admonished Soviet-Poland and Czecho-Slovakia to carry out their mass deportations of Germans and Hungarians (from Slovakia) in a "humane and orderly" manner. Anne O'Hare McCormick, in an article in the New York *Times,* referring to the expulsion of the German population from Sudetenland, stated: "The exodus takes place under nightmarish conditions, without any international supervision or any pretense of humane treatment. We share responsibility for horrors only comparable to Nazi cruelties."

To complete the picture of the developments in

Hungary I wish to quote as a final note a statement of Prime Minister Ferenc Nagy of Hungary made to the press upon his arrival in the United States as a refugee. The harsh treatment of Hungary at the peace conference and the consistent pressure and terrorism of the Russian power of occupation has finally broken the backbone of that brave little nation and has forced it temporarily to play the inglorious role which Stalin and the politbureau have assigned it.

The statement made to the press on June 17 by Premier Nagy appeared in the New York *Times* of June 18, 1947 as follows:

A year ago, when I first came to Washington, I was the leader of the freely elected majority in the Hungarian National Assembly and the head of a coalition government. Since that time, the majority has been overruled by the joint pressure of Soviet Russia and the Communists in Hungary; some of my closest collaborators have become actual or virtual prisoners; others are sharing exile with me. The only duly elected government in Russian-occupied southeastern Europe has fallen victim to totalitarian aggression.

The Hungarian coalition government was broadly representative, as required by the Yalta Agreement, and made strenuous efforts to be friendly with Soviet Russia. While trying to maintain the independence of the country and to establish freedom and democracy, the paramount aim was to assure a peaceful evolution to the Hungarian people, worn out by the hardships of war and the armistice period. It was our earnest hope that, with the coming into effect of the peace treaty, a political and economic system based on Western concepts of democracy would be consolidated.

Although my party had won a clear-cut majority in the elections of November, 1945, we decided to maintain the coalition government and, taking into consideration the facts that the sovereignty of Hungary was limited by the armistice agreement and the country was occupied by the Red Army, we were ready to make concessions to the minority as well as to the Soviet Government.

I admit to having appeased the Communists and Soviet Russia, in the hope of being able to save my people from further troubles, meanwhile maintaining the basic political structure as it had resulted from the elections. But I must emphasize that on several occasions I also resisted; the best proof thereof is that, until the recent coup, political and economic conditions in Hungary differed greatly from those prevailing in other oppressed countries in southeastern Europe.

Our position was extremely difficult, however. The rigged Rumanian elections in November, 1946, further consolidated the Russian position in southeastern Europe; and the way toward cooperation with Czechoslovakia was blocked by the ruthless treatment of the Hungarian minority in that country. Thus we were isolated, the more so because the Allied Control Commission, the supreme authority under the armistice agreement, was actually a Russian agency.

When the Foreign Ministers agreed on the definite terms of the peace treaty, in spite of all of its undue hardships and shortcomings, we hoped that the treaty would soon come into effect. This would have enabled the duly elected majority to proceed with greater freedom toward the achievement of its aims: to consolidate the radical reforms in our economic and political life and to make Hungary a country of happy, free and self-governing human beings.

But our hopes did not materialize. In December, 1946, the Communist-controlled police discovered an alleged conspiracy to overthrow democracy in Hungary. At first the police produced evidence and statements which made me agree to the prosecution of the case. However, now that I can have no further doubts as to the methods and aims of the Communists and their police, I can say that I do not believe in the existence of a conspiracy aimed against the democratic form of government.

Among those accused there might have been some people who had talked and written fantastic and childish things, but the leaders or the rank and file of the Smallholders party did not plot against the country.

The signature and eventual coming into force of the peace treaty being in sight, I had to play for time once more, and with the inter-party truce of March, 1947, we still succeeded to save the basic results of the elections: The majority in the National Assembly.

As a result of the direct intervention of the Soviet Union, however, I was ousted from my office, and a new Government was imposed upon the Hungarian people.

The events in Hungary, as well as in many other countries in southeastern Europe, make it definitely clear that the Soviets and Communists do not seek fair and genuine cooperation, but dominance. To them, the coalition is only a means to save the appearance of representative government, and nothing short of unconditional surrender is considered by Russia as a friendly gesture.

As a consequence of Russian and Communist conspiracy, Hungary has lost her independence. The Hungarian people are no longer responsible for the words or deeds of their imposed rulers. Whatever might be said or done on behalf of Hungary by her present and eventual rulers, the Hungarian people, deprived of their freedom, are no longer responsible.

I sincerely hope that American public opinion, having been fully informed by the American press on present events in Hungary, will judge with more understanding and sympathy the very similar events which forced her in Hitler's time into the same degrading situation in which she has been placed now, mainly because of her geographical position and the policy of appeasement on the part of the Western powers.

6

AMERICA'S RESPONSIBILITY

IN THE American and British zones of occupation, the trend is to provide a way for the people to make their own living—directly the reverse of the Russian policy. It had looked as though we had settled down to a long occupation with the idea that the

American taxpayer would indefinitely furnish food and supplies, not only for inhabitants of our zones of occupation, but also for those of the Russian zone.

Before the war fifty percent of the exports of Czechoslovakia went to Germany. In the case of other Danubian countries, the percentage was even larger. The exports of England, France, Belgium, Holland and the Scandinavian countries to Germany were very important to the economies of those countries. With Germany prostrate, not even able to support herself, and divided up into zones with no common purpose in mind, this could not but affect adversely the recovery of all of Europe. Should a central section of the U.S.A. containing eighty million people be permanently ruined, the rest of the country would very soon be in the same condition.

In keeping Germany prostrate the Allies pretended fear where the danger no longer existed, in order to appease Stalin, who determined our attitude. He too is no longer afraid of Germany. His aim apparently is to push Soviet rule forward into the very heart of Europe, and for this reason he needs a new order which brings, in reality, anarchy.

The economic conditions of Europe are inherently at variance with the doctrines of the Morgenthau plan. They offer the development of German agriculture as a substitute for German industry. But they forget that German agriculture cannot be developed without German industry, because the farmer would stop producing for the market if he were unable to buy industrial articles with his proceeds. He could buy foreign articles, but would we or England be prepared to deliver these in exchange for German foodstuffs? As a matter of fact, German agriculture was so highly developed before the war that there remains a very small margin for future improvement.

Europe, despite its political fissures, was an economic unit. For the rest of the European continent, Germany was the decisive buyer and seller. If this situation had not been in existence, Hjalmar Schacht would not have been able to misuse it for the purpose of furthering Germany's war economy. That situation is not unalterable. But it cannot be changed by the economic destruction of Germany which does not enrich, but impoverishes Europe—including Great Britain.

The striking similarity between the situation that existed before the last war and that which exists today cannot be ignored. The difference is that today there is only one supreme power in Europe, Russia, and opposition to her is still hesitant and disorganized. Europe itself is prostrate. Generally speaking, all over eastern Europe, particularly in Soviet-occupied countries, the importance of the individual has been reduced. He has never been respected there as in the Anglo-Saxon world, but the evil teaching of Hitler's state worship, superseded by the Soviet denial of basic human rights and care for the masses, in which the individual hardly figures, has made men and women desperately conscious of their insignificance. Nazi Germany has been defeated, but true democracy meets everywhere practically insurmountable difficulties. Millions of people live in a lamentable state. Not only are there incredible physical sufferings in consequence of the hardships of war, but there are moral sufferings which are much greater and harder to bear.

In all these huge regions of Europe under Soviet domination, no one is sure of his life, his liberty or his property. There is no more human dignity. As one Hungarian diplomat has written me, ". . . the Bolsheviks take our women, our children, our homes, our daily bread, and yet we dare not complain. You are obliged to be delighted and to thank these profane Red liberators." Freedom from want, the prerequisite of normal behavior, cannot be said to exist in eastern Europe, and freedom from fear is a phrase that has become a mockery.

Some people are perhaps wondering why the communists, who are now in the saddle in Warsaw, Belgrade, Bucharest, Sofia, Prague (and as of May 1947, Budapest), are taking such great pains to mislead us. Why all the camouflage? Why do they not openly confess what they are doing? The reason is that they are still in need of our help. To me, the most charming feature of Marxism has always been the admission that socialism must take over the nation at the highest peak of capitalistic prosperity. This does not express great self-confidence. The Poles, Czechs and Yugoslavs who are telling us that the economic chaos left by the Germans can only be overcome by socialistic planning and regimentation are, at the same time, stormy applicants for American gifts and loans. They are quite certain that we shall feed the serpent which yearns to bruise our heels. Perhaps they are right. Did the UNRRA not obey Tito's orders?

We Americans cannot get over the idea that if we do not want war, we won't have it. Certainly, no sane human wants war. We did not go to war with Germany and Japan because we wanted war; we went to war because finally we realized that we had no choice. It is hard for the man on the street to believe that some incident which happens in Iran is of any particular importance so far as he is concerned. Russia wants oil. Well, what does he care? To the man on the street, oil is of interest only to big capitalists; it has nothing to do with him. So, why bother? Actually, these incidents are of greatest importance because of what they portend. Time after time, Hitler could have been stopped, and the second World War could have been prevented, if we had faced facts instead of believing in what we wished to be true. A third World War is certainly not improbable, in fact it is quite possible. It can be avoided; but not by the same methods that we used with Hitler, which would prove futile all over again.

Our diplomatic service is certainly equal to or better than that of any other country. Our greatest difficulty, however, is that our foreign policy is subjected to internal politics. Consequently, shifts and changes occur where stability is needed. It was heartbreaking to see a great leader, as President Roosevelt had been, sacrificing American principles for the sake of political expediency. After his death, in the decisive period when the war came to an end, when everything was still fluid, weak leadership and internal leftist opposition within the Democratic Party deprived this country of its freedom of action, stalemated its efforts to bring about a measure of international justice and transformed our military victory into the biggest political disaster we ever suffered.

Stalin's will became supreme, for he alone knew what he wanted and could pursue his policy of imperialism and oppression with determination, while

America was desperately trying to appease his insatiable greed. On February 9, 1946, Stalin's blunt speech revealed the futility of the American policy of appeasement. Since then, we have established a foreign policy which is grounded on American principles and is accepted on a bipartisan basis by the majority of the nation. But can anything be done this late? Can peaceful methods be applied where force has already accomplished so many brutal facts?

The world has not been, since the Dark Ages, in such a chaotic and distressed condition. A moral force is needed, and what country other than the United States could supply it? We are in the focus where the desperate hopes of a tortured humanity converge. To what other place on earth could they be directed? Certainly not to Moscow, the main source of oppression. Perhaps to London, where the voice of decency has never been silenced. But Great Britain has to climb a steep path to her own recovery. Only we have some practical, surplus strength left. The manner in which we use it will decide whether we shall reap humanity's curse or humanity's blessing. The responsibility to a large degree is ours because we are the one nation that could bring order out of chaos. Upon whether, when, and how we meet that responsibility the future of the world depends.

APPENDICES

Appendix I

THE TEXT OF THE SECRET PROTOCOL OF
THE RUSSO-GERMAN NONAGGRESSION
PACT OF 1939

O N MAY 22, 1946, the St. Louis *Post-Dispatch* published the
following article by its correspondent at Nuremberg, Mr.
Richard L. Stokes:

The *Post-Dispatch* presents herewith what purports to be
the authentic text of the famous "Secret Protocol" for partitioning Poland and disposing of the Baltic states which was
signed by Foreign Commissar V. M. Molotov and Foreign
Minister Joachim von Ribbentrop at Moscow on the night of
Aug. 23, 1939. It is followed by an amendment transferring
Lithuania to Russia with recompense for Germany in Poland
which the same statesmen executed at Moscow on Sept. 28,
1939.

The existence of the "Secret Protocol" was first mentioned
during the defense of Rudolf Hess. It was brought into notice
by Dr. Alfred Seidl, attorney for Hans Frank, Nazi Governor
General of Poland. At the insistence of the Russian prosecution, which has always shown itself acutely sensitive in this

matter, Seidl was stopped in his tracks. Some weeks later he returned to the attack and after a vehement struggle was permitted to place in evidence the so-called "Gauss affidavit." This was an account of the contents of the documents which was drafted from memory by Dr. Wilhelm Gauss, legal adviser of the Nazi Foreign Office, who drew up the nonaggression treaty between the Reich and the Soviet Union.

On the witness stand of the international military tribunal yesterday and this morning was a diplomat of the old school, Ernst von Weizsaecker, who served at the Foreign Office during the ministries of Constantin von Neurath and Ribbentrop and who then became the last German ambassador at the Vatican. Weizsaecker is a man with abundant white hair and a thoughtful, scholarly face.

After his direct examination was concluded, the court president, Lord Justice Sir Geoffrey Lawrence, asked as usual whether other defense counsellors had questions they wished to put. Among the first to reach the microphone was the indomitable Dr. Seidl. He flourished several typewritten sheets. Like a hand grenade he tossed the following interrogation into the arena:

"On Aug. 23, 1939, were there other agreements between the German and Soviet governments which are not contained in the nonaggression pact?"

The chief Russian prosecutor, Gen. Roman Rudenko, was instantly on his feet. He asked that the question be ruled out on the ground that it had nothing to do with the defense of the Grand Admiral Erich Raeder. Lawrence instructed Seidl to go ahead. The witness replied that there was a secret protocol containing agreements which he himself saw and read in his capacity as state secretary in the Foreign Office.

"I have before me," Seidl continued, waving his papers, "a text in which there can be no doubt that these agreements are faithfully and authentically reproduced. I shall have this text submitted to you."

The attorney explained to the court that he wished to read the documents into the record and then ask the witness whether to the best of his recollection the original text of the agreements was accurately given.

Rudenko protested that the tribunal is hearing the case of German war criminals and not examining the treaties of Allied countries.

Seidl was asked the source of the documents. He answered: "I got it a few weeks ago from a man on the Allied side who seems entirely reliable to me, but I received it only on condition that I would not divulge the exact source."

Rudenko objected that the papers were of unknown and anonymous origin. He was supported by the American deputy prosecutor, Thomas J. Dodd, who suggested, however, that Weizsaecker should be permitted to relate the contents of the agreement from memory. The magistrates agreed to reject the documents but to hear the version as recollected by the witness. In general, Weizsaecker's testimony corroborated the Gauss affidavit. At the writer's request Dodd obtained a German copy of the agreements from Dr. Seidl and arranged for their translation into English.

The first is dated Moscow, Aug. 23, and bears this purported superscription: "For the German Government, J. Ribbentrop; on behalf of the Government of the U.S.S.R., V. Molotov."

The text is as follows:

On the occasion of the signing of the nonaggression treaty between the German Reich and the Union of Socialist Soviet Republics the undersigned representatives of the two parties discussed in a highly confidential conversation the problem of the demarcation of the spheres of influence of either party in Eastern Europe.

This conversation has the following result:

1. In the case of a politico-territorial change in the territories belonging to the Baltic States—Finland, Estonia, Latvia and Lithuania—the northern frontier of Lithuania shall form also the demarcation of the spheres of interest between Germany and the U.S.S.R. Both parties recognize the interest of Lithuania in the Wilno territory.

2. In the case of a politico-territorial change in the territories belonging to the Polish state, the spheres of interest between Germany and the U.S.S.R. shall be divided approximately following the line on the rivers Narow, Vistula and San. The question as to whether the interests of both parties make it desirable to maintain an independent Polish state, and how the frontiers of this state should be fixed, can be clarified in a final manner only in the course of further political developments. In any case, both governments will solve this question by way of a friendly understanding.

3. With respect to southeastern Europe, the U.S.S.R. emphasize their interest in Bessarabia. Germany declares her complete political disinterestedness in this area.

4. This protocol shall be treated by both parties in a strictly secret manner.

The second agreement with the title "Secret Agreement," is dated Moscow, Sept. 28, 1939 and is signed identically with the first. The text runs:

The undersigned plenipotentiaries state that there is an agreement between the governments of the German Reich and the U.S.S.R. as follows:
Paragraph No. 1 of the secret protocol of Aug. 23, 1939 is modified in that the territory of the Lithuanian state shall fall within the sphere of interest of the U.S.S.R., whereas, on the other hand, the district of Lublin and parts of the district of Warsaw shall fall within the sphere of interests of Germany. As soon as the government of the U.S.S.R. shall take special measures on Lithuanian territory for the protection of her interests, the present German-Lithuanian frontier will be rectified in order to accomplish a natural and simple frontier so that the Lithuanian territory lying in the southwest of the line marked on the attached map shall belong to Germany. Furthermore, it is stated that the economic agreements presently in force between Germany and Lithuania shall not be impaired by the measures of the Soviet Union mentioned above.

When Ribbentrop was on the stand he told of German-Russian negotiations that followed the signing of the secret agreements. These culminated, he related, in a proposal by Hitler for a virtual military alliance, to which Stalin replied with three conditions which Hitler in turn rejected. According to Ribbentrop these were:

1. Russian occupation of Finland; 2. Soviet domination in Bulgaria; 3. Russian control of the Dardanelles and Russian access to ice-free ports in the Baltic, including a foothold in the Skagerrak.

The Gauss affidavit to which Mr. Stokes referred, is worth

recording here. The text as published by the *New Leader* on November 30, 1946, follows:

My name is Friedrich Gauss . . . Until the end of the war I was legal adviser to the Foreign Office in Berlin, my last rank was of Ambassador Extraordinary.

1. In the early Summer of 1939 . . . the then Reich Minister of Foreign Affairs, von Ribbentrop, asked the then Secretary of State of the Foreign Office, von Weizsaecker, and myself to come to his estate, Sonnenburg, near Freienwalde an der Oder, and informed us that Adolf Hitler had for some time been considering an attempt to establish better relations between Germany and the Soviet Union. This had been the reason why, as we might have noticed ourselves, the extremely sharp polemics of the German press against the Soviet Union had for some time been greatly reduced. . . .

2, Sometime afterward Herr von Ribbentrop surprised me one day in Fuschl by letting me read a document which contained the draft of a special message from the Reich Government to the Soviet Government and amounted to a proposal to initiate negotiations for a political treaty. After preliminary remarks on the evolution of German-Russian relations up to that time and on the antagonism of the two systems of government, the idea was emphasized that the interests of the two states were intimately connected, but did not overlap. . . . A telegram was sent to the German Ambassador in Moscow instructing him to transmit the message and, a short time afterwards, the answer of the Soviet Government arrived; it did not reject in principle the idea of putting German-Russian relations on a new political basis, though it pointed out that extensive examination and diplomatic preparation would have to precede the initiation of direct negotiations.

A second German message was promptly sent to Moscow which expressed Germany's urgent wish immediately to initiate negotiations. . . . This second message—or perhaps the first one—proposed immediately to dispatch the Reich Foreign Minister to Moscow for the purpose of beginning political conversations. To this message an affirmative answer from the Soviet Government was received—I think on August 21—which, as I was able to observe personally, caused great rejoicing to Hitler and his entourage. If my memory does not deceive me, both German messages had the outward form of an immediate personal message from Hitler to Mr. Stalin and the preliminary correspondence was confined to an exchange of messages on these two occasions.

3. On August 23, around noon, the plane of the Reich Foreign Minister, whom I had to accompany as legal adviser in view of the planned negotiations for a treaty, arrived in Moscow. In the afternoon of the same day the first meeting of Herr von Ribbentrop and Mr. Stalin took place. . . .

The Reich Foreign Minister returned very satisfied from this meeting, which had lasted a long time, and expressed the opinion that an accord was as good as certain on the agreements aimed at by Germany. . . .

I personally participated in the second meeting and, also, Count Schulenburg, and Embassy Councillor Hilger. The Russians were represented in the negotiations by Messrs. Stalin and Molotov who were assisted by Mr. Pavlov, as interpreter.

Agreement on the text of the German-Soviet Non-Aggression Pact was reached promptly and without difficulty. . . .

In addition to the Non-Aggression Pact a longer negotiation took place on a special secret document which, as far as I remember, was designated as "Secret Protocol" or "Secret Additional Protocol" and whose contents amounted to a delimitation of the spheres of interest of both parties in the European territories situated between the two states . . . In the document Germany declared that she was politically disinterested in Latvia, Estonia, and Finland, but she considered Lithuania part of her sphere of interest. At first there was a controversy with regard to the political disinterestedness of Germany in the two Baltic countries mentioned inasmuch as the Foreign Minister, according to his instructions, wanted to exclude a certain part of the Baltic territories from this political disinterestedness; this was, however, not accepted by the Soviets, especially because of the ice-free ports which were situated precisely in this part of the territory.

The Reich Foreign Minister had put in a long distance call to Hitler because of this point which, apparently, had already been discussed during his first meeting (with the Russians). The long distance call did not come through until during the second meeting, and, in a direct conversation with Hitler, the Reich Foreign Minister was empowered by him to accept the Soviet point of view. For the Polish territory a line of demarcation was decided upon. . . .

In regard to the Balkan countries it was established that

Germany had only economic interests there. The Non-Aggression Pact and the secret document were signed the same night at a rather late hour. . . .

(In a second affidavit, Gauss corrected himself: Not the Balkan States but Bessarabia was excluded from the German sphere of interest.)

4. During the time when copies of the final text were being prepared, refreshments were served; a conversation developed during which Herr von Ribbentrop told how a public speech by Mr. Stalin, which he made in the Spring, had contained a sentence which, though Germany was not expressly mentioned, had been understood by Hitler as a hint on the part of Stalin that the Soviet Government considered it possible or desirable to establish better relations also with Germany. (Ribbentrop obviously referred to Stalin's report to the Eighteenth Congress of the Communist Party in March, 1939.) Mr. Stalin answered by a short remark which, according to the translation by the interpreter Pavlov, meant: "That was the intention." In this connection Herr von Ribbentrop also mentioned that Hitler had recently shown to him a film of a public ceremony in Moscow and that he, Hitler, found this film and the Soviet personalities shown in it "very likable" (sympathisch). An additional matter which deserves to be mentioned, since I have also been questioned about it, is the fact that, both during these conversations and the official negotiations, the Reich Foreign Minister chose his words so as to represent a military conflict between Germany and Poland not as something that had been definitely decided upon, but only as a probable possibility. The Soviet statesmen did not make any utterances in regard to this point which would have amounted to approval of such a conflict or encouragement of it. In this connection the Soviet representatives merely took note of the statements of the German representatives.

5. During the negotiations on the second German-Soviet political treaty, which took place about a month later, the second document . . . was modified, in accordance with the proposal submitted by the Soviet Government to Berlin on an earlier date; by this modification Lithuania, with the exception of a small "tip" adjoining Eastern Prussia, was also taken out of the German sphere of interest, while in exchange the line of demarcation on Polish territory was shifted farther to the East. As a result of later negotiations through diplomatic

channels, which, as far as I remember, did not take place until the end of 1940 or the beginning of 1941, this Lithuanian "tip" ultimately was also renounced by Germany.

Appendix II

REGENT HORTHY'S RADIO PROCLAMATION:

OCTOBER 1944

T HE TEXT of Admiral Horthy's armistice proclamation broadcast to the people of Hungary on October 15, 1944, follows. Made soon after Rumania's and Bulgaria's withdrawal from the war, it nevertheless required much courage on Horthy's part, for Hungary was still regarded as part of Hitler's "inner fortress"; and it precipitated Horthy's arrest:

Ever since the will of the nation put me at the helm of the country, the most important aim of Hungarian foreign policy was, through peaceful revision, to repair, at least partly, the injustices of the Peace Treaty of Trianon. Our hopes in the League of Nations in this regard remained unfulfilled.

At the time of the beginning of a new world crisis, Hungary was not led by a desire to acquire new territories. We had no aggressive intention against the Republic of Czecho-Slovakia, and Hungary did not wish to regain territories taken from her by war. We entered Bacska only after the collapse of Yugoslavia and at that time in order to defend our blood brethren. We accepted a peaceful decision of the Axis powers regarding the eastern territories taken from us in 1918 by Rumania.

Hungary was forced into war against the Allies by German pressure, which weighed upon us owing to our geographical situation. But even so we were not guided by any ambition to increase our own power and had no intention to snatch as much as a square meter of territory from anybody.

Today it is obvious to any sober-minded person that the German Reich has lost the war. All governments responsible for the destiny of their countries must draw pertinent conclusions from this fact, for, as a great German statesman, Bismarck, once said: 'No nation ought to sacrifice itself on the altar of an alliance.'

Conscious of my historic responsibility, I have the obligation to undertake every step directed to avoiding further unnecessary bloodshed. A nation that would allow the soil inherited from its forefathers to be turned into a theater of rearguard actions in an already lost war, defending alien interests out of a serflike spirit, would lose the esteem of public opinion throughout the world.

With grief I am forced to state that the German Reich on its part broke the loyalty of an ally toward our country a long time ago. For a considerable time it has launched ever-new formations of Hungarian armed forces into the fight outside the frontiers of the country against my wish and will.

In March of this year, however, the Fuehrer of the German Reich invited me to negotiation in consequence of my urgent demand for the repatriation of Hungary's armed forces. There he informed me that Hungary would be occupied by German forces and he ordered this to be carried out in spite of my protests, even while I was retained abroad. Simultaneously German political police invaded the country and arrested numerous Hungarian citizens, among them several members of the legislative assembly as well as the minister of the interior of my government then in office.

The Premier himself evaded detention only by taking refuge in a neutral embassy. After having received a firm promise from the Fuehrer of the German Reich that he would cancel acts that violated and restricted Hungary's sovereignty, in case I appointed a government enjoying the confidence of the Germans, I appointed the Sztojay government.

Yet the Germans did not keep their promise. In the shelter of German occupation the Gestapo tackled the Jewish question in a manner incompatible with the demands of humanity, applying methods it had already employed elsewhere. When war drew near the frontiers, and even passed them, the Germans repeatedly promised assistance, yet again they failed to honor their promise.

During their retreat they turned the country's sovereign territory into a theater of looting and destruction. Those actions, contrary to an ally's loyalty, were crowned by an act of open provocation when in the course of measures for the maintenance of order in the interior of Budapest, Corps Com-

mander Field Marshal Lieutenant Szilard-Bokay was treacher-
ously attacked and abducted by Gestapo agents who exploited
the bad visibility of a foggy October morning when he was
getting out of his car in front of his house.

Subsequently German aircraft dropped leaflets against the
government in office. I received reliable information that
troops of pro-German tendency intended to raise their own
men to power by using force to effect a political upheaval and
the overthrowing of the legal Hungarian government which
I had appointed in the meantime (Premier Lakatos) and that
they intended to turn their country's territory into a theater
of rearguard actions for the German Reich.

I decided to safeguard Hungary's honor even in relation to
her former ally, although this ally, instead of supplying the
military help he had promised, meant to rob the Hungarian
nation finally of its greatest treasure—its freedom and independence.

I informed a representative of the German Reich that we
were about to conclude a military armistice with our previous
enemies and to cease all hostilities against them.

Trusting your love of truth, I hope to secure in accord with
you the continuity of our nation's life in the future and the
realization of our peaceful aims.

Commanders of the Hungarian army have received corresponding orders from me. Accordingly, the troops, loyal to
their oath and following an order of the day issued simultaneously, must obey the commanders appointed by me. I appeal
to every honest Hungarian to follow me on the path beset by
sacrifices that will lead to Hungary's salvation.

Appendix III

SWISS LEGATION REPORT OF THE RUSSIAN
INVASION OF HUNGARY IN THE
SPRING OF 1945

THE MEMBERS of the Swiss legation and consulate, accompanied by a group of Swiss subjects—as an aggregate about sixty persons—left Budapest in 1945 at the end of March and beginning of April. The following is a summary condensed from their reports, drafted on May 24, 1945, in Switzerland.

During the siege of Budapest and also during the following fateful weeks, Russian troops looted the city freely. They entered practically every habitation, the very poorest as well as the richest. They took away everything they wanted, especially food, clothing and valuables. Looting was general and profound, but not always systematic. It happened, for instance, that a man was deprived of all his trousers, but his jackets were left to him. There were also small groups which specialized in hunting up valuables, using magnetic mine detectors in search of gold, silver and other metals. Trained dogs were also used. Looting became more general after the Russians had gutted the city, for they did not object to proletarians, who previously had been looted by them, looting the city for themselves. Thus every apartment, shop, bank, etc. was looted several times. Furniture and larger objects of art, etc. that could not be taken away were frequently simply destroyed. In many cases, after looting, the homes were also put on fire, causing a vast total loss.

Bank safes were emptied without exception—even the British and American safes—and whatever was found was taken. Cash found in the banks was confiscated (in the Commercial Bank 120,000,000 pengoes; in the Credit Bank 80,000,-000 pengoes). The Russians use their own currency with the inscription "Red Army" but the peasants are unwilling to accept this currency. In commercial rating, 1,000 Russianlabeled pengoes are worth only 800 normal pengoes. The Swiss franc was rated 60 to 80 centimes against 100 pengoes. The Hungarian National Bank has again started circulation of the previously withdrawn 20-pengo banknote in order to alleviate the shortage of banknotes on the market.

After several weeks, looting stopped; today it is the Hungarian police who watch over public security. But Russian soldiers often arrest passersby, relieving them of the contents of their pockets, especially watches, cash and even papers of identity.

Rape is causing the greatest suffering to the Hungarian population. Violations are so general—from the age of 10 up to 70 years—that few women in Hungary escape this fate. Acts of incredible brutality have been registered. Many women prefer to commit suicide in order to escape monstrosities. Even now, when order is more or less re-established, Russian soldiers will watch houses where women live and raid them at night, knocking down anybody who opposes them. The women generally are not killed, but kept for several hours, if not for days, before being liberated. Misery is increased by the sad fact that many of the Russian soldiers are ill and medicines in Hungary are completely missing. Cases have been reported where Russian women serving in the Red army or in the Russian police force have been guilty of rape. Men have been beaten up by such women for not having submitted themselves to their wishes.

Only a few political executions are known to have taken place, including those of some extremist officers who have "distinguished" themselves in the persecution of Jews. On the other hand, complete uncertainty prevails concerning the fate of very many people. The reason for this incertitude is that many persons escaped at the approach of the Russians. Hungarians were evacuated or deported in large numbers by the Germans; many were killed during the siege; and large numbers changed their addresses as their habitations were destroyed. All means for the search of such persons is lacking. Uncertainty is increased by the Russian practice of assuring labor for necessary public works by simply halting people in the streets or raiding certain blocks of houses for workers. (In the beginning everybody was treated this way. Later this treatment was restricted to men below sixty and women below forty years of age.) By these methods, thousands and thousands of people in the provinces as well as Budapest proper are forced to work. These people usually are returned after more or less time, but are never given a chance to inform their families of their whereabouts. For instance, the present cabinet minister for public instruction, Count Geza Teleki, and one of the mayors of the city of Budapest, were seized without warning, forced to work and found only after two days, when a Russian officer with whom they could speak finally released them. The richest man of the country, Prince Paul Eszterhazy, was found in a graveyard burying dead horses.

Near the town of Godollo, a large concentration camp has been erected where some forty thousand internees are being held and from where they are being deported for an unknown destination toward the Orient. It is known that these internees get very little food unless they sign an agreement to engage as volunteers in the Red army or accept a contract for work in Russia. Very few details are known concerning this camp, as nobody is allowed to approach it. Especially are those people being held here who are suspected by the Russians of having fought against them, or who have been denounced as pro-Nazi. But not all of the pro-Nazis are being persecuted. It is known, for instance, that a member of the guards of the general head-quarters of the Hungarian Nazis, was arrested by the Russians, but was released very shortly after having joined the Communist Party. The case of Mr. Juhasz, president of the Gamma factory for precision instruments, can be cited. He is generally known as an extreme rightist and anti-Semite. After his arrest, laborers of his factory visited the Russian authorities and assured them that they were satisfied to work under his guidance. The Russians immediately released him, and he is working today in his old post.

The population of Germanic origin from the age of two up to the age of seventy is deported en masse to Russia.

To force diplomatic missions still residing in Budapest (the Swiss, Swedish, Turkish and Papal legations) and also foreigners living in Hungary to rejoin their own countries, the Russians have declared that all foreigners who stay in Budapest will be treated exactly as if they were Hungarians. The departure of the Swiss legation was properly organized by the Russians; second and third class railway cars were made accessible to them. During their journey to Istanbul, which lasted forty-eight hours, all the travelers were strictly forbidden to contact the outside world. In Bucharest, for instance, they could not speak to anybody, not even to the members of the Swiss legation in Bucharest who had come to the railway station to meet them. Several Swiss citizens could not leave Budapest within the allowed twenty-four hours as they did not possess papers of identity, Russian patrols having previously halted them in the streets and confiscated all their documents. The passports issued by the Swiss legation have not been accepted as valid by the Russians.

The Hungarian government has no power whatsoever. It is simply tolerated by the Russians.

The chief of the Swiss legation, Mr. Feller, and its chancellor, Mr. Mayer, were arrested by the GPU shortly after the entry of the Russians. Nobody has heard a word about them since. On the other hand, the rumor that two ladies of the same legation had disappeared was not found to be true. During the looting of the premises of the legation, one of four occasions, the Russians put a rope around the neck of Mr. Ember, an employee of the legation, in order to force him to hand over the keys of the official safe. As he refused to do so, even in his plight, they pulled the rope around his neck until he lost consciousness. Then they took the keys from his pocket, emptied the safe and took away all the deposits, amounting to several millions.

The Committee of the International Red Cross had two delegates in Budapest. One of them, Mr. Born, was ordered to leave the country immediately. The other, Mr. Weyermann, after having been arrested for two days (when all his documents were also destroyed) was allowed to stay on; but he has no liberty of action and can do very little.

A big safe of the Swedish legation which the Nazis had unsuccessfully tried to remove was removed by the Russians with all its contents. This affair will have a diplomatic sequence as the Swedes propose to protest to Russia.

Jewish refugees within the neutral legations succeeded in escaping extermination by the German Gestapo. They were apparently saved because of the hardships imposed on the Germans by the siege. A member of the Swiss legation reports that the Jews whom they had been taking care of are generally safe. There were only three Jewish-inhabited houses under Swedish protection which were occupied by the Germans, their inhabitants being killed and their corpses thrown into the Danube. There is also reassuring news concerning several persons protected by the legation of Portugal. Unfortunately, Mr. Zoltan Farkas, attorney of the Spanish legation, charged with the protection of that legation, was killed.

Generally speaking, the Russians do not treat the Jews any better than the rest of the population.

It is estimated that more than half of the city of Budapest is destroyed. The commercial district and the hills of Buda (the Fortress and the Rozsadomb) have suffered most. There are certain parts in the city which, according to the Russians, have suffered more than Stalingrad. The quays on the Danube and especially the Elizabeth Bridge and the Chain Bridge have been almost completely destroyed. In the Fortress there is almost no house standing. The Royal Palace was burned down. The Coronation Church collapsed. The Parliament Building is severely damaged, but its skyline has remained intact. The hotels Ritz, Hungaria, Carlton, Vadaszkurt, and Gellert are all in ruins. The Vaczi-utca has suffered very much. The house of Gerbeaud is damaged, but still stands. A stable was set up during the siege in the great hall of the confectionery store. The Commercial Bank is more damaged than the Credit Bank. The buildings housing the other banks, Moktar, Adria, the National Casino, were burned down completely. The French legation was entirely destroyed by the Germans. The house of the Hubay family next to the French legation also suffered a lot during the siege.

Only the waterworks on the Pest side function, not yet those in Buda. There is no gas. Electricity can only be granted to factories working for the Russians and to offices and habitations of the forces of occupation. Two film theaters playing Russian films have been granted electricity. All other customers' meters have been sealed. The trams had started circulation, but on account of the lack of current, they have been halted and those blocking traffic on the roads have been removed by tractors. For civilian use there is no other means of communication than a few horse- or mule-driven carriages. Within the city the post already functions, but in order to send a letter to the provinces you have to take your letter to some suburb from which trains start, the central railway station being entirely destroyed. Travel in the provinces is only allowed with special permission from the Russian authorities and only in freight cars. All the radios in town have been requisitioned by the Russians.

The Franz Josef Bridge and the Nicholas Horthy Bridge have been repaired with wooden constructions. There is also a pontoon bridge which the Russians built at the head of Margaret Island. The food situation in town is disastrous due to the lack of transportation. In the provinces the situation is distinctly better. The bread ration in Budapest is 100 grams daily per person, or 70 grams of flour. Potatoes are granted: two pounds per person per week, but even these rations are received infrequently. The black market is considered legal and prices are not controlled. If any person succeeds in slipping through the Russian city control with his products, he can sell them freely. By this system, the fabulous prices that existed throughout the siege have been lowered (for instance, two pounds of flour has fallen from 200 pengoes to 50 or 70).

The factories are working exclusively for the Russians. Laborers receive a threefold food ration. In order to maintain this ration the Russians are compelled to transport a limited quantity of food to Budapest.

During the siege the population had to live exclusively on whatever stocks or reserves it had piled up. Toward the end of the siege, the situation was disastrous and the corpses of horses dead for several weeks (often flattened by tanks that passed over them) had also been eaten up.

Hygienic conditions are very saddening. There are several epidemics (especially typhus). Sanitary service has been fairly well organized. Every block of houses has one doctor for surveillance against epidemics, but on the other hand, pharmaceutical products and medicines are completely missing, although the Russians have given some disinfectants for the population of Budapest. The pharmacies were completely looted by the Germans, the Hungarian Nazis and the Russians. Medicines are highly in demand; you can exchange against aspirin and especially against antiseptic products very favorably for food and other products.

The Russian troops that entered Budapest first made a distinctly good impression as they were very well equipped. The troops coming later were much less well equipped and very poorly clad, except for their armaments which were just as good as with the elite troops. Almost all the infantry is armed with machine guns. Discipline is very questionable. The soldiers will only obey the officers of their own detachment. The officers are not greeted by the soldiers and detachments on the march resemble a band of excursionists. Many of the Russian soldiers do not understand Russian as there is an immense variety of races among them. Propaganda plays the supreme role in the Russian army. For instance, the castle of Seregelyes, belonging to Count Bela Hadik—the Russian shock troops removed all the furniture and destroyed all the installations within the castle, poured gasoline over the mass of things and ignited it. The castle was then refurnished by the Russian soldiers with straw beds in order to prove to the troops following them in what misery even the bourgeoisie were living. The same procedure was followed in the villages and in the peasants' habitations.

Appendix IV

SECRET CONTACTS BETWEEN KING
ALEXANDER OF YUGOSLAVIA
AND MUSSOLINI

PRECEDING HITLER's advent to power several attempts were made to bring about better understanding between neighboring nations which within a few years were to become victims of Nazi aggression. Italian-Yugoslav animosity was an inheritance of the Paris peace conference. It had led to serious incidents between Italy and Yugoslavia even before the advent of Mussolini to power.

The Corfu incident almost destroyed Mussolini's dictatorship in 1924 and from that time on he proceeded more carefully with his schemes concerning imperialistic expansion in the Balkans. Nevertheless, he distinctly favored disruptive tendencies aimed at the splitting up of Yugoslavia into separate national units, especially at the separation of the Croats from the Serbs. The resulting tension extending over all of the

Adriatic coastline interfered with the general stability in southeastern Europe and affected the situation both in Vienna and in Budapest.

King Alexander reacted very firmly against Croat separatism. He even went much too far by establishing his personal dictatorship in Yugoslavia (1930) but credit must be given him for his tenacious attempts at coming to a better understanding with Mussolini.

The following excerpts from the file of my Italian friend, whose name I prefer not to divulge, are evidence of Alexander's good faith and of Mussolini's shady intentions. To my mind, this document is of interest as a behind-the-scenes example of the play of forces which swayed events in central Europe.

The conversations began late in 1930 when King Alexander discovered that my friend had direct access to Mussolini. On many occasions the king did not ask him to convey direct messages to Mussolini but merely expressed his opinions vehemently, confident that my friend would repeat them to the Duce. Much of the record is repetitious; much of it expresses Alexander's indignation against the Italian press, as on January 1, 1931:

The papers continue with their attacks and when they have nothing to say, they invent. Recently they published the statement that there had been discovered here a conspiracy of generals, and that I don't know how many had been shot and hanged. There was not a word of truth in it, for at all events with our army, which is well disciplined, we are absolutely safe. I cannot understand why Italy acts this way to create difficulties for us when both our countries could obtain great advantages from a good friendship, since we are an agricultural and Italy an industrial country.

We are accused of desiring war! Thanks! That would indeed be the last straw for the whole world. We have just come out of a war, and we know what it means. And what good would it do? What would we get? I assure you that I can think of no conceivable reason for desiring a war, for even if I had a ninety percent chance of winning it, I would not risk the ruin of my country.

In 1921 our relations with Italy were most cordial and we were entirely willing that Italy should be free to do what she pleased anywhere except in the Balkans, where any question could have been settled after a reciprocal agreement. And then Italy goes and signs a treaty at Tirana without giving us the slightest warning. From 1920-21 on, France was determined to persuäde me to sign a treaty of alliance and she was pressing me as hard as she could. I had steadily refused to sign, out of regard for Italy with whom I desired good relations, but as soon as I learned of the Treaty of Tirana I instructed my minister at Paris to sign. Subsequently, Italy signed a second treaty at Tirana, and after that we strengthened our ties with France; now we are committed to following the French line.

People are astonished that we are arming when the threat of treaty revision is always present. Does anyone believe that I would submit to treaty revision being discussed at a table? My entire country would turn on me in a fury! Those who wish revision must fight for it. It is just as though someone came to take away belongings from your own home. It is because of this continual threat that we are compelled to arm. Do you suppose that I am pleased at having to spend billions to buy cannon, aeroplanes and weapons in Czechoslovakia and France when all this money might remain in my own country which needs so many things? This year alone I have bought nine hundred cannon and it has cost me an incredible sum of money.

Before the annexation of Fiume, I received a message that Mr. Mussolini desired to come to an agreement with me on the basis of a policy of sincere and frank friendship, providing I would not raise difficulties in this question of Fiume. I was delighted to seize this opportunity, and I replied that if the friendship of Italy and particularly of Mr. Mussolini were involved, I would yield in the matter and undertake to raise no difficulties. I myself accepted the entire responsibility and likewise I courted the displeasure of my entire country. . . . I expected that the press would cease its attacks in order to prepare the ground and public opinion; but the press has not stopped its attacks, nor has anyone to date said another word about discussions or agreements. You know I believe that Italy is now no longer free: she must have commitments, of which I am not aware, with other powers binding her so that she can no longer come to an agreement with us.

Had the spirit of King Alexander been able to appear at the League of Nations trial concerning his assassination, there can be little doubt as to whom he would have accused. On February 12, 1931, lamenting the recent bomb incident at Zagreb, he said: ". . . the bomb attempt was hatched and paid for by Italy."

To my friend's protest that he must be mistaken, he replied: "But my dear fellow, we now have the whole organization in our hands and we are well aware through our excellent police that *lire* were received in payment for the business."

My friend protested that if Italy had actually been behind the matter she would probably have paid in dollars. But the king was insistent:

. . . on Italy's side it is really a policy of obstinacy; Italy is determined to create obstacles for us, but they will have no success. . . . If I, as a soldier, wished to capture a position, I would, of course, do everything possible to that end; but once persuaded that I could not capture it and that I would merely lose my men and ammunition, I would withdraw. . . . Italy should now realize that she cannot bring catastrophes upon us and that her policy of obstinacy is costing her a great deal of money without any results.

It would be much better to decide on a good policy of frank and loyal friendship from which we would draw great reciprocal advantages . . . leaving aside sentiment, one could, from a purely selfish point of view, come to a commercial agreement; . . . why should we not make an experiment of this kind, let us say for three years, and try to obtain the greatest possible advantages from such a commercial arrangement, at the same time practicing a frank and loyal policy? The policy of hostility can always be resumed if it is found to be more advantageous and if the commercial arrangement does not work . . . I particularly believe that this hostility is created entirely artificially, for neither among our people nor among yours is it a part of popular sentiment.

Late in February, when my friend asked the king whether he would be interested in meeting with Mr. Mussolini, his reply was emphatic:

You may well imagine that I would be delighted, for you must remember that I have always spoken to you of Mr. Mussolini with admiration, understanding, and I would even say enthusiasm, and I would like to speak to him calmly and frankly; but I would wish to be sure that on his side he had a firm intention and disposition to find a way of agreement, and —when found—the desire to follow it.

I would not wish our conversation to share the fate of all the other conversations between our respective ministers, which after having given us hope never led to anything. I am convinced that Mr. Mussolini is, generally speaking, not well informed. I do not say that Mr. Galli (the previous Italian minister to Belgrade) does not keep him properly informed, for Mr. Galli is a man of the best type—a real 'gentleman'— whom I hold in the greatest esteem; but he likewise is in a difficult position here, since he must carry a very heavy load left by his predecessor. Informers often make reports and shape them according to what they think will please the persons who receive them, thus hoping to do well for themselves; or else they exaggerate to create the belief that they are extremely well informed even about the most confidential matters.

I saw Mr. Galli after the marriage of the Prince of Piedmont and he told me that he had spoken with Mr. Mussolini and Mr. Grandi at Rome and that he was under the impression that Rome was extremely well disposed toward us—but nothing more ever came of it. Later Mr. Grandi met Mr. Marinkovic in Switzerland, but after four hours of conversation the same negative results followed.

If I could speak with Mr. Mussolini I wish we could push forward without being discouraged at the first difficulties, for I can well understand that after all the fuel which has been thrown on the fire by the filthy press, any suggestion of agreement would at first be most unpopular in both countries. Soon, however, the material and moral usefulness of an agreement would be realized and satisfaction would follow. As for myself, I know definitely that I could obtain its willing acceptance, for, in my own country I am esteemed and well-liked and above all they know very well that I have no other thought nor aim than the welfare of the nation.

In Italy they believe absolutely that our country is under the domination of Zifkovic—another matter wherein they are badly informed, since I have everything in my hands, and I myself brought in Zifkovic as prime minister for the simple reason that I wished a man in that position who had nothing to do with politics. General Zifkovic has no political ambitions and he serves his king as a faithful servant with intelligence and devotion; but he is ready to leave his place and go back to his regiment whenever I wish.

As far as General Zifkovic's political ambitions were concerned, the king was certainly mistaken. General Zifkovic tried to seize power in Yugoslavia immediately following the death of King Alexander. He was prepared to go so far as to provoke a war against Hungary to serve his political ambitions. He was prevented from doing so by the foresighted action of Mr. Jeftic —who had succeeded him as prime minister before Alexander's death—in settling the Marseilles affair through the instrumentality of the League of Nations.

Alexander went on:
Mr. Mussolini has often declared in favor of treaty revision without particularly stressing that such revision must necessarily be directed against Yugoslavia. If we could converse, we could most probably reach an agreement on this delicate and important question—perhaps the most delicate and the most important of all—but naturally until that time I am on the side of those who are against revision. It is said that because of this we are the vassals of France. We are nobody's vassals, but we have with France treaties which bind us reciprocally, and it is scarcely surprising that we are and continue in agreement with those who, like ourselves, are interested in preventing treaty revision. . . .

Late in March 1931, the king spoke of France again:

As I told you, I have a treaty with France and we are reciprocally bound. If sometimes France uses a somewhat high-handed tone to Italy, she does so because she believes you isolated and because she knows that she is supported by us and —of course—by the entire Little Entente. She would no longer do it if Italy had with us—and naturally with the Little Entente—a frank and loyal agreement. Isolation is to be avoided; what does Italy think she will get out of alliances with Hungary, Albania, Bulgaria, etc? All these people tie on to Italy in the hope of getting her to pull the chestnuts out of the fire; but these alliances will cost Italy appalling amounts, and in her day of need she will get nothing from them: believe me, it is a bad investment.

An interesting sidelight on Hungary's ceaseless attempts to break up the Little Entente is a note which appears in my friend's file concerning a conversation he had in Budapest on his way back to Italy at this time. The Italian minister to Hungary, Mr. Arlotta, told him that "Count Bethlen and also the Hungarian minister of war, Mr. Gombos, would be far from displeased with an agreement with Yugoslavia and Rumania isolating Czechoslovakia" and authorized him to tell that to Mr. Mussolini.

In May definite plans were made for the king to meet Mussolini in Italy that summer. The king was impatient for the meeting to take place. At this time the Yugoslav minister Marinkovic was meeting in Geneva with Mr. Grandi, and Alexander had high hopes that the meeting would bring about constructive results which could be the subject of discussion with Mussolini.

But Marinkovic sent a discouraging report of the meeting and the king was much grieved.

Returning to the discussion of the necessity for an agreement between Italy and Yugoslavia Alexander said:

You see, an agreement with Italy means changing my whole policy and turning it completely up-side-down. My present policy is based on the possibility of a war: it is the policy of treaties of alliance securing defense in case of attack, the policy of armament. Doubtless it is a good policy and, in view of present circumstances, we are compelled to follow it—but there is a far better one. The present-day policy is a negative and ruinous one; a policy which destroys the riches of our countries, which compels us to spend billions, mostly abroad, for armaments.

On the other hand, the policy which we could pursue if we had an agreement with Italy would be a positive one, a policy creating riches in the line of commerce and industrial development. We could reduce our expenses for armaments, without counting the enormous benefits which we would reap through tranquility and confidence once the danger of war in Europe had been averted: for, after all, we have no other enemies to fear except Italy, and Italy has none except ourselves. If we

continue—and let us call a spade a spade—as enemies, the day
will come when war will be inevitable, even with the best will
to avoid it; for we will be in such a state of excitement as to
be at the mercy of some mad Dalmatian or Croat, who, without being able to avoid it, will fire the powder magazine on
account of a mere nothing. The war would inevitably be a
world war—or at least a European war—and this would be
the last straw for Europe: what a result! Heaven preserve us!

Let us suppose that Italy makes war and wins it: what
would she get from it? At most she would be able to take from
us Dalmatia. If we suppose a victory for Yugoslavia, we might
get Albania, Istria, and Trieste; but, as I have already told
you, I would not take Albania as a gift; Istria isn't worth
much, and Trieste we could not hold because of German pressure, since the Germans wish to get it so as to have their own
port on the Mediterranean. Even if we could hold it, it would
only yield expense and worries for us, since we already have
our hands full with Susak and Split, and Trieste would be for
us a port with a passive balance—just as it now is for Italy.

One of the capital questions is the question of Albania. Italy
concluded the Treaty of Tirana to protect and defend the independence and integrity of Albania; but on this point I am
in complete agreement and I have also expressly declared in
public that I myself am likewise ready to guarantee the integrity and independence of Albania. . . .

In June, discussing the proposed meeting still further—for
despite his discouragement over Marinkovic's report he still
wished to meet with Mussolini—Alexander again brought up
the subject of Albania as the most important one between
himself and Mussolini. He remarked that "Italy constitutes a
real military base against us in Albania which is like an arrow
in our body." Stating that one "could not find a better time
for reaching an agreement than the present when there are no
parliaments to begin an endless fire of interpellations," he
went on: "At present the matter only depends on the two of
us. . . . Once an agreement has been reached it doesn't matter who comes into power; unless they are completely mad
they cannot but approve my action and maintain the agreement."

In July, on my friend's return from Italy where he had con-
veyed the king's earnest desire for a meeting, Alexander

wanted to know what had been said about the Albanian question. When my friend replied that Mr. Grandi had said Italy would not renounce the mandate which had been given her and which had been affirmed both by the League of Nations and by the Conference of Ambassadors, Alexander exclaimed: "But don't you see that this is a mistake! It is not a question of a *mandate:* Italy was given the mission of protecting Albania *in case of attack by third parties,* but if Albania is not attacked . . . and besides, by whom should she be attacked if not by us?"

Mr. Mussolini had sent word to the king at this time that the proposed meeting would not be convenient to him until September 1931. To this delay Alexander readily agreed.

On the following day the king explained his political point of view concerning the situation in Europe and all over the world:

As regards our neighbors, the Hungarians, the Rumanians, the Bulgarians, etc., it is believed in Italy—on the basis of I do not know what kind of reports—that we have aggressive and invading tendencies . . . I can assure you that this is absolutely false because, since we have already obtained by the treaties all that we could desire, we ask nothing better of our neighbors than to live in peace with them and to develop as far as possible our good relations of vicinage, commerce and peace; we do not covet their territory, nor do we desire to mix in their affairs.

As regards the international political field, we have no expansionist ambitions as we do not desire either colonies or mandates. Our policy is a local policy since we have many provinces which, like Montenegro and others, are large and incredibly poor. Nothing grows in them and we must provide for them and send them wheat, corn and everything else. . . . We are only interested in central European questions which may have a reflex action on us. Italy, being a great power, must pursue a world policy; she must be interested in Asiatic and African questions, etc.—all matters concerning which we will never have anything to say and regarding which there will consequently never be any conflict between us. As regards European and particularly central European questions, we will have the same interests to maintain once we have reached an agreement.

Mr. Grandi once said that he wanted to make Albania another Belgium; a neutral state guaranteed by treaties. I would accept this idea willingly and I am ready to give to this end any guarantees which might be desired. Is this still the intention of Italy? I wish to be informed exactly of the political point of view of Italy on this question of Albania, as it is the only one which is of capital importance between us.

As this is a complex question I would suggest to Mr. Mussolini either to send me here with you a person thoroughly and technically conversant with the matter, or to allow me to send to Rome with you the person whom I consider best adapted to this purpose and who, having been with me a number of years, knows my ideas on this subject. I am speaking of Mr. Jeftic, the minister of the Royal House, who officially has nothing to do with politics and who is a most discreet and loyal person.

Nobody in my entourage is aware of our discussions, for even Mr. Marinkovic is ignorant of them. Once the meeting has taken place and the agreement has been reached, I will say to Mr. Marinkovic: 'This is the policy to be pursued'—and he will pursue it.

Mr. Jeftic's subsequent visit to Rome proved to be completely futile, as he was not even received by Mr. Mussolini. King Alexander was incensed. "Our propositions," he complained, "are neither intangible nor unchangeable; why then are we met with this attitude of unwillingness to discuss them? We drew up our ideas in writing: why did Italy not do likewise?"

The September meeting did not take place. But early in 1932, the king had a visit from Mr. Galli, Italian minister to Yugoslavia, who was just back from Rome and came as the bearer of an agreement "complete in every detail."

The king described the interview to my friend upon his arrival in Belgrade on February 21, 1932. When Alexander had asked Galli whether he had spoken with Mussolini regarding the Albanian question, the latter had replied: "Naturally, Your Majesty, but on this point Italy cannot renounce its rights. . . ."

"At this point I really lost patience," the king told my friend. "This was really making fun of me, as it was the only matter on which I had asked Italy to yield. In all other matters I am ready to accept the Italian point of view completely."

King Alexander discussed the problem further on the following day:

If Albania is a free and independent country such as, for instance, Greece or Hungary, then there is no reason why Italy should mix in its internal affairs, just as Italy would not think of sending troops if tomorrow the Greeks and the Hungarians were to quarrel among themselves.

If Albania is an Italian colony, then I am faced with another Italian front in Albania. If we are enemies I can look at it in that way, but if we are good allies I cannot admit that Italy should keep the right to send troops on that part of the frontier whenever she pleases and on some pretext which can always be found.

If Italy refuses to consider this point of view, she must inevitably be concealing ulterior motives hostile to us, either to leave herself an opening to pounce on us or to take Albania definitely for herself. In such case it would be useless to talk of a loyal agreement.

The agreement between us must be either absolute and complete or cannot exist at all. We are too close to each other, and our interests have too much in common; we must either be very good friends or enemies: there is no middle course.

In Italy they say: 'The Adriatic must be ours.' Is it not yours? Can we with our four ships compete with Italy? 'Italy must have the key of the Adriatic,' but has she not already got it with the islands? And once we are united by a good friendship, will we not have the same interest to guard together the key of the Adriatic? In that case I would be willing to give you the Bocche di Cattaro, to defend together our common interests in the Adriatic against third parties.

Finally, on being reassured that Mussolini had expressed definitely a wish to go on with the meeting while my friend was last in Italy, Alexander said: "Go and see Mr. Mussolini and tell him my general ideas," and he proceeded to outline them as follows:

Foreign Policy: Peace and cordial agreements with our neighbors and with distant countries. Full liberty for Italian expansion. Italy naturally needs to expand, because of the too great density of its population, either in Africa or in Asia. If other great powers wish to block these aspirations of Italy, we will always be ready to support her. We have no colonial aims, as we have sufficient to occupy us at home.

League of Nations: We undertake to support the Italian policy and to 'pull together' in all questions. The agreement would bring disarmament as its immediate and automatic effect, for we are arming exclusively against yourselves. We could, therefore, support at Geneva Mr. Mussolini's ideas on disarmament.

France: We have nothing against France, and I will not do anything against her because I am under too many obligations toward her; but I will merely say to her frankly and freely: 'We are very good friends, but I have also other good friends, our neighbors the Italians'—and that is all. France will have nothing to say.

Internal Policy: We have nothing to change, nor any pretensions to territorial enlargement. War to the death against any possible Bolshevik infiltrations into the country. No tolerance nor indulgence nor asylum for any Italian anti-fascist emigres. Encouragement of cultural and commercial development, etc., reduction of armaments to the strictly necessary amount, and employment of our enormous military investments for the benefit of peace industries.

Commercial and Financial Policy: We are ready to undertake to buy all Italian products, excluding by customs tariff the products of other countries.

We are disposed even to go as far as a kind of customs union and abolish frontiers, even bringing Hungary into the combination, since we have no special or serious reasons for conflict with her. Encouragement and protection for the organization of Italian banks in the country; preference for Italian capital. If the agreement becomes a fact, it will be as though a partition-dam were opened in a water reservoir: the waters will mix naturally and inevitably and will require no one to make them do so. Manufactured products, money, everything will go from one country to the other according to needs and natural interests—and this will be a real and sensible and thorough agreement. After all, individual interests make up the general interest of a people and the bonds of interest are the most natural and the most durable.

Albania: On this subject I have already spoken to you sufficiently, but I repeat and I declare that I have no pretensions and no concealed ulterior aims regarding Albania; I repeat that I will have none of Albania nor of the Albanians. I am ready to guarantee with Italy the integrity, the liberty and independence of Albania in the most thorough fashion which Italy could ask—even by bringing in a third great power (England) as a party to the contract. The formula adopted with and for Belgium should be ideal for Albania.

Generally speaking, I think that we are in agreement with Italy. I might add that England has informed me through her minister that she would see with satisfaction an agreement with Italy and a drawing-away from France; that the most influential persons in Yugoslavia are all favorable to such an agreement.

It seems to me that I have said everything. Go and see Mr. Mussolini and give him my assurances of good will and confidence in him; but I would ask you to tell him from me that I *entreat* him to take the matter into his *own* hands: we have had enough of 'spokesmen'.

In reply to these statements my friend was given the following message by Mr. Mussolini in an interview on March 1, 1932:

Tell His Majesty that I first listened to and subsequently carefully read the very interesting statements which he has transmitted to me and ask him now to leave me the time to formulate an agreement which shall be for our common interest and gratification.

As a preamble to this agreement we must first say that it is derived from the desire for peace not only between our two peoples, but for the peace of *Europe*.

To this end:

1) Italy and Yugoslavia declare that for the purposes of this peace, they have the same common interest in the integrity and independence of Albania.

2) Yugoslavia, however, declares that Italian interests *prevail* in Albania, as has, moreover, been acknowledged by the treaties and by the Conference of Ambassadors.

3) Italy undertakes not to avail herself of the rights granted her by the treaties in any way which might be harm-

ful to the interests of Yugoslavia or might weaken the pact
of friendship.

In regard to having a third power guarantee the agreements,
Mussolini said: "There are only two of us in the Adriatic and
it is best to avoid any pretext which might allow a third great
power to stick its nose in there."

In regard to the treaties of commerce, which would be
drawn up by technical experts and which might even go so far
as the possibility of a customs union, Mussolini expressed the
opinion that there should also be constituted a *single* Italo-
Yugoslav port authority for Fiume and Port Baross. "As it is
now," he explained, "Fiume cannot live because it has no
'hinterland', and Port Baross cannot live because its 'hinterland' is not sufficient."

Mussolini went on:

This draft of a treaty will be drawn up within a month and
will afterwards be submitted to His Majesty for approval; then
our meeting can immediately be arranged.

Tell His Majesty the King that he will find me in the best
possible good will, as this agreement must be complete, loyal
and productive of results if it is to be a lasting one.

Toward the end of the month you will come to me to get the
drafts; but let me know immediately the opinion of His
Majesty on these general matters.

On March 15, King Alexander dictated a reply to Mussolini's statement, which my friend had presented to him ten
days before:

We acknowledge with pleasure the clearness of thought and
the loyalty with which Mr. Mussolini has treated the essential
elements of a lasting agreement between our two countries. As
it seems that we are in agreement on the general lines, it only
remains for us to reach a definite agreement by drawing up a
clear and precise draft.

To our regret, however, point No. 2 of the preamble proposed by Mr. Mussolini, namely,

'that Yugoslavia, however, declares that Italian interests prevail in Albania, as has, moreover, been acknowledged by the
treaties and by the Conference of Ambassadors,'

does not seem to us in conformity with the principles of the independence of Albania, recognized by the two guarantor countries. We could not in principle recognize such a *prevalence* of Italian interests in Albania. We see therein a constant danger to our agreement. This 'prevalence' is vague and ambiguous: it will lead to distrust. Undoubtedly, the economic and financial interests of Italy in Albania are greater than those of Yugoslavia, and in the future will be even more so; we do not deny this *de facto* situation and *we can undertake to do nothing to interfere with* (or, perhaps, 'endanger') *Italian interests in Albania.*

Since our agreement must be perfect, loyal and deeply sincere, the Albanian question automatically disappears; hence we see no reason for any special acknowledgment of the *prevalence* of Italian interests in Albania.

As regards the remaining questions we are in agreement and we share Mr. Mussolini's point of view. We are awaiting with great hopes and will receive with the best good will the treaty draft which Mr. Mussolini expects to send us.

The king discussed the question of Italy's wisdom in leaving armaments in the hands of a childish people like the Albanians, and went on:

We will do something great. Even France, once she knows that we are entirely reconciled with Italy in a lasting and loyal way, will feel the need likewise to draw nearer to Italy. Ours will be the first really serious and *positive* step which will set the good example; one must not mark time too long on a given spot, and if we decide, the others must inevitably follow us. Although the questions which divide Italy and France are much more serious—for they comprise colonial questions, the question of Tunisia, the question of naval parity, etc.—I do not doubt that after our agreement France will be much less exacting.

When I was in Paris I spoke to Mr. Laval, who told me that he intended to get on better terms with Italy and asked me— as did Mr. Tardieu—if I objected or at any rate would be displeased. Naturally I answered that I had nothing against it and that it would give me great pleasure. The French minister at Belgrade asked me the same thing the other evening, and I gave him the same answer.

When asked what he thought of the Tardieu proposal for a Danubian agreement, Alexander replied:

I am very sceptical and I do not think that anything will come of it. I think, however, that as the world does not know that we have been preparing our agreement for a long time, it might be believed in France that we had hastily thrown it together to torpedo Mr. Tardieu's plan for a Danubian understanding. As for myself I am not in the least disturbed about what may be said or thought: I am entirely indifferent and I hope that Mr. Mussolini will think as I do.

Besides, as I said before, I am sceptical. We are too much accustomed to hearing every minute of new proposals which are given out without any solid preparation—and then there follows conference after conference always with the same result: disillusion. I think one should do the opposite, as we have done: prepare beforehand, study the details and interests involved, discuss them, and when everything is prepared, present a positive, concrete, vital and definite achievement. This is the great difference.

Ask Mr. Mussolini to give you the draft which I await with hope, confidence, and good will—just as I await with impatience the setting of a date for our meeting. Go, then, and may God be with you.

However, the draft did not arrive, nor was a meeting arranged.

In October 1932, when my friend saw the king the day after he had received from his ministry of the interior reports on the recent riots at Lika, he found him very much aroused because the report was drafted in such a way as to indicate clearly that the propaganda, the weapons and the bombs had come from Italy. Alexander firmly believed this and his remarks at this time were prophetic:

. . . I am disgusted; this is what the Italians are constantly doing to us; they try to stab us in the back and they hope to obtain success with these disloyal attacks. Is it possible for a country like Italy to use such means in trying to increase the troubles in our country and provoke us! Do they believe in Italy they will get anywhere with such pitiful methods unworthy of a great and self-respecting people? They will not obtain any radical political success by stirring up some poor ignorant peasants and killing some farmer who asks nothing better than to live! Tell them that in Italy, and say to Mr. Mussolini from me that to stir up serious disorders in Yugoslavia or to obtain a change of regime they will have to shoot at me and be very sure to kill me, for only in that case will there be any changes here; I repeat that you will have to kill me and kill me thoroughly! You may say also that if it were necessary for the good of the country to shed rivers of blood I would be ready to do so, for I am conscious above all of my duty and of the responsibility of my position. I desire the welfare of my country.

Chronology

TREATIES AND AGREEMENTS MADE AND BROKEN, AND TERRITORIAL READJUSTMENTS AFFECTING HUNGARY, FROM 1933 TO 1945

February 15, 1933: Implementation of the Little Entente Accord (concluded in 1921) signed at Geneva: Expresses determination to resist all efforts to destroy existing treaties. No member of the Little Entente will sign a treaty with an outside power before consulting the other two.

June 7, 1933: Four Power Pact initialed by Britain, France, Italy, Germany.

September 2, 1933: The British government agrees to the establishment of a special Austrian force of 8,000 men to meet "grave circumstances." France and Italy have consented before.*

September 29, 1933: Little Entente meeting at Sinaia: King

---

* Agreements concerning Austria have been included in this chronology because, since the advent of Hitler to power, the maintenance of Austrian independence became a primary issue for all powers interested in the stability of Europe.

Alexander, King Carol, Benes, Titulescu and Jeftic. They
decide to rebuild Danubian countries and base their plan
upon "an intimate co-operation of Czechoslovakia, Yugoslavia, Rumania, Hungary, Bulgaria and Austria."

February 6, 1934: Hungary recognizes the Soviet government
by establishing diplomatic relations with Russia.

March 17, 1934: Three Power Pact: Italy, Austria and Hungary envisage common consultation; an increase of mutual
exports by means of bilateral treaties. They set up a permanent commission of three trade experts. Austrian goods shall
receive preferential treatment in Italy.

June 15, 1934: After a Mussolini-Hitler meeting, Count Ciano
declares: "We have agreed to grant to Austria the means of
making her livelihood on the basis of the full recognition
of her independence."

July 26, 1934: In reaction to Dollfuss assassination: England's
Sir John Simon, France's Premier Doumergue and Mussolini declare their respective country's support of Austrian
independence.

January 7, 1935: French-Italian Pact: initialed in Rome by
Laval and Mussolini. It fixes the frontiers in North Africa
and defines the status of Italians in Tunisia. Furthermore:
"The two governments declare that they are in agreement
in recommending to those states most interested the conclusion of a pact of noninterference in their respective internal
affairs. . . . The above-mentioned agreement should be
signed by Italy, Germany, Hungary, Czechoslovakia, Yugoslavia and Austria, that is to say by the countries which border on Austria and by Austria herself.

April 14, 1935: Foundation of the Stresa Front: Stresa Conference of Italy, Britain and France reaffirms the consultation
pacts concerning threats to Austria's independence. Also reaffirms the Locarno obligations.

May 2, 1935: Franco-Russian mutual assistance pact initialed
in Moscow by Laval.

May 16, 1935: Soviet-Czecho-Slovak mutual assistance pact
signed: Aid is pledged on condition that the victim of aggression is assisted by France.

June 18, 1935: Anglo-German Naval Agreement: conceded to

Germany a fleet representing 35% of the British navy in each category regardless of constructions of other powers.

July 26, 1935: Italy proposes to Austria and Hungary, and France proposes to the members of the Little Entente to make a Danubian Pact on the following lines: a) Affirmation of Austria's independence; b) affirmation of mutual noninterference; c) nonaggression agreement; d) consultation in case of violation of a, b, or c.

September 9, 1935: Foreign ministers of Austria and Hungary conclude a Hungarian-Austrian Agreement concerning the proposed Danubian Pact. Hungary opposed to mutual assistance pacts. Both will observe a common attitude toward requesting military equality. (Abrogated by the Paris Peace Treaties.)

March 7, 1936: German troops march into Cologne, Coblenz, Frankfort, Mainz, Trier and Saarbruecken.

July 11, 1936: German-Austrian Agreement: "Austria's general policy and its policy toward Germany in particular shall be constantly guided by the principle that Austria recognizes herself as a German state. The Rome Protocol of March 1934, together with its additional clauses of 1936, and the relations of Austria with Italy and Hungary as partners of that protocol are not hereby affected."

September 12/14, 1936: A Bratislava meeting of the foreign ministers of the Little Entente resolves that: a) Political treaties with outside countries shall only be concluded with the consent of the other two members of the Little Entente; b) expresses hope that Little Entente relations with Italy and Poland will improve; c) regrets that Austria violated the military clauses of St. Germain; d) agrees on necessity of opposing Hungary's rearmament; e) regrets German press attacks on Czechoslovakia because of Russian airdromes there, calling them a "pure invention."

October 20, 1936: Italo-German Agreement: Berlin recognizes annexation of Ethiopia.

November 1, 1936: Mussolini at Milan: "The Italo-German Entente forms a vertical line Berlin-Rome. This line is not a partition but is rather an AXIS around which all European states can collaborate."

January 4, 1937: The Mediterranean Agreement, signed by Sir Eric Drummond and Count Ciano: "Anglo-Italian Gentlemen's Agreement," indirect recognition of Mussolini's Impero. Governments recognize that "the freedom of entry into, exit from and transit through the Mediterranean is a vital interest both to the different parts of the British Empire and to Italy and that these interests are in no way inconsistent with each other. . . ."

March 26, 1937: Count Ciano and Premier Stoyadinovitch of Yugoslavia sign at Belgrade a political and economic agreement and a nonaggression pact. They undertake to respect their common frontiers on land and on the Adriatic Sea.

December 12, 1937: Italy withdraws from League of Nations.

January 12, 1938: Daranyi, Schuschnigg and Ciano, representing signatories of the Rome Protocol, hold a conference at Budapest: Austria and Hungary express friendly feelings toward the Axis, their antagonism to communism and sympathy for German, Italian, Japanese Anticomintern Pact. Austria and Italy pronounce themselves in favor of Hungary's military equality.

March 12, 1938: Germany occupies Austria.

March 14, 1938: German government through Goering and their minister to Prague, assure the Czech government of their determination to respect territorial integrity of Czechoslovakia.

March 25, 1938: Hungarian Foreign Minister de Kanya declares that the spirit of the Rome Protocol will survive the end of one of its partners. Hungary will continue her efforts to improve her relations with the Little Entente.

April 16, 1938: Anglo-Italian Agreement: concerning good neighbor relations in East Africa, the evacuation of Spain, and the Naval Treaty of London; signed by Count Ciano and British Ambassador Lord Perth.

July 24, 1938: The British government, with the consent of Prague and Paris, sends Lord Runciman on an unofficial mission to Prague to act as an impartial standing adviser to the Czech government in negotiations with the German minority.

August 23, 1938: The Little Entente recognizes Hungary's

right to rearm on the basis of a mutual renunciation of all recourse to force between Hungary and the Little Entente. The agreement, however, will be signed after settlement of minority problems.

September 9, 1938: The Czech government publishes the so-called Fourth Plan for a settlement of the nationality question. Language laws will be modified on the basis of the equality of the German, Russian, Ruthenian, Hungarian and Polish languages with the Czechoslovak language. The principle of national self-government is to be admitted in the form of cantons.

September 21, 1938: The Czechs accept the amputation of German regions from Czechoslovakia.

September 30, 1938: Four Power Agreement of Munich signed. Czech Prime Minister Sirovy accepts Munich agreement.

October 1, 1938: Czechs cede Teschen to Poland.

October 5, 1938: President Benes of Czechoslovakia resigns, having nominated Frantishek Chvalkovsky foreign minister.

October 9, 1938: The Ruthenians of the Carpatho-Ukraine decide on autonomy within the framework of the Czechoslovak state.

October 21, 1938: Foreign Minister Chvalkovsky tells the Soviet minister in Prague that Czechoslovakia is no longer interested in her mutual assistance pact with Russia.

October 26, 1938: The Czechs accept German-Italian arbitration in their territorial dispute with Hungary.

November 2, 1938: Ribbentrop and Ciano meet in Vienna to give their award: Hungary gets most of her territorial claims satisfied in this first Vienna Award, but not Bratislava and Nitra and not the Carpatho-Ukraine.

November 11, 1938: Hungarian troops enter Kassa, completing occupations following Vienna Award.

January 15, 1939: Count Csaky informs Germany, Italy and Japan that Hungary has decided to accept the invitation to join the Anticomintern Pact.

February 2, 1939: Russia severs diplomatic relations with Hungary because of the latter's joining the Anticomintern Pact, accusing Hungary of having abandoned her political independence.

February 24, 1939: Csaky signs a protocol registering Hungary's entry into Anticomintern Pact.

March 14, 1939: Slovakia proclaims her independence.

March 15, 1939: President Hacha, summoned to Berlin, places fate of Czech people into the hands of Hitler. German troops enter Prague.

Following Slovak declaration of independence, the Hungarian government presents an ultimatum to the Czech minister in Budapest demanding withdrawal of all Czech troops in the Carpatho-Ukraine within twenty-four hours . . . Ultimatum accepted by Prague. Hungarian troops cross the frontier and reach the Polish border on March 16.

March 16, 1939: Count Teleki announces the return of Carpatho-Ukraine to Hungary and granting of autonomy to her.

Slovakia becomes a German protectorate.

March 22, 1939: Lithuania cedes Memel to Germany after an ultimatum.

April 7, 1939: Italy invades Albania.

April 11, 1939: Hungary withdraws from the League of Nations, but not from the ILO and the Hague Court.

April 13, 1939: Britain and France give Rumania and Greece a pledge of assistance in case they would consider it vital to resist actions threatening their independence.

April 28, 1939: Hitler declares that "the basis for the naval treaty with Great Britain has been removed."

July 9, 1939: Bulgarian Premier Kiosse Ivanoff on his way home from Berlin meets Foreign Minister Cincar-Markovic at Bled. They confirm the Yugoslav-Bulgarian Pact of Eternal Friendship, economic collaboration, a policy of independence and neutrality and of friendship with all neighbors.

August 23, 1939: Soviet Russia and Germany conclude a non-aggression pact (containing a secret protocol for the partition of Poland).

September 1, 1939: Germany invades Poland from East Prussia and Slovakia.

September 3, 1939: Prime Minister Chamberlain declares that Britain is at war with Germany.

September 4, 1939: Hungarian government declares its attitude will not undergo the least change because of the outbreak of war. This is considered a declaration of neutrality.

September 5, 1939: Yugoslavia declares strict neutrality.

September 17, 1939: Soviet troops invade Poland.

September 24, 1939: Soviet Russia agrees to resume diplomatic relations with Hungary.

September 28, 1939: Stalin and Ribbentrop fix a "frontier between the interests of their respective states in the territory of the former Polish state."

October 16, 1939: Germany declares her military operations in Poland completed and annexes western Poland.

November 1, 1939: Soviet Russia annexes the western Ukraine and, the next day, western White Russia (from Poland).

November 17, 1939: The French government of Daladier recognizes a group of Czechs and Slovaks in London as a Czechoslovak National Committee headed by Benes.

December 20, 1939: The British government recognizes the Czechoslovak National Committee.

January 16, 1940: Hungary and Germany conclude a new trade agreement. Hungary rejects Germany's demand for a more favorable pengo-mark exchange rate, but agrees to reduce official dollar quotation to prewar level.

April 9, 1940: Germany invades Denmark and Norway.

May 10, 1940: Germany invades the Netherlands, Belgium and Luxembourg.

June 10, 1940: Italy declares war on Great Britain and France.

June 20, 1940: France asks for an armistice.

June 24, 1940: Yugoslavia and Russia resume diplomatic relations. (They had been suspended since the Russian revolution of 1917.)

June 26, 1940: Soviet Union demands in a twenty-four hour ultimatum that Rumania cede Bessarabia and Northern Bukovina. Rumania says she is willing but asks for negotiations. Moscow rejects plea and demands evacuation within four days. On June 28, Rumania yields.

July 1, 1940: Rumanian Premier Tatarescu renounces formally the Anglo-French guarantee to his country and states that future Rumanian policy will be aligned within the "new orientation in Europe."

July 11, 1940: Rumania withdraws from League of Nations.

August 21, 1940: Rumania cedes the Southern Dobrudja to Bulgaria, thus restoring the frontier of 1912.

August 30, 1940: Premiers Teleki of Hungray and Gigurtu of Rumania are called to Vienna to receive second award. Hungary gets northern half of Transylvania.

October 7, 1940: Rumanian legation in Berlin announces that German troops have been sent to Rumania with consent of the latter "to reorganize the Rumanian army with all equipment necessary for modern warfare."

November 11, 1940: In a joint declaration the Polish and Czech governments in exile affirm their intention to collaborate closely after the war, forming a confederation.

November 23, 1940: General Antonescu, Rumanian premier, signs his country's adherence to the Anticomintern Pact in Berlin. Tuka, premier of Slovakia, signs too.

December 12, 1940: Count Csaky and Yugoslav Foreign Minister Cincar-Markovic sign, at Belgrade, a pact of lasting peace and eternal friendship. The pact provides for consultation on all questions of mutual interest.

February 10, 1941: Great Britain severs diplomatic relations with Rumania, stating that the latter has become a military base of Germany without protest.

March 1, 1941: Professor Filoff signs Bulgaria's adherence to the Axis Pact in Vienna. German troops occupy Bulgaria.

March 2, 1941: Filoff declares that presence of German troops in Bulgaria does not change her policy of peace. Britain severs diplomatic relations, pointing to the German menace against Greece.

March 25, 1941: Yugoslav Premier Tsvetkovitch and Cincar-Markovic sign adherence to the Tripartite Pact. Ribbentrop promises that Germany will respect at all times the sovereignty and territorial integrity of Yugoslavia, and that Yugoslavia will not be asked to permit the passage of German troops.

March 27, 1941: General Simovitch stages a *coup d'état*. King Peter II takes over in Yugoslavia.

April 6, 1941: Russia announces conclusion of Yugoslav-Soviet Friendship Pact: "Should one of the contracting parties be subjected to aggression by a third state, the other party will preserve its policy of friendship."
Germany invades Yugoslavia and Greece.

April 8, 1941: The British government informs the Hungarian minister in London that the British legation in Budapest is being withdrawn because Hungary has become a base for military operations against the Allies.

April 10, 1941: Croatia proclaims her independence.

April 11, 1941: Hungary occupies Yugoslav territory.

April 15, 1941: Bulgaria breaks off her relations with Yugoslavia.

April 23, 1941: Greece severs diplomatic relations with Bulgaria.

May 14, 1941: Croatia is constituted as a totalitarian state with Ante Pavelitch as leader.

June 14, 1941: Croatia enters the Axis Pact.

June 21, 1941: Hitler's armies attack Russia.

June 24, 1941: Hungary severs diplomatic relations with Russia.

June 27, 1941: Hungary declares war on Russia.

July 18, 1941: Great Britain recognizes Benes' provisional government in London.

July 31, 1941: The United States does the same.

August 17, 1941: The Soviet government accepts Zdenko Fierlinger as minister of the Benes government.

November 10, 1941: The Czecho-Slovak-Polish Co-ordination Committee meets in London and agrees that the Polish Czech Federation will be the nucleus of political and economic organization in that part of Europe and will constitute an indispensable element in the new European democratic order. Benes, speaking at Aberdeen, says that Austria and Hungary and perhaps Rumania will be invited to join, but that Hungary will have to give up her territorial gains.

December 6, 1941: British government declares that from December 7 Britain will be at war with Finland, Rumania, and Hungary owing to their refusal to cease hostilities against Russia.

December 7, 1941: Japanese attack on Pearl Harbor.

December 12, 1941: The Slovak government declares war on Britain and the United States.

Hungary severs her diplomatic relations with the United States.

December 13, 1941: Croatia and Bulgaria declare war on Britain and the United States.

December 28, 1941: Britain announces that she is at war with Bulgaria.

March 9, 1942: Premier Bardossy of Hungary resigns. New premier is Nicholas de Kallay.

August 8, 1942: Benes broadcasts that Russia has recognized Czechoslovakia's pre-Munich frontiers.

July 25, 1943: Mr. Ghyczy becomes foreign minister of Hungary.

December 12, 1943: Russo-Czech "alliance" is signed during Benes' visit to Moscow.

March 18/19, 1944: German troops occupy Hungary.

March 24, 1944: Former Premier Kallay calls the new Sztojay government illegal. He and Horthy are retained.

May 21, 1944: The Bulgarian cabinet Bojiloff resigns twenty-four hours after receiving Russian note warning Bulgaria of consequences of her assistance to Germany.

May 29, 1944: Bulgarian Regent Filoff returns from Berchtesgaden with an ultimatum demanding more co-operation and a friendly government.

June 1, 1944: Ivan Bogrianoff, a pro-German, forms a new Bulgarian cabinet.

July 8, 1944: Yugoslav cabinet Subasitch nominated.

August 5, 1944: Hungary rejects Germany's demand to break with Turkey.

August 25, 1944: Moscow states: "The USSR has no desire to acquire any part of the Rumanian territory, to modify the social order in Rumania or to limit in any fashion the independence of Rumania."

August 26, 1944: Radio Sofia announces Bulgaria's withdrawal from the war.

September 3, 1944: The Soviet Tass agency alleges that Bulgaria's neutrality is used to cover the exodus of German troops; Russia concentrates troops along the Danube on Rumanian soil.

September 5, 1944: The new Bulgarian premier Muravieff states that his government is resolved to restore freedom and democracy; announces a rigorous policy of neutrality involving disarmament of Germans irrespective of Berlin's attitude. . . .

The same evening, Russia declares war on Bulgaria.

September 6, 1944: Bulgaria asks Russia for an armistice.

September 8, 1944: Russia invades Bulgaria.

September 9, 1944: Colonel Kimon Georghieff forms a new government in Bulgaria, composed of members of the Fatherland Front which includes the Zveno Group, the communists and left wing agrarians and socialists.

September 10, 1944: Russia announces that hostilities in Bulgaria have ceased.

September 13, 1944: The Bulgarian government sends an armistice delegation to Marshal Tolbukhin.

Moscow announces an armistice with Rumania.

October 16, 1944: A national socialist coup follows Horthy's plea for an armistice. Major Szalasi heads the new Hungarian "government." Horthy is seized by the Gestapo and taken to Berlin.

October 28, 1944: Bulgaria signs an armistice in Moscow.

November 11, 1944: Hungarian General Staff Chief Voeroes escapes to Russian lines, orders army to join Russians and declares that the Horthy regime is the legal one.

December 24, 1944: Russia announces that a Hungarian National Assembly has been set up in Debrecen. General Voeroes appears as defense minister, Colonel General Miklos as premier.

January 21, 1945: Hungarian Premier Miklos signs an armistice with Russia, United States, and Great Britain.

January 31, 1945: The Czechoslovak government in London recognizes the Lublin Committee as the provisional government of Poland.

February 1, 1945: The Polish government in London severs

its relations with the Benes government and states that it has long recognized that the Czechoslovak government is not independent. . . .

February 12, 1945: The siege of Budapest is ended and Russian forces occupy Budapest, accompanied by Mathias Rakossi, who returns from twenty-five years' service in the Soviet to become the dictator of Hungary.

BOOKS DEALING WITH HUNGARY

Andrassy, Count Julius, Jr., *Bismarck, Andrassy and Their Successors.* London, 1927.

Apponyi, Count Albert, *Lectures in the U. S. on the Peace Problems and on the Constitutional Growth of Hungary.* Budapest, 1921.

Apponyi, Count Alexander, *Hungarica* (Works about Hungary printed in Western countries. 16th-18th century). 4 vols. 1900.

Baker, R. Stannard, *Woodrow Wilson and the World Settlement,* 3 vols. New York, 1923.

Balanyi, George, *The History of Hungary.* Budapest, 1930.

Bandholtz, Harry Hill, *An Undiplomatic Diary.* New York, 1933.

Bethlen, Count Stephen, *Hungary in the New Europe.* Foreign Affairs, 1924.

———, *The Treaty of Trianon and the European Peace.* London, 1934.

Buday, Laszlo, *Dismembered Hungary.* London, 1923.

Burian, Count Stephen, *Austria in Dissolution.* New York, 1925.

Czako, Stephen, *How the Hungarian Problem Was Created.* Budapest, 1934.

Deak, Francis, *The Hungarian-Rumanian Land Dispute.* New York, 1928.

——— and D. Ujvary, *Papers and Documents Relating to the Foreign Relations of Hungary, vol. I., 1919-1920.* New York, 1939.

Eckhart, Francis, *A Short History of the Hungarian People.* London, 1931.

English State Papers: *Correspondence Relative to the Affairs of Hungary.* London, 1850.

Fay, Sidney Bradshaw, *Origins of the World War.* New York, 1928. Vol. II.

Ferenczi, Imre, *International Migration,* 2 vols. New York, 1929, to 1931.

Fest, Alexander, *The Sons of Edmund Ironside at the Court of St. Stephen.* Budapest, 1938.

Gathorne-Hardy, G. M., *A Short History of International Affairs, 1920 to 1938.* London, 1939.

Glaise-Horstenau, Edmund, *The Collapse of the Austro-Hungarian Empire.* London, 1930.

Gooch, G. P. and H. M. Temperley, *British Documents on the Origins of the War, 1898-1914.* London, 1926, et seq.

Gorgey, Arthur, *My Life and My Acts in Hungary in 1848-1849.* London, 1852.

Gratz, G. *The Era of Revolutions.* Budapest, 1935.

Hengelmuller, Laszlo, *Hungary's Fight for National Existence, 1703-1711.* London-New York, 1913.

Homan, Balint, *Hungary 1301-1490.* Cambridge Medieval History. 1923.

———, *King Stephen, the Saint.* Budapest, 1938.

House, Edward Mandell, *The Intimate Papers of Colonel House.* (Arranged by Ch. Seymour). 4 vols. Boston, 1926-28.

The Hungarian Peace Negotiations. (Publ'd. by R. Hung. Ministry For. Affairs). 3 vols. Budapest, 1920-22.

Hungarian Quarterly, Budapest, 1936 et seq.

Janossy, Denis, *Great Britain and Kossuth.* Budapest, 1937.

———, *The Kossuth Emigration in America.* Hung. Hist. Soc., Budapest, 1940.

Jaszi, Oscar, *Revolution and Counter-Revolution in Hungary.* London, 1924.

———, *The Dissolution of the Habsburg Monarchy.* Chicago, 1929.

Kaas, Albert, *Bolshevism in Hungary.* London, 1931.

Kende, Geza, *Hungarians in America, 1583-1926.* 2 vols. Cleveland, 1926.

Klapka, George, *Memoirs of.* London, 1850.

Kornis, Julius, *Education in Hungary.* New York, 1932.

———, *Hungary and European Civilization.* Budapest, 1938.

Kosary, Dominic, *Gabriel Bethlen.* Slavonic Review, London, 1938.

———, *A History of Hungary.* Cleveland-New York, 1941.

Kovacs, Aloys, *The Development of the Population of Hungary since the Cessation of the Turkish Rule.* Budapest, 1920.

Leiningen-Westerburg, Count, *His Letters and Diary,* ed. by Henry Marczali. 1920.

Lloyd George, David, *The Truth about the Peace Treaties.* 2 vols. 1938.

Lockhart, Bruce, *Seeds of War.* London, 1926.

Lukinich, Imre, *A History of Hungary.* Budapest, 1937.

Lybyer, A. Howe, *The Government of the Ottoman Empire in the Time of Suleiman the Magnificent.* Cambridge, 1913.

Macartney. C. A., *The Magyars in the Ninth Century.* Cambridge, 1930.

———, *Hungary.* London, 1934.

———, *Hungary and Her Successors.* Royal Inst. of Internat'l Affairs. Oxford, 1937.

———, *Studies on the Early Hungarian Historical Sources.* Budapest, 1940.

Malyusz, Elemer, *The Fugitive Bolsheviks.* London, 1931.

Marczali, Henry, *Hungary in the 18th Century.* Cambridge, 1910.

———, *Papers of Count Stephen Tisza, 1914-1918.* Amer. Hist. Rev., 1924.

Miller, David Hunter, *My Diary at the Conference of Paris.* 20 vols. Privately printed, 1928.

Nagy, Ivan, *Hungarians of the Five Hemispheres.* Budapest, 1935.

Nicolson, Harold, *Curzon, Peacemaking, 1919.* Boston, 1933.

Pivany, Eugene, *Hungarian American Connections.* Budapest, 1927.

Pribam, Alfred Francis, *Austrian Foreign Policy, 1908-1918.* London, 1923.

———, *The Secret Treaties of Austria-Hungary* (Eng. ed. by A. Coolidge) Cambridge, 1920-21.

Riedl, Frederick, *A History of Hungarian Literature*. London, 1906.

Rutter, Owen, *Regent of Hungary*. London, n.d.

Schmitt, B. E., *The Annexation of Bosnia, 1908-9*. Cambridge, 1937.

Seton-Watson, R. W., *Racial Problems in Hungary*. 1908.

———, *The Southern Slav Question in the Hapsburg Monarchy*. London, 1911.

———, *German, Slav and Magyar*. London, 1916.

Sproxton, Charles, *Palmerston and the Hungarian Revolution*. Cambridge, 1929.

Stiles, W. H., *Austria in 1848-49*. 2 vols. New York, 1852.

Szasz, Zsombor, *The Minorities in Rumanian Transylvania*. London, 1927.

Szentkiralyi, Joseph, (Education in) *Hungary*. The Phi Delta Kappan, Nov. 1939.

Teleki, Count Paul, *The Evolution of Hungary and Its Place in European History*. New York, 1923.

Toulmin, J. Smith, *Parallels between England and Hungary*. London, 1849.

———, *Louis Kossuth*. London, 1852.

Toynbee, Arnold Joseph, *Survey of International Affairs, 1924*. London, 1926.

Tyler, *Reports, Financial Position of Hungary*. Geneva, 1931-1933.

United States, Department of State, Papers Relating to Foreign Relations of the United States, 1918. Supplement I. Washington, 1933.

Vasvary, Edmund, *Lincoln's Hungarian Heroes*. Washington, 1939.

Ward, A. W. — Gooch, G. P., *The Cambridge History of British Foreign Policy*. Vol. 2. London, 1922.

INDEX

More Books of Interest on Hungary and East-Central Europe

AUTHOR	**TITLE**
Sisa, Stephen	The Spirit of Hungary
Baross, Gabor	Hungary and Hitler
Bibo, Istvan	Democracy, Revolution, Self-determination
Biro, Sandor	The Nationalities Problem in Transylvania
Bogdan, Henry	From Warsaw to Sofia
Borsody, Stephen	The New Central Europe
Borsody, Stephen ed.	The Hungarians. A Divided Nation
Cadzow, Ludanyi, Elteto	Transylvania. The Roots of Ethnic Conflict.
Chaszar, Edward	Decision in Vienna. The Czechoslovak-Hungarian Border Dispute
Chaszar, Edward	The International Problem of National Minorities
Chaszar, Edward	International Protection of Minorities:
Cseres, Tibor	Titoist Atrocities in Vojvodina 1944-1945
DuNay, Andree	The Early History of the Rumanian Language
Hogye, Michael	The Last Satellite? Hungary's Destiny at the End of WW.II
Illyes, Elemer	National Minorities in Romania. Change in Transylvania.
Illyes, Elemer	Ethnic Continuity in the Carpato-Danubian Area
Janics, Kalman	Czechoslovak Policy and the Hungarian Minority. War & Society, etc. Vol. IV.
Kertesz, Stephen D.	The Last European Peace Conference
Kertesz, Stephen D.	Between Russia and the West. Hungary and the Illusion of Peacemaking.
Kiraly, Pastor, Sanders	Total War and Peacemaking. A Case Study of Trianon. War & Society, Vol. IV
Kostya, Sandor	Northern Hungary. A Historical Study of the Czechoslovak Republic
Kosztin, Arpad	The Daco-Roman Legend
Lote, Louis L. ed.	Transylvania
Major, Mark Imre	American-Hungarian Relations 1918-1944
Romsics, Ignac ed.	Wartime American Plans for a New Hungary
Sakmyster, Thomas L.	Hungary, the Great Powers and the Danubian Crisis, 1936-1939.
Szent-Ivanyi	Janos Esterhazy (A Hungarian Leader in Czechoslovakia)
T.V.F. & Danubian R.	Genocide in Transylvania
Wagner, Frances S.	Toward a New Central Europe
Wagner, Frances S.	Hungarian Contributions to World Civilisation
Wojatsek, Charles	From Trianon to the First Vienna Award.

[Continued from front flap]
essential for us to know if we still hope
to construct a decent, a just peace. Here
are the facts not only about Hungary herself, but as they relate to the Balkans and
to Middle-Europe as well. Here too are
the diplomatic maneuverings of Germany,
Russia, Italy, Great Britain, France and
the United States — an absorbing nar-
rative.

Hungary, The Unwilling Satellite
brings what has been a very confusing
picture into sharp and lucid perspective.
To it John Montgomery contributes an intimate knowledge of his subject, an objective viewpoint and a deeply American
desire to seek out and make known the
truth.
_____

JOHN FLOURNOY MONTGOMERY comes
from Missouri where he learned at an
early age to apply his state's slogan "Show
me."

His natural quest for truth about the
small countries of Europe was made use
of by Roosevelt, who encouraged him to
travel extensively and report on what he
found. His reports were evidently carefully digested by the President and used
in Cabinet meetings.

Born in Sedalia, Missouri, on September 20, 1878, he received his early education there. In 1904 he married Hedwig
Wildi. Much of his life has been spent in
business enterprises. He has been largely
interested in the dairy industry, in which
he obtained international recognition.

Before entering the diplomatic service
at President Roosevelt's request, he spent
a great deal of time, for business and personal reasons, in various parts of Europe,
particularly in the decade preceding 1933.
Being interested in international politics,
he watched the European political situation which foreshadowed the momentous
events he later observed from his preferred position in Budapest.